Gender ['dʒɛndɐ], das Substantiv, Neutrum, Geschlechtsidentität des Menschen als soziale Kategorie (z.B. im Hinblick auf seine Selbstwahrnehmung, sein Selbstwertgefühl oder sein Rollenverhalten)

gender ['dʒen.dɚ], noun, human's gender identity as a social category (e.g. in terms of self-awareness, self-esteem, or role behaviour)

Nicht mein Ding – Gender im Design
Not My Thing – Gender in Design

HfG-Archiv Ulm

Herausgegeben von / *Published by:*
HfG-Archiv / Museum Ulm
/ Katharina Kurz, Pia Jerger

Mit Beiträgen von / *With contributions from:*
Olivia Daigneault Deschênes, Axel Städter,
Susanne Umscheid und Christiane Wachsmann

avedition

Inhalt / Content

6	Vorwort / *Foreword* / Stefanie Dathe		62	Pink oder Blau, Entweder-oder / *Pink or blue, either-or*
9	Einleitung / *Introduction* / Katharina Kurz		62	Das pinke Rennauto / *The Pink Racing Car*
16	**Öffentlicher Raum** / *Public Space*		64	**Medizin und Gesundheit** / *Medicine and Health*
18	Für alle? / *For all?*		66	»Mothers: Buy Flavored Bayer Children's Aspirin!«
20	Über Piktogramme: Goldstandard und kulturelle Zeichen / *On Pictograms: Gold Standard and Cultural Symbol*		68	Das Undenkbare gestalten: / *Designing the Unthinkable:* The Andro Chair
23	»Was ist Ihr Ding?« / *»What's your thing?«*		70	The Tampon Book: »Warum ist Menstruation Luxus, Kaviar aber nicht?« / *»Why is menstruation considered a luxury, but caviar not?«*
24	OpenMoji – Emojis für alle! / *OpenMoji – Emojis for all!*		72	Herrensattel, Damenrad – Fahrradfahren für alle / *Men's Saddles and Women's Bikes – Cycling for All*
26	Lounge-Möbel / *Lounge Furniture*		74	»Breast is best«?
28	heer – Stillen in der Öffentlichkeit? / *heer – Breastfeeding in public?*		76	Anti-Rauch-Kampagne auf HfG-isch / *Ulm School of Design (HfG Ulm) Anti-Smoking Campaign*
30	Gender – Space – Architecture		79	Gender-Marketing: Nein, danke! Gendermedizin: Ja, bitte! / *Gender Marketing: No, thanks! Gender Medicine: Yes, please!*
32	Machtsymbol Geld: das Projekt »Womoney« / *Power Symbol Money: The »Womoney« Project*			
34	Ein Hijab für den Leistungssport? Der Nike Pro Hijab / *A Hijab for Competitive Sports? The Nike Pro Hijab*		82	**Haushalt und Wohnen** / *Household and Living*
36	Designer in Residence		84	My Home is my Castle
			86	System-Design an der HfG Ulm / *System Design at the HfG Ulm*
40	**Spielen und Erziehung** / *Play and Education*		90	Einrichtungsspiel: »Wie könnte Ihre Wohnung aussehen?« / *Furnishing Game: »How could your apartment look like?«*
42	Jungensachen, Mädchenkram? / *Boys' things and girly stuff?*		92	Butler und Dienstmädchen sind von gestern? / *Butler and maid are of yesteryear?* Q– The First Genderless Voice
44	The Pink and Blue Project		94	Küche vs. Werkstatt / *Kitchen vs. Workshop*
46	spiel gut – Gutes Spielzeug / *spiel gut – Good Toys*		96	Der Akita Multitask Future 2000 / *The Akita Multitask Future 2000*
52	LEGO gestern und heute / *LEGO: Past and Present*		97	Visualisierung von Gendernormen im Design: Bohrer »Dolphia« und Stabmixer »Mega Hurricane« / *Visualising Gender Norms in Design: »Dolphia« Drill and »Mega Hurricane« Mixer*
54	LEGO & Gender		100	Bosch »IXO«
55	Vom Frisieren und Schießen / *On Shooting Guns and Styling Hair*		104	Gestaltung eines »genderneutralen« Produktes / *Design of a »Gender-Neutral« Product*
57	Killing Boys, Killing Girls			
58	Puzzles für Kindergartenkinder / *Jigsaw Puzzles Designed for Nursery School Children*			
59	Puzzlen leicht gemacht? / *Jigsaw puzzles made easy?*			
60	Wer ist es? / *Guess who?*			
61	Who's She?			

106	**Kosmetik und Gender-Marketing** / *Cosmetics and Gender Marketing*
108	Pink stinks?
110	Pinkstinks Germany e.V.: »Werbemelder*in« und / *and* »Pinker Pudel«
111	Rasieren: Braun und Gillette / *Shaving: Braun and Gillette*
114	Unisex, oder was? / *Unisex or what?* 4711 Echt Kölnisch Wasser, NIVEA, BASIK
118	Gestaltung von »genderneutralen« Kosmetikverpackungen / *Design of »Gender-Neutral« Cosmetic Packagings*
120	**Design: Ausbildung und Beruf** / *Design: Education and Profession*
122	Gender im Design
125	Frauen und Männer an der HfG – Lebensentwürfe der 1950er und 1960er Jahre / *Women and Men at the Ulm School of Design (HfG Ulm) – Life Planning in the 1950s and 1960s* / Christiane Wachsmann
130	Selbstbehauptungen – Frauen an der hfg ulm / *Assertiveness – Women at the hfg ulm*
131	notamuse – A New Perspective on Woman Graphic Designers in Europe
132	Design for …
134	AIGA Gender Equity Toolkit
135	Gestaltungsfaktoren / *Design Factors*
139	Zig Zag, Tulip & Co. – Stuhldesign-Klassiker, mal anders befragt / *A Different Take on Classic Chair Designs*
143	Confused, Ir/regular and In/correct – De-gendering Everyday Life
144	Durch die HfG-Brille: Entwicklung einer standardisierten Brillenfassung / *The Development of a Standardised Eyeglass Frame*
148	**Vorwort Teilprojekte** / *Foreword Subprojects* / Pia Jerger
152	**Schulprojekt mit einer 9. Klasse der Realschule Dornstadt** / *School project with 9th grade pupils from Realschule Dornstadt*
154	Rückblick / *Review* / Susanne Umscheid
161	Interview mit / *with* Michaela Settele-Jakob
166	**Produktdesignkurs des Aicher-Scholl-Kollegs** / *Product design course of the Aicher-Scholl-Kolleg*
168	Interview mit / *with* Judith Hoerder / »Küche vs. Werkstatt« / *»Kitchen vs. Workshop«*
173	Interview mit / *with* Anna-Lotta Dechow / »Das pinke Rennauto« / *»The Pink Racing Car«*
174	Interview mit / *with* Tabea Wegelin »Killing Boys, Killing Girls«
176	Interview mit / *with* Anton Sievert / »Ulmer Hocker« / *»Ulm Stool«*
178	**Designer in Residence** / *Stipendiatin:* / *Resident:* Olivia Daigneault Deschênes
180	Zeig' mir wie du isst und ich sag' dir, wer du bist / *Show me how you eat, I will tell you who you are* / Olivia Daigneault Deschênes
194	**Gender – Space – Architecture** / Ausstellung mit Fotografien von Juliane Peil in der PUTTE / *Exhibition with photographs by Juliane Peil in the PUTTE*
196	Gender – Ein Schaufenster in die Gesellschaft / *A Display Window into Society* / Axel Städter
204	Biografien / *Biographies*
206	Literatur / *Literature*
209	Bildnachweise / *Image Credits*
210	Dank / *Acknowledgements*
211	Impressum / *Imprint*

Vorwort
/Foreword

Stefanie Dathe \ Als Wiege des Nachkriegsdesigns zählte die Hochschule für Gestaltung Ulm in den 1950er und 1960er Jahren zu den international fortschrittlichsten Ausbildungsstätten für Design und Umweltgestaltung. Das Archiv der HfG – seit 1993 eine Abteilung des Museums Ulm – verfolgt in seiner Doppelfunktion als Archiv und Museum das Ziel, einerseits die Geschichte der HfG zu dokumentieren und andererseits durch Ausstellungen, Publikationen und Veranstaltungen neue Impulse für eine lebendige Auseinandersetzung mit dem Design heute zu entwickeln und eine breite Öffentlichkeit für aktuelle gesellschaftsrelevante Gestaltungsfragen zu interessieren.

Museen leisten einen unerlässlichen Beitrag in unserer Gesellschaft: Sie bewahren und vermitteln Geschichte, dokumentieren aktuelle Entwicklungen, schaffen Wissen, erspüren zukünftige Trends und legen bisweilen den Finger in die Wunden der Gesellschaft, um Diskussionen und Diskurse anzuregen. Zum ersten Mal im deutschsprachigen Raum hat sich am HfG-Archiv eine Ausstellung mit der Frage nach Gender im Design befasst, mit soziokulturell geprägten Geschlechterrollen, die sich als prägendes Element der menschlichen Identität in allen Lebensbereichen des Alltags bis hin zum Design mal mehr, mal weniger offensichtlich bemerkbar machen. Dieses Buch dokumentiert die von Pia Jerger und Katharina Kurz konzipierte Ausstellung, die überregionale Resonanz erfahren hat und als Projekt von nationaler Relevanz durch Vermittlung von Martin Gerster, MdB auch in der Landesvertretung Baden-Württemberg in Berlin gezeigt werden kann.

Zukunft braucht Herkunft. Mit seinem Ausstellungsauftrag versteht sich das HfG-Archiv als eine Agentur der Öffentlichkeit, als lebendiger Ort

A cradle of post-war design, Ulm School of Design (HfG Ulm) was one of the most progressive institutions internationally for education in design and environmental design. In its twin role as an archive and a museum, the HfG-Archiv – a part of Museum Ulm since 1993 – pursues the goal to document the history of the HfG, while developing new impulses for a lively engagement with presentday design through its exhibitions, publications, and events and attracting broad public interest for contemporary design issues in society.

Museums provide an indispensible contribution to society: They preserve and convey history, document current developments, produce knowledge, identify future trends, and sometimes touch a sore spot in society in order to spur discussions and discourse. For the first time in the German-speaking region, the HfG-Archiv has addressed the topic of Gender in Design with an exhibition that delves into socially and culturally prescribed gender roles, a key facet of human identity that has distinct impacts – sometimes more, sometimes less visible – in all realms of daily life, including design. This book documents the exhibition conceived by Pia Jerger and Katharina Kurz, which received excellent response all across Germany and, as a project with national relevance, can now also be presented in the Baden-Württemberg State Representation Office in Berlin, thanks to the efforts of Martin Gerster, Member of the Bundestag.

Future needs origins. In its mission as an exhibition house, the HfG-Archiv sees itself as an agency of the public, a vibrant site for the exchange of ideas, for questions about the future, free opinion making and participation in processes that shape

des Gedankenaustausches, der Zukunftsfragen, der freien Meinungsbildung und Teilhabe an kulturellen Gestaltungsprozessen. So geht es bei der Betrachtung und Hinterfragung geschlechtsspezifischer Designs um Vergangenheit und Gegenwart zugleich, wenn die Ausstellung historische Studien- und Diplomarbeiten zum Thema aus den Beständen des HfG-Archivs in einem bereichernden Dialog aktuellen Positionen internationaler Designbüros, Firmen, Museen und Privatpersonen gegenüberstellt. Ihnen sei an dieser Stelle herzlich gedankt für die großzügige Überlassung der Exponate.

Viele Ideen aus der Vergangenheit der Hochschule für Gestaltung Ulm haben ihre Zukunft noch vor sich. Sie bieten Anregungen und Antworten auf Fragen zu unserer industriellen Massenkultur, zu ökologischen, ökonomischen und soziokulturellen Problemen.

Mit dem von Katharina Kurz initiierten Designer in Residence-Programm verfolgt das HfG-Archiv auch über die Ausstellung hinaus das Ziel, das eigene Erbe unter gegenwärtigen Fragestellungen zu betrachten und die Doppelfunktion als Museum und Archiv in den Räumen der einstigen Ausbildungsstätte mit zeitgenössischer Designforschung zu verbinden. Den dreimonatigen Aufenthalt der ersten Stipendiatin Olivia Daigneault Deschênes auf dem Campus der ehemaligen HfG unterstützte die Stiftung HfG Ulm. Julia Hanisch und Alexander Wetzig sei hierfür größter Dank ausgesprochen, ebenso wie für die Förderung dieser Publikation, deren Realisierung ohne die wertvolle Unterstützung von Christina und Marina Bauernfeind, des Vereins der Freunde des Ulmer Museums sowie durch den erheblichen finanziellen Beitrag der Rudolf und Clothilde Eberhardt-Stiftung nicht möglich gewesen wäre.

Vor dem Hintergrund des musealen Bildungsauftrages hat das HfG-Archiv als identitätsstiftender Ort der Begegnung mit diesem Projekt erstmals konsequent partizipative Prozesse in das Vermittlungskonzept einfließen lassen und die Ergebnisse aus den Projektkursen des Aicher-Scholl-Kollegs und der Realschule Dornstadt unter Leitung von Michaela Settele-Jakob, Susanne Umscheid, Fabian Karrer und Uli Häussler sichtbar in der Ausstellung präsentiert. Dank sei hier allen beteiligten Akteurinnen und Akteuren, Schülerinnen und Schülern ausgesprochen sowie »lab.Bode – Initiative zur Stärkung der Vermittlungsarbeit in Museen«, einem gemeinsamen Programm der Kulturstiftung des Bundes und der Staatlichen Museen zu Berlin, das nicht nur das Schulprojekt und das wissenschaftliche Volontariat im Bereich Bildung und Vermittlung ermöglicht und finanziell unterstützt hat, sondern auch wertvolle Denkanstöße auf dem Weg zu einem »offenen Museum« lieferte.

Eine lokale Verankerung und Sichtbarmachung des gesellschaftsrelevanten Gender-Themas im Ulmer Stadtraum wurde möglich durch die Zusammenarbeit mit dem Verschwörhaus e.V. Ulm,

culture. So the contemplation and investigation of gender-specific design involves both the past and the present – for instance, the exhibition juxtaposes historical studies and theses on the subject from the inventories of the HfG-Archiv in an enriching dialogue with contemporary positions of international design offices, companies, museums, and private persons. Here a mention of great thanks for their generous contribution of the exhibits.

Many ideas from the past of Ulm School of Design still have their future in front of them. They offer inspiration and answers to questions about our industrial mass culture, to ecological, economic, and sociocultural problems.

With the Designer in Residence programme, initiated by Katharina Kurz in the run-up to the exhibition, the HfG-Archiv aims to view its own heritage in the context of contemporary issues and to connect the dual function as museum and archive with contemporary design research in the spaces of the former school. The three-month stay on the HfG campus of the first resident Olivia Daigneault Deschênes was supported by the HfG Ulm Foundation. Many thanks to Julia Hanisch and Alexander Wetzig in this respect as well as for the funding of this publication, whose realisation would not have been possible without the valuable support of Christina and Marina Bauernfeind, the Association of Friends of Museum Ulm, and the substantial financial contribution by the Rudolf and Clothilde Eberhardt Foundation.

Against the backdrop of the museum's educational task, the HfG-Archiv, as an identity-building place of encounters, took this exhibition project as a first opportunity to integrate participative processes into the educational concept and to prominently showcase the results from the project courses of the Aicher-Scholl-Kolleg and Realschule Dornstadt, which were held under the guidance of Michaela Settele-Jakob, Susanne Umscheid, Fabian Karrer, and Uli Häussler. Thanks goes to all of the protagonists and students as well as to »lab.Bode – Initiative to Strengthen Museum Education in Museums«, a joint programme of the German Federal Cultural Foundation and the Staatliche Museen zu Berlin, which not only facilitated and financially supported the school project and the scientific volunteer work in the realm of education and mediation, but also provided valuable input on the road to becoming an »open museum«.

A local foothold and visibility for the socially relevant gender theme in the city of Ulm was made possible through cooperations with the Verschwörhaus e.V. Ulm, which helped realise the projects by designer in residence Olivia Daigneault Deschênes, and with PUTTE, a non-profit project space for contemporary art in Neu-Ulm. Here the exhibition »Gender – Space – Architecture« with photographic works by Juliane Peil explored the stereotypical representations of masculinity and femininity in daily life.

das die Realisierung der Projekte der Residence-Stipendiatin Olivia Daigneault Deschênes unterstützt hat, und mit der PUTTE, einem Non-Profit-Projektraum für aktuelle Kunst in Neu-Ulm. Dort hat die Ausstellung »Gender – Space – Architecture« mit fotografischen Arbeiten von Juliane Peil den stereotypen Darstellungen von Männlichkeit und Weiblichkeit im Alltag nachgespürt.

    Ein solch vielschichtiges partizipatives Ausstellungsprojekt bedarf vielfältiger Unterstützung und helfender Hände. So geht mein abschließender Dank an alle Beteiligten, die mit Rat und Tat vor und hinter den Kulissen zur Seite gestanden sind.

Such a multilayered, participative exhibition project requires multifaceted forms of support and many helping hands. So my last words of thanks go to all of those who were involved for their advice and assistance on stage and behind the scenes.

Einleitung
/Introduction

Katharina Kurz \ Gender Studies, Gender Pay Gap, Gender-Sternchen, Gender Mainstreaming … und jetzt auch noch Design? »Nicht mein Ding!«, könnte man antworten – weitaus förderlicher ist es dagegen, in einen Dialog über einen Gegenstand zu treten, der uns alle persönlich betrifft.

»Gender« (engl.) bezeichnet unsere sozial geprägte Geschlechtsidentität. Gemeint ist, wie wir uns selbst und andere im Hinblick auf ihr Rollenverhalten wahrnehmen. Das deutsche Wort »Geschlecht« dagegen beschreibt in erster Linie die biologische Geschlechtsidentität (engl. »sex«). Das binäre, also das zweigeschlechtliche System aus männlich und weiblich ist tief in der (west-)europäischen Kultur verwurzelt, während es in anderen Kulturen durchaus mehr als zwei Geschlechter gibt. Die Einführung des dritten Geschlechts »divers« in Deutschland (2018) wird in vielerlei Hinsicht als Errungenschaft gefeiert. Menschen, die sich dem binären System nicht zugehörig fühlen, ist damit eine Alternative geboten.

Doch was hat Gender mit Design zu tun? Der universelle Ausspruch »Menschen formen Dinge, Dinge formen Menschen« fasst es prägnant zusammen. Alles nicht Natürliche ist von Menschen gestaltet. Der Umsetzung widmet sich Design auf professionelle Weise. Die ehemalige HfG Ulm war eine Gestaltungshochschule, an der das Berufsbild im Feld des Designs, wie wir es heute kennen, geprägt wurde. Das genannte wechselseitige Prinzip, dass Menschen Dinge formen und Dinge Menschen, dürfte auch in Ulm nicht unerkannt gewesen sein – wie sonst hätte mit der Intention, eine Gesellschaft über Gestaltung prägen zu wollen, eine ganze Hochschule aufgebaut werden

Gender studies, gender pay gap, gender neutrality, gender mainstreaming … and now design, too? »Not my thing!« one might answer – hence, it makes all the more sense to start a dialogue about a subject that personally concerns us all.

»Gender« refers to our socially informed gender identity. Namely, how we perceive ourselves and others in terms of their role behaviour in this respect. In contrast, the German word »Geschlecht« describes first and foremost the biological gender identity – »sex« in English. The binary two-gender system of male and female has deep roots in (Western) European culture, whereas other cultures recognise that by all means there are more than just two genders. In Germany the introduction of the third sex »diverse« in 2018 was celebrated in many respects as an achievement. People who feel that they do not belong in a binary system are now offered an alternative.

But what does gender have to do with design? The universal claim »what we design, designs us back« sums it up concisely. Everything that is not natural is made by humans. Design is there as a profession to implement this process. The former Ulm School of Design (HfG Ulm) was a design institution that helped to establish design as a professional field as we know it today. The mentioned reciprocal principle, that people design things and things people, apparently was not unfamiliar in Ulm either – how else could have the intention to shape society through design led to the establishment of a complete college? »From the coffee cup to the housing estate,« that's how Max Bill, the first rector of the HfG, described the design standards for the advancing mass culture of the 1950s.

können? – »Von der Kaffeetasse bis zur Wohnsiedlung«, so beschreibt Max Bill als erster Rektor der HfG Ulm den Gestaltungsanspruch für die voranschreitende Massenkultur inmitten der 1950er Jahre. Diese Formulierung deutet gleichzeitig an, was und für wen gestaltet werden soll: Alltagsgegenstände und -räume – industrielle Massenfertigung statt Kunsthandwerk – und das für alle. Dass wiederum der Begriff »Gender« zu jener Zeit nicht existierte, heißt nicht, dass es keine soziokulturellen Rollen der Geschlechter gab – es heißt nur, dass das Bewusstsein für Geschlechterrollen und deren Bedeutung sich gewandelt hat. Heute, über 60 Jahre nach Gründung der HfG Ulm und nach dem ausgiebig gefeierten Gründungsjubiläum des Bauhauses, sind wir auf dem Höhepunkt der globalisierten Konsumkultur angekommen und Rollenbilder haben sich stark gewandelt – oder nicht? Gegenwärtige gesellschaftliche Debatten über das Thema »Gender« verweisen darauf, dass dies in einigen Bereichen mehr, in anderen weniger der Fall ist. Wir befinden uns in einem vielschichtigen Aushandlungsprozess.

Auch die Frage »Wie wollen wir leben?« war bereits am Bauhaus und der HfG Ulm eine sehr zentrale, die dem Funktionalismus als grundlegende Überlegung und Prinzip einer Gestaltung »für alle« diente. Zugleich ist es symptomatisch, dass diese Frage an den beiden Gestaltungsschulen mit ihrem demokratischen Anspruch einen so hohen Stellenwert einnahm. Diese gilt es nicht abschließend zu beantworten, sondern sie begleitet stets unsere zeitgenössischen Umwälzungsprozesse, und als demokratische Gesellschaft müssen wir uns ihr immer neu stellen. Oder, um es mit den Worten eines Verfechters der »Offenen Gesellschaft«, Harald Welzer, zu sagen: »Demokratie [ist] ein Projekt, das nur dann funktionieren kann, wenn beständig und mit Blick auf die Zukunft daran gearbeitet wird.«[1] Entsprechende Antworten für die Zukunft anhand der uns umgebenden Dinge, dem Jetzt, und der sehr persönlichen Kategorie Geschlecht zu verhandeln, kann im Feld der bisher vor allem abstrakt geführten Gender-Debatten neue Perspektiven eröffnen.

»Man mag solche Positionen, die Design als Modus des politischen Handelns und der Zukunftsgestaltung postulieren, visionär finden, anmaßend oder schlicht naiv – sicherlich aber sind sie von einer aufschlussreichen Ambivalenz durchzogen.«[2]
Claudia Mareis

Was den Ansatz von »Gender Design« oder »Gender-im-Design«[3] anbelangt, so unterscheidet er sich aus wissenschaftlicher Sicht im Wesentlichen dadurch von anderen Beispielen einer Design-Kritik, als dass Gender eine soziale Kategorie neben »Race« und »Class« ist, die mit der Verteilung von Machtverhältnissen verbunden ist. Damit handelt es sich unweigerlich auch um ein politisches Thema.[4] Überhaupt ist es kennzeichnend für Ansätze wie Social, Universal, Eco oder eben Gender Design, dass sie einerseits Kritik an Design, dessen Prozessen sowie an Produktions- und Konsumlogiken üben und – wie Design überhaupt immanent – einer Lösung nachzugehen suchen. Diesen gestaltungskritischen Ansätzen wohnt, wie schon der

This formulation also indicates what should be designed and for whom: everyday objects and spaces – industrial mass production instead of arts and crafts – and for all. In turn, the fact that the term »gender« was not commonplace at this time does not imply that there were no sociocultural roles of the sexes – it only means that the awareness of gender roles and their significance has changed. Today, more than 60 years after the founding of the HfG Ulm, and following the widely celebrated 100th anniversary of the Bauhaus, we have arrived at the pinnacle of globalised consumer culture, and the understanding of the roles has changed – or hasn't it? Contemporary debates in society on the topic of gender indicate that this is more so the case in some realms and less so in others. We find ourselves in a multifarious process of negotiation.

The question »How do we want to live?« was already a very central issue at the Bauhaus and the HfG Ulm, which underpinned functionalism as a fundamental cornerstone and principle of a design for all. At the same time, it is symptomatic that this question had high priority at the two design schools with their democratic claims. However, it does not demand a conclusive answer, rather it continues to accompany transformation processes in our present, and, as a democratic society, we must confront it time and again. Or to say it in the words of a proponent of the »open society«, Harald Welzer: »Democracy is a project that can only work when it is continuously elaborated with a view to the future.«[1] Negotiating answers for the future on the basis of the things that surround us now and the very personal category of gender can open new perspectives into heretofore predominantly abstract gender debates.

»Positions that postulate design as a mode of political action can seem visionary, pretentious, or simply naïve – but they are quite definitely permeated by a revealing ambivalence.«[2]
Claudia Mareis

When looking at »gender design« or »gender in design«[3] from a scholarly viewpoint, it differs significantly from other forms of design critique as gender, a social category like »race« and »class«, is bound to power relations. Inevitably, we are dealing with a political topic.[4] It is a general characteristic of approaches like social, universal, eco, or also gender design to criticise design, its processes, as well as the logics of production and consumption and – integral to design – to search for a solution. Intrinsic to these claims, as was already the case with »good form« [die Gute Form], is to link design with moral and democratic ideals. There is an implicit dimension of design that challenges, in the spirit of critique, how we want to live, and not only from the standpoint of the designer (as producer) but increasingly from the perspective of the user (as consumer) as well. In this context, gender is a category that accompanies

»Guten Form«, ein Anspruch inne, der Design mit moralischen und demokratischen Idealen verknüpft. Implizit enthalten ist eine Dimension von Design, die die Frage danach stellt, wie wir leben wollen – oder auch im Sinne einer Kritik infrage stellt – nicht nur von Seiten der Designer*innen (als Produzent*innen), sondern zunehmend auch seitens der Nutzer*innen (als Konsument*innen). Dabei ist die Kategorie »Gender« wohl diejenige, die uns alle ganz persönlich und alltäglich begleitet; so gewohnt, dass wir es nicht immer bewusst wahrnehmen.

Und diejenigen, die Dinge entwerfen? Welche Rolle spielt Geschlecht in der Ausbildung und den Berufsfeldern des Designs? Designphilosoph Daniel Martin Feige zeigt auf, vor welchem Determinismus[5] die Praxis des Gestaltens sich durchaus abspielt: »Ob Designer*innen wollen oder nicht: Auch dann, wenn sie ganz profane Alltagsgegenstände entwerfen, gestalten sie damit immer schon mehr und anderes als bloß diese Gegenstände. Sie arbeiten nämlich implizit auch an den kulturellen Praktiken mit, im Rahmen deren diese Gegenstände gebraucht werden.«[6] Vor diesem Hintergrund ergeben sich zentrale Anknüpfungspunkte der Ausstellung sowie der vorliegenden Publikation: Fragen nach Gender im Design nachzuspüren, aber auch dem, was es überhaupt heißt, genderspezifisch, -sensibel oder gar -neutral zu gestalten. Gibt es überhaupt eine Gestaltung »für alle«?

Angesichts der dargelegten Zusammenhänge scheint es kaum begreiflich, dass die Themen Gender und Design nicht »irgendjemandes Ding« sein können. Dies führt mithin zu einem weiteren Motiv für die Umsetzung dieser ersten musealen Ausstellung zu Gender im Design. Wenn die Diskurse um diese beiden Felder zu abstrakt geführt werden, dann ist es eine Aufgabe von Kulturinstitutionen, Anlässe zur Auseinandersetzung zu bieten. Das bedeutet Räume zu schaffen, in denen wir gegenwärtige Zustände durchleuchten und sowohl fragen: »Wie ist es?«, aber auch Gedankenräume für ein »Wie soll es sein?« öffnen. Daher haben meine Kollegin der Vermittlung Pia Jerger und ich uns für ein Konzept von gemeinsamem Ausstellen und Vermitteln entschieden, sowie für eine inhaltliche Gliederung, die im Alltag verortet ist und somit vielfältige Anknüpfungspunkte bietet. Teilhabe zu ermöglichen, stand hierbei von vornherein als ein bedeutendes Ziel fest, weshalb wir mehrere Projekte bereits im Vorfeld der Ausstellung initiierten und deren Ergebnisse Bestandteil der kuratorischen Strategie für ein partizipatives Ausstellungs- und Publikationsprojekt sind (siehe Teilprojekte, ab S. 148). Zudem haben wir den vertrauten, aber eher stadtfernen Ulmer Kuhberg verlassen und sind mit einem Schaufenster in das urbane Zentrum vorgedrungen: Der Off-Space die PUTTE stellte zeitweilig fotografische Arbeiten von Juliane Peil aus, die auf ihren Streifzügen durch die Zweilandstadt Ulm und Neu-Ulm mehr oder weniger offenbare Genderstereotype im öffentlichen Raum erkundete.

us all personally and on a daily basis; so familiar that we do not consciously perceive it at all times.

And what about those who design things? What role does gender play in the education and profession of design? Design philosopher Daniel Martin Feige reveals the determinism[5] that the design practice is subject to: »Whether designers want to or not: Even when they design the most profane everyday objects, they are always designing more than just these objects. Namely, they are inherently also at work on the cultural practices in which these objects will be used.«[6] Against this backdrop emerge the main points of reference for the exhibition and the publication before you: to investigate the subject of gender in design, but also what gender-specific, gender-sensitive, or even gender-neutral design really means. Does a design »for all« even exist?

Given the abovementioned factors, it is hard to imagine that the topics of gender and design could not be »someone's thing«. This leads to another motif in the realisation of a first museum exhibition on gender in design. When the discourse about the two fields is too abstract, then it is the task of cultural institutions to offer occasions for discussion and interaction. This implies creating spaces where contemporary conditions can be examined and asking »How is it?« while also pointing to a visionary terrain for the question »How should it be?« With this in mind, my colleague from art education Pia Jerger and I chose a combined concept of exhibiting and educating, and to organise the contents in a manner that is rooted in the everyday and thus offers a diverse array of access points. From the very beginning, promoting participation was one of the most important goals – a reason why we already initiated a number of projects in the run-up to the exhibition, whose results form an integral part of the curatorial strategy for a participative exhibition and publication project (see Subprojects, from p. 148). Additionally, we took a step and left the trusted yet remote Kuhberg area of the HfG, and advanced to the urban centre with a public display window: the off-space PUTTE accommodated a temporary exhibition of the photographic works of Juliane Peil, who explored the more or less obvious gender stereotypes on her forays through the public space of the twin city Ulm and Neu-Ulm.

Another curatorial aspiration in this project at the former Ulm School of Design was to integrate contemporary designers and the collections of the HfG, and in this way examine the heritage of the legendary school in the present. To this end, we could initiate a project – which is important to me personally – in association with the exhibition project and with the kind support of the HfG Ulm Foundation: the Designer in Residence programme. Our ambition is for this programme to continue in the future, for the results our first resident Olivia Daigneault Deschênes produced under the gender design focus are impressive. She was inspired by Max Bill's design of the HfG canteen, which led to her project »Show me how you eat, I will tell you

Ein weiteres Anliegen für die Umsetzung dieses Projektes an der ehemaligen HfG Ulm ist die Einbeziehung derjenigen, die gestalten und auch die Sammlung und damit das Erbe der einstigen Schule in der Gegenwart zu befragen. Ein mir persönlich wichtiges Projekt konnten wir deshalb in Anknüpfung an das Ausstellungsprojekt und mit freundlicher Unterstützung der Stiftung HfG Ulm realisieren: Die Initiierung eines Designer in Residence-Programms. Dieses wird wünschenswerter Weise fortgeführt werden, denn die Ergebnisse, die unsere Stipendiatin Olivia Daigneault Deschênes unter dem Fokus Gender Design produziert hat, sind beeindruckend. Sie hat sich von Max Bills Gestaltung der HfG Mensa inspirieren lassen und ihr Projekt »Zeig' mir wie du isst und ich sag' dir wer du bist« ist eine angewandte Designforschung zum Thema Essen und Tischkultur (die Ergebnisse finden Sie im Katalogabschnitt zu den Teilprojekten ab S. 178 sowie angegliedert an den thematischen Bereich Öffentlicher Raum, S. 36). Dieser ist der erste Bereich des Alltags, in dem wir neben der Stillbank »heer« des Designstudios 52hours unter anderem auch Otl Aichers Piktogramme für Leitsysteme neben den heute für die digitale Kommunikation so relevanten Emojis betrachten. Die Stillbank »heer« (2018) ist ein exzellentes Beispiel für eine Gestaltung, die gesellschaftlich relevante Fragen – zum Stillen im öffentlichen Raum – anhand von Gestaltung buchstäblich in den Raum holt und so Anlass zur Diskussion bietet. Weitere Bereiche sind die Themen Spielen und Erziehung, wo Teile des einprägsamen Fotografie-Projekts der Südkoreanerin JeongMee Yoon neben Positionen der 1950er Jahre stehen und die dazu verleiten zu fragen, ob wir wirklich in den 1950er Jahren stärker in Rollenklischees verhaftet waren als heute. Diese wechselseitigen Wirkungen, sowie die Frage danach, wo Design und Marketing ineinander übergehen oder wie Antworten auf eine gendersensible oder -spezifische Gestaltung aussehen, finden Sie in den Bereichen Medizin und Gesundheit, Haushalt und Wohnen sowie Kosmetik und Gender-Marketing. In Bezug zur ehemaligen HfG Ulm spielen zudem der Designberuf und die -ausbildung eine Rolle, wie auch der zeitliche Kontext der 1950er und 1960er Jahre. Das Nebeneinander dieser und zeitgenössischer Designpositionen zusammen mit Ergebnissen aus den vier Teilprojekten, dem Produktdesignkurs (Aicher-Scholl-Kolleg), der Projektwoche (Realschule Dornstadt) und dem genannten Designer in Residence-Programm, regt, so denken wir, zu einem Dialog an, der über die Ausstellung hinweg andauert und zu dem diese Publikation ein entsprechender Beitrag ist.

Es bleibt – last but not least – einen großen Dank auszusprechen. Die Ausstellung und die Publikation sind das Ergebnis einer intensiven Teamarbeit und mehrerer gelungener Kooperationen, zu denen auch die Teilprojekte gehören. Dem Team des Museums Ulm und des HfG-Archivs sprechen wir den herzlichsten Dank für die Zusammenarbeit aus, sowie Stefanie Dathe, Martin Mäntele und Christiane Wachsmann für ihr Vertrauen und die Unterstützung. Für die Förderung durch Mittel, durch die die Umsetzung

who you are«, an applied design research on the topic of eating and table culture (see Subprojects p. 178 and the thematic chapter Public Space, p. 36). In Public Space, our first section of the everyday, we find the »heer« breastfeeding bench by the design studio 52hours and Otl Aicher's pictograms for guidance systems beside the indispensible emojis of our digital communication. »heer« (2018), a breastfeeding bench for public space, is an excellent example of a design that literally takes socially relevant topics to the street and puts them up for discussion. Other sections include Play and Education in which parts of the captivating photography project by South Korean artist JeongMee Yoon are contrasted with positions from the 1950s, prompting the question whether we were more strongly rooted in role clichés back then than we are today. These interrelationships, the question where design and marketing flow into one another, or examples of what gender-sensitive or specific design can look like can be found in the sections Medicine and Health, Household and Living, and Cosmetics and Gender Marketing. With reference to the former Ulm School of Design, the design profession and education come into play, along with the historical context of the 1950s and 1960s. The juxtaposition of that day and age with contemporary design positions, together with the results from the four subprojects – the product design course (Aicher-Scholl-Kolleg), the project week (Realschule Dornstadt), the Designer in Residence programme, and the exhibition in the off-space PUTTE – inspire a dialogue, in our opinion, which transcends the exhibition itself and is captured in this publication.

Last but not least, a few words to express our gratitude. The exhibition and publication are the result of intensive team work and many successful cooperations, among them also the subprojects. We would like give our heartfelt thanks to the team of Museum Ulm and the HfG-Archiv for their collaboration, and to Stefanie Dathe, Martin Mäntele, and Christiane Wachsmann for their trust and support. Our utmost thanks for their financial support go to Christina and Marina Bauernfeind, the HfG Ulm Foundation, lab.Bode – Initiative to Strengthen Museum Education in Museums, the Rudolf and Clothilde Eberhardt Foundation, the Association of Friends of Museum Ulm, and PlayWood. We are equally as grateful for the numerous loans from museums, companies, design offices, and private persons, which enabled the concept to be realised in this manner and for the exhibition to be shown in a new context. Hence, a sincere thank you to Martin Gerster, Member of the Bundestag, and to Andreas Schulze and Petra Beckmann – we look forward to presenting the exhibition in the Baden-Württemberg State Representation Office, a place of encounters and a public forum in Berlin. Furthermore, our gratitude goes to our cooperation partners for their openness, collaboration, and support in the subprojects: the Aicher-Scholl-Kolleg of the vh ulm,

ermöglicht wurde, möchten wir uns bei Christina und Marina Bauernfeind, der Stiftung Hochschule für Gestaltung (HfG Ulm), lab.Bode – Initiative zur Stärkung von Vermittlungsarbeit in Museen, der Rudolf und Clothilde Eberhardt-Stiftung, dem Freundesverein des Ulmer Museums und PlayWood außerordentlich bedanken. Ebenso dankbar sind wir für die vielen Leihgaben von Museen, Unternehmen und Designbüros sowie Privatpersonen, die es ermöglichten, das Konzept derart umzusetzen und die Ausstellung andernorts zu zeigen. Daher auch ein ausdrücklicher Dank an Martin Gerster, MdB, sowie Andreas Schulze und Petra Beckmann – wir freuen uns, die Ausstellung in der Baden-Württembergischen Landesvertretung zu zeigen, einer Begegnungsstätte und einem Schaufenster in Berlin. Für die Offenheit und Zusammenarbeit hinsichtlich der Teilprojekte sei außerdem allen Kooperationspartnern wärmstens für ihre Unterstützung gedankt: dem Aicher-Scholl-Kolleg der vh ulm, Andreas Lörcher sowie den Kollegiat*innen und Uli Häussler, der Realschule Dornstadt sowie den Schüler*innen, Susanne Umscheid und Fabian Karrer, Matthias Schmiedel, Michaela Settele-Jakob und Martin Böhnisch, erneut der Stiftung HfG Ulm, Julia Hanisch, Alexander Wetzig, Olivia Daigneault Deschênes, Uta Brandes, Burak Ertem, dem Verschwörhaus der Stadt Ulm und Stefan Kaufmann sowie Miriam und Robert Albrecht, wie auch der PUTTE, Axel Städter und Juliane Peil. Christine Schöffler und Peter Blakeney, Charlotte Maconochie und Clemens Marschall, sowie Susanne Dickel sprechen wir unseren großen Dank für die Übersetzungsarbeit aus, wie auch Petra Kiedaisch für die Zusammenarbeit und das Verlegen dieser Publikation. Fabian Karrer haben wir die Gestaltung, das Gesicht von »Nicht mein Ding« zu verdanken – er hat in einer für das Archiv der HfG Ulm so wichtigen, aussagekräftigen Weise und mit dem Museumsteam ein einzigartiges, treffendes Erscheinungsbild der Ausstellung und Publikation geschaffen – möge es noch viele Menschen ansprechen, irritieren, neugierig machen.

[1] Welzer, Harald. 2018. »Generation 2018«. In DIE ZEIT, Nr. 2 / 2018, 03.01.2018, https://www.zeit.de/2018/02/demokratie-zukunft-generation-fluechtlinge-klimapolitik-rechtspopulismus/seite-2, zul. abgerufen am 17.11.2019.
[2] Mareis, Claudia. 2016 [2014]. Theorien des Designs, hier: S. 216.
[3] Brandes, Uta. 2017. Gender Design, hier: S. 16.
[4] Während die Gleichstellung der Geschlechter und deren Förderung im deutschen Grundgesetz verankert ist, fordert die 2017 erstmals in den Bundestag eingezogene Partei »Alternative für Deutschland« (AfD) die unverzügliche und ersatzlose Beendigung des Gender Mainstreamings als einem politischen Leitprinzip und einer Querschnittsaufgabe staatlichen Handelns auf allen Ebenen, Parteiresolution der AfD Baden-Württemberg zu Gender Mainstreaming, https://afd-bw.de/partei/resolutionen/gender-mainstream (zul. abgerufen am 23.06.2018); sie führen dafür den Begriff der »Gender-Ideologie« an, die verfassungsfeindlich sei, siehe Wahlprogramm der AfD, Bundestagswahl 2017,

Andreas Lörcher and the students along with Uli Häussler, the Realschule Dornstadt and the pupils along with Susanne Umscheid and Fabian Karrer, Matthias Schmiedel, Michaela Settele-Jakob and Martin Böhnisch, once again the HfG Ulm Foundation, Julia Hanisch, Alexander Wetzig, Olivia Daigneault Deschênes, Uta Brandes, Burak Ertem, the Verschwörhaus of the City of Ulm and Stefan Kaufmann, Miriam and Robert Albrecht, and naturally PUTTE – Axel Städter and Juliane Peil. To Christine Schöffler and Peter Blakeney, Charlotte Maconochie and Clemens Marschall, and Susanne Dickel, great thanks for their translation work, and also to Petra Kiedaisch for the collaboration and publishing this book. And we have Fabian Karrer to thank for the design, the face of »Not My Thing« – he created a unique, striking visual look and feel for the exhibition and publication in a manner that was so very important and meaningful for the HfG-Archiv and the museum team – may it speak to, irritate, and intrigue many more people.

[1] Harald Welzer, »Generation 2018,« DIE ZEIT 2 (2018), Jan. 3, 2018, https://www.zeit.de/2018/02/demokratie-zukunft-generation-fluechtlinge-klimapolitik-rechtspopulismus/seite-2. Translated for this publication.
[2] Claudia Mareis, Theorien des Designs. Zur Einführung (Hamburg: Junius, 2014), 216. Translated for this publication.
[3] Uta Brandes, Gender Design. Streifzüge zwischen Theorie und Empirie. (Basel: Birkhäuser, 2017), 16.
[4] While gender equality and its promotion are anchored in the German Constitution, in 2017 the party »Alternative für Deutschland« (AfD – Alternative for Germany), who had entered the German Bundestag for the first time, demanded the immediate termination of gender mainstreaming as a political guiding principle and cross-sectional task of state action on all levels. Cf. Party resolution of the AfD Baden-Württemberg on Gender Mainstreaming, https://afd-bw.de/partei/resolutionen/gender-mainstream. They used the term »gender ideology«, which they declared unconstitutional. Cf. Election programme of the AfD, 2017 Parliamentary Elections, http://www.bundestagswahl-bw.de/wahlprogramm_afd_btwahl2017.html, section 6.6, p. 22: »For a clear picture of family – gender ideology is unconstitutional.« Such right-wing populist positions, in the first instance, have nothing in common with the strategy of gender mainstreaming, which was instigated by the UN World Conference on Women (1985) and rooted in European Union law since the late 1990s. Nevertheless, it seems that the name of the strategy as well as the term »gender« increasingly have a negative connotation or are at least misunderstood, even interpreted in the sense of an abolition of sexes. The conceptual bridge made in English between the biological and social gender does not seem to be recognised in a broader social discourse. Yet, gender as a sociocultural category (and in the fluid parallel to biological sex) can inspire diverse perspectives upon social realities.
[5] What is meant here is a sense of powerlessness, of having no influence on certain contexts because of their predetermined nature. Along the same lines in the design profession, the powerlessness is rooted in the inescapability of shaping as well as not being able to shape cultural practices, as

http://www.bundestagswahl-bw.de/wahlprogramm_afd_btwahl 2017.html, Abschnitt 6.6 »Für ein klares Familienbild – Gender-Ideologie ist verfassungsfeindlich«, S. 22 (zul. abgerufen am 23.06.2018). Solche rechtspopulistischen Positionen haben zwar zunächst nichts mit der Strategie des »Gender-Mainstreamings« gemein, die von der UN-Weltfrauenkonferenz (1985) angeregt und seit den späten 1990er Jahren im Recht der Europäischen Union verankert wurde. Trotzdem ist zu beobachten, dass die Benennung der Strategie sowie der Begriff »Gender« zunehmend negativ konnotiert oder zumindest missverstanden scheint, gar im Sinne einer Abschaffung der Geschlechter ausgelegt wird. Die gedankliche Brücke, die die englische Sprache zwischen biologischem und sozialem Geschlecht schlägt, scheint nicht im gesamtgesellschaftlichen Diskurs angekommen zu sein. Dabei eröffnet Geschlecht, im Sinne des engl. ›gender‹ als soziokulturelle Kategorie (und im fluiden Neben zum biolog. ›sex‹) vielfältige Perspektiven auf gesellschaftliche Realitäten.

[5] Gemeint ist hier eine gefühlte Ohnmacht, auf bestimmte Zusammenhänge aufgrund ihrer Vorbestimmtheit keinen Einfluss zu haben. Analog zum Designberuf ist es die Ohnmacht vor dem Hintergrund, immer auch kulturelle Praktiken mitzugestalten respektive nicht nicht-gestalten zu können, ähnlich wie es Daniel M. Feige beschreibt. Siehe auch Kap. 6, Design: Ausbildung und Beruf, S. 120.

[6] Feige, Daniel Martin. 2018. Design: Eine philosophische Analyse, hier: S. 203.

Daniel Martin Feige describes. See also: Chapter 6, Design: Education and Profession, p. 120.

[6] *Daniel Martin Feige, Design. Eine philosophische Analyse (Berlin: Suhrkamp, 2018), 203. Translated for this publication.*

Öffentlicher Raum
/*Public Space*

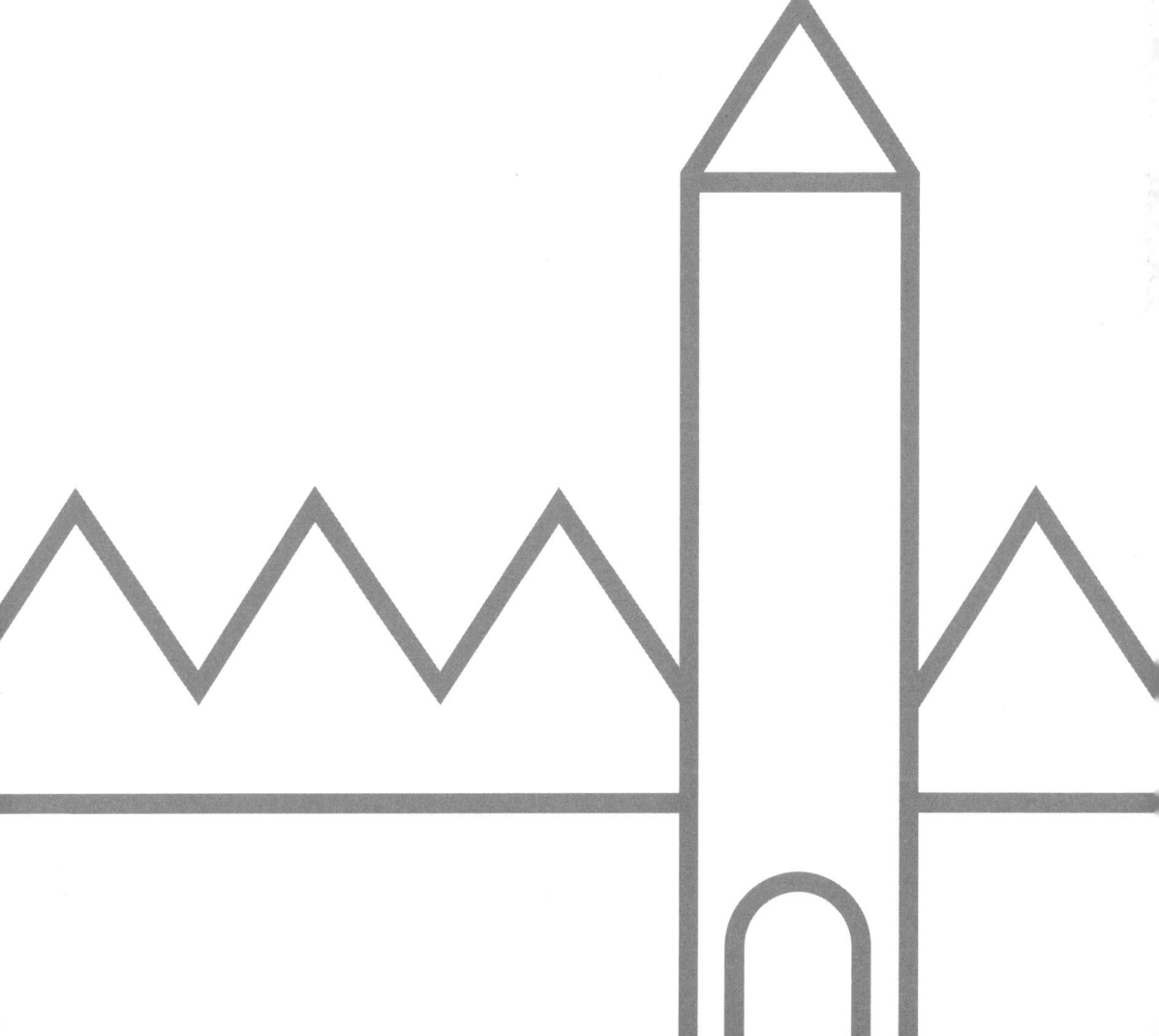

Für alle? Wie unser privater Rückzugsort, das eigene Zuhause, gestaltet ist, hängt individuell von verschiedenen Faktoren ab. Der öffentliche Raum hingegen ist ein Bereich, der von der öffentlichen Hand geplant wird und wesentlicher Teil des Alltags ist: Bei diesen Planungen geht es vor allem um die Nutzung und Aufteilung von Flächen wie beispielsweise Wohnraum, Handel und Gewerbe, Infrastruktur für Mobilität sowie Grün- und Spielflächen. Neben räumlichen gehören damit auch soziale Strukturen zur Stadt- und Regionalplanung dazu. Verhaltensweisen zueinander sowie Wege und Räume werden organisiert und deren Gestaltung soll möglichst für alle bzw. ohne Ausgrenzung funktionieren. Aber inwieweit ist das möglich?

Um die Stadt als Ort gesellschaftlichen Miteinanders auszubauen, streben die Verantwortlichen an, Gender-Mainstreaming zu implementieren. Ein Beispiel dafür ist die Barrierefreiheit. In diesen Bereich fällt auch das Leitliniensystem für sehbehinderte und eingeschränkte Menschen. Leitsysteme aus Piktogrammen, die wiederum zur Orientierung für sehende Menschen in öffentlichen Gebäuden und Räumen dienen, sind international gängig. So finden wir schnell den Weg zum nächsten Aufzug oder den nach Geschlechtern getrennten Toiletten an Bahn- oder Flughäfen. Das von Otl Aicher für die Olympischen Spiele (1972) und anschließend für die Firma ERCO entwickelte Piktogramm-System wird als zeitlose Gestaltung gepriesen. Es wird auch heute noch gern eingesetzt, aber auch kopiert.

Als Erweiterung des öffentlichen Raums ist der virtuelle Raum durch Emojis bestimmt, die unsere digitale Kommunikation prägen. Für beide gilt es, durch Reduktion eindeutig und schnell lesbare Systeme durch Gestaltungsrichtlinien zu schaffen, die bestimmte Tätigkeiten, Informationen oder Emotionen repräsentieren. Nicht nur Mechanismen von Ein- und Ausschluss sind hier relevant, sondern auch, wer diese Systeme gestaltet. So entwickelten Daniel Utz und Benedikt Groß an der HfG Schwäbisch Gmünd das Projekt OpenMoji (2017–2018) und fragten: »Warum überlässt die Design-Community es den großen Tech-Companies […] wie Emojis für Milliarden von Menschen aussehen?«

Manch andere Designinnovation, die genderspezifische oder -sensible Ansätze verfolgt, zeigt auf, dass sie bestehende öffentliche Räume verändern und damit zur Mobilität und Vielfalt beitragen kann: Eine Bank zum Stillen im öffentlichen Raum, wie die »heer«-Bank (Studio 52hours, 2018), hebt die theoretische Diskussion anhand von konkreter Gestaltung in die Alltagswelt. Das Design und die breite Vermarktung eines funktionalen Hijabs für den Leistungssport durch den Global Player Nike eröffnen wiederum Möglichkeiten für spezifische Personengruppen und treiben die Auseinandersetzung über Ein- und Ausschluss anhand von Design voran. Dass insbesondere auch Verhaltensweisen zur Alltagspraxis und Performance von geschlechtlicher Identität gehören, führt das Projekt »Zeig' mir wie du isst und ich sag' dir wer du bist« von Designer in Residence-Stipendiatin Olivia Daigneault Deschênes vor Augen: Die Mensa

For all? The design of our private place of retreat, one's own home, depends on various personal factors. Public space, on the other hand, is a realm that is planned by public authorities and forms an important part of daily life: These plans involve, above all, the usage and allocation of space for housing, trade and commerce, infrastructure for mobility, and green and play areas. Besides spatial infrastructures, also social provisions form a part of city and regional planning. The corresponding relationships as well as the paths and spaces are organised, and their design should work for as many people as possible without excluding anyone. But to what extent is this possible?

In order to further enhance the city as a space of social cohesion, the responsible parties are striving to implement gender mainstreaming. One example is accessibility. Tactile paving for the visually impaired falls under this category. Guidance systems using pictograms, which in turn serve sighted persons for orientation in public buildings and spaces, are internationally recognised. That's how we quickly find our way to the next elevator or toilet specified by gender in train stations and airports. The pictogram system designed by Otl Aicher for the 1972 Olympic Games and subsequently developed for the company ERCO is celebrated as timeless design. It is still in use to this day and often copied.

As an extension of public space, the virtual realm is populated by emojis, which have a strong impact on our digital communication. Like pictograms, it is about using reduced design guidelines to create clear and easy to read systems, which represent specific activities, information, or emotions. Mechanisms of inclusion and exclusion are important factors here, but also who designs these systems. For example, Daniel Utz and Benedikt Groß developed the project »OpenMoji« (2017–2018) at Schwäbisch Gmünd University of Design and asked: »Why is the design community leaving it to the big tech companies how the emojis for billions of people look like?«

Other design innovations that employ gender-specific or gender-sensitive approaches demonstrate that they are capable of changing existing public space and thereby make a contribution to mobility and diversity: A bench for breastfeeding in public like the »heer« bench by design studio 52hours (2018) transfers a theoretical discourse into everyday life with a concrete design proposal. The design and widespread marketing of a functional hijab for competitive sports by global player Nike, in turn, offers possibilities for specific target groups and furthers the discussion on inclusion and exclusion by means of design.

The project »Show me how you eat, I will tell you who you are« by designer in residence Olivia Daigneault Deschênes is a concise illustration that especially behavioural patterns belong to the everyday practice and performance of gender identities.

der ehemaligen HfG Ulm als öffentlicher Ort war Ausgangspunkt ihrer angewandten Designforschung zum Thema Essen und Tischkultur in Relation zur Ausübung von Geschlechterrollen.

Als Schaufenster der Ausstellung »Nicht mein Ding« im städtischen Raum fungierte die Ausstellung »Gender – Space – Architecture« im Off-Space die PUTTE, an der Grenze der »Zweilandstadt« Ulm und Neu-Ulm. Die Fotografien von Juliane Peil sind das Ergebnis ihrer Streifzüge durch den urbanen Raum und zeigen, wenngleich als subjektive Momentaufnahmen, dass die Straßenzüge auch durch die werbenden Schaufenster des Handels mitgestaltet werden.

The design of the HfG canteen as a public space was the departure point for her applied design research on the topic of eating and table culture in relation to the performance of gender roles.

The exhibition »Gender – Space – Architecture« in the off-space PUTTE, located nearby the twin city border, served as a display window in urban space for the exhibition »Not My Thing«. The photographs of Juliane Peil are the result of her forays through public space, which illustrate – albeit as subjective snapshots – that the advertising display windows of commerce co-author the design of the streets.

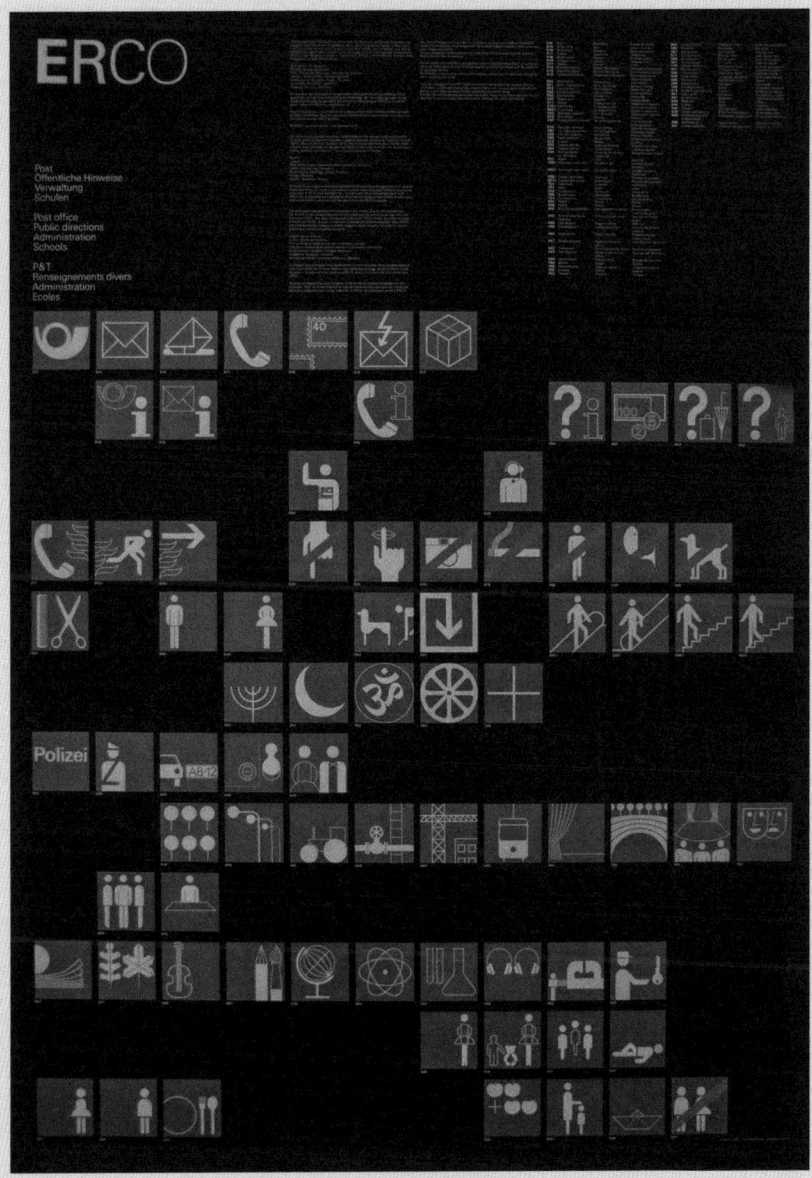

1

Über Piktogramme: Goldstandard und kulturelle Zeichen

Piktogramme prägen unseren Alltag heute ganz selbstverständlich, indem sie uns z. B. an Flughäfen oder Bahnhöfen den Weg zur nächsten Toilette im nicht-privaten Raum weisen. Doch geben Piktogramme auch Verhaltensweisen vor. Was muss ein Piktogramm dafür »können«? Es ist ein visuelles Zeichen, grafisch stark zum Symbol reduziert, welches in der Regel ohne Sprache, daher z. B. auch interkulturell und auf Fernwirkung hin funktioniert. Anders als ein Markenzeichen, das als ein singuläres Symbol für ein Produkt bzw. eine Firma steht, sind Piktogramme Teil eines einheitlichen, visuellen Kommunikationssystems, das strikten Gestaltungsregeln folgt. In manchen Ländern, insbesondere solchen mit einem hohen Anteil an Analphabet*innen, kommen auch bei Wahlen Piktogramme zum Einsatz: Menschen, die nicht oder wenig lesen und schreiben können, soll damit der Zugang zu Informationen und eine Beteiligung ermöglicht werden. Von den weltweit 780 Millionen Analphabet*innen sind laut Bundeszentrale für politische Bildung fast zwei Drittel Frauen.[1] Nehmen diese wegen fehlender Bildungschancen nicht an Wahlen teil, dürfte klar sein, dass sich das gesamtgesellschaftlich auswirkt. Ganz eigene Piktogramm-Systeme kommen auch für Sportevents zum Einsatz, wofür als Beispiel immer wieder die Gestaltung des Erscheinungsbildes für die Olympischen Spiele 1972 in München durch Otl Aicher und sein Team angeführt wird. In der Weiterentwicklung für und mit der Firma ERCO eröffnet sich ein ganzes Aicher'sches Piktogramm-Universum, auf das noch heute und weltweit vielfach zurückgegriffen wird.

Gerade diese reduzierten Zeichen sind auch ein Zeugnis und Spiegel menschlicher Kultur. Betrachtet man die auf den ERCO-Plakaten thematisch zusammengefassten Piktogramme zu öffentlichen Hinweisen, gibt es einige, die schnell erkannt werden, und andere, die weniger geläufig sind. Woran liegt das? Zwei Beispiele: Das Posthorn als Piktogramm (s. Abb. 1) ist in Deutschland nicht zuletzt deshalb geläufig, weil es auch von der Deutschen Post AG verwandt wird. Dabei ist dies nicht mehr zeitgemäß bzw. entspricht längst nicht mehr dem Postwesen, hat sich aber als Symbol etabliert und ist zeitgleich Beleg von etwas Vergangenem. Zwar ist das Posthorn auch in anderen Ländern geläufig, jedoch keineswegs universell, sondern vor allem ein Zeichen und Teil westlicher Kultur. Ein anderes Piktogramm im Bereich »Geschäfte, Branchen, Gewerbe« stellt einen entblößten Frauentorso dar (s. Abb. 2). Hierzu mögen eventuell Assoziationen entstehen, geläufig ist das Piktogramm dagegen eher nicht – zugleich der Grund dafür, warum wir es nicht genauso schnell einordnen können wie das Posthorn. Damit ein Piktogramm eben ohne Sprache funktioniert, muss es auch Eingang in unsere Zeichenwelt gefunden haben. Die Legende klärt auf: Das Piktogramm steht für »Sex Shop«. Sogleich eröffnet sich eine weitere Deutungsebene. Dass der nackte Frauentorso als stellvertretendes Zeichen gewählt wurde, unabhängig davon, ob wir es in

On Pictograms: Gold Standard and Cultural Symbol

Today, pictograms are a natural part of our day-to-day lives, guiding us on our way to the next public toilet, for instance, in airports or train stations. But pictograms prescribe behavioural patterns as well. What must a pictogram be able to »do«? It is a visual sign, its graphics strongly reduced into a symbol, which generally has to work without language and thus also interculturally and with a long-distance effect. Unlike a trademark, a singular symbol that stands for a product or company, pictograms are part of a unified visual communication system that follows strict design rules. In some countries, especially those with a high percentage of illiterate people, pictograms are also used in elections: People with insufficient or no reading and writing skills should have access to information and be able to participate. According to the German Federal Agency for Civic Education, amongst the worldwide 780 million illiterate people, almost two-thirds are women.[1] When this group does not participate in the elections due to lacking educational opportunities, it is clear that this has an effect on society as a whole. Standalone pictogram systems are also used for sport events. The design of the visual appearance of the 1972 Olympic Games in Munich by Otl Aicher and his team is often cited in this regard. The further development phase for and with the company ERCO led to a complete Aicherian universe, which is still relied on today around the world.

Precisely these reduced symbols serve as a testimony and reflection of human culture. Taking a look at the thematically grouped pictograms for public notices on the ERCO posters, one discovers that some are easy to recognise and others are less common. Why is that? Two examples: The post horn pictogram (fig. 1) is common in Germany because it is also used by the Deutsche Post AG postal service corporation. Even though it is no longer an up-to-date representation of the postal system, it is widely recognised as a symbol, and at the same time it is a testament to something past. Indeed, the post horn is also common in other countries, yet in no case universal – above all, it is a symbol and a part of Western culture. In the section »Shops and Markets« another pictogram depicts a naked female torso (fig. 2). It might provoke certain associations, but in contrast this pictogram is not so familiar – the reason why we cannot categorise it so quickly as we can with the post horn. For a pictogram to work without language, it has to have entered into our world of symbols. The legend reads: The pictogram stands for »sex shop«. This immediately leads to another level of interpretation. The fact that a naked female torso was chosen as a representative symbol, regardless if we can categorise its function, reflects a cultural viewpoint – one in which the object of desire, the commodity of the erotic business, is the female body. As a continuation of this heteronormative viewpoint, the assumption can also be made

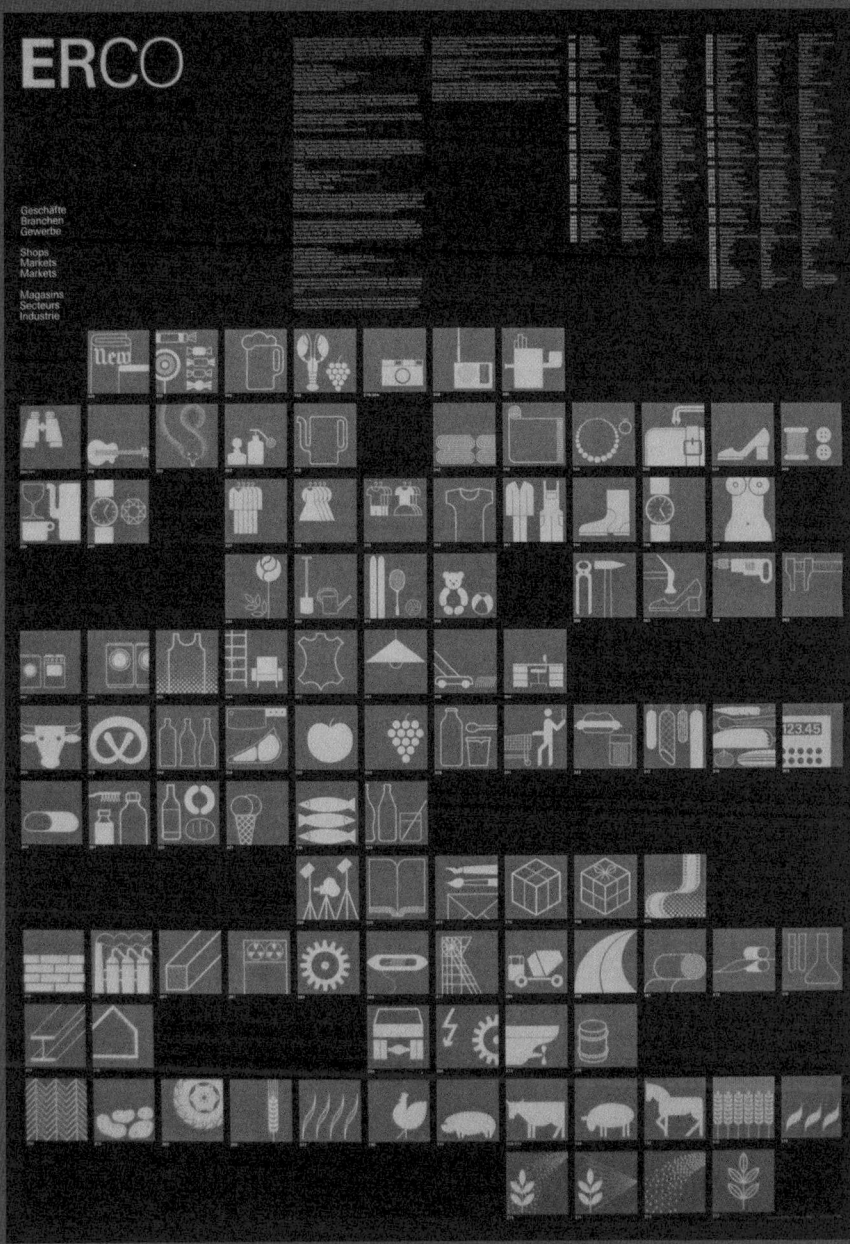

1–2 **Piktogrammsystem** / *Pictogram system*
ERCO / DE ab / *from* 1976 / Plakate: Post,
Öffentliche Hinweise, Verwaltung, Schulen;
Geschäfte, Branchen, Gewerbe / *Posters:
Post office, Public directions, Administration,
Schools; Shops and Markets* / Otl Aicher
/ Sign. Ai.G.1404, Ai.G.1405 / HfG-Archiv /
Museum Ulm

seiner Funktion einordnen können, spiegelt eine kulturelle Sichtweise wider – eine, in der das Objekt der Begierde, die Ware des Erotikgeschäftes, der weibliche Körper ist. Mutmaßlich kann als Weiterführung der heteronormativen Sichtweise auch die Vorstellung angeschlossen werden, dass zugleich die Unterstellung eingeflossen ist, dass diejenigen männlich sind. Somit lässt das Piktogramm begründete Vermutungen zu, die aber vor allem oder gar nur deshalb möglich sind, weil das Piktogramm keinen Eingang in unser alltägliches Zeichenrepertoire gefunden hat. Recherchen in den Akten des Gestaltungsbüros von Otl Aicher haben Aufschluss darüber gegeben, dass das Piktogramm 1975 ergänzt wurde.[2] Dies wirkt besonders erhellend vor dem Hintergrund, dass die ersten Sexshops in der BRD Anfang der 1960er Jahre von Beate Uhse gegründet wurden – damals unter dem klangvollen Namen »Fachgeschäft für Ehehygiene«. Ein Beginn der sexuellen Liberalisierung, die mit den Umwälzungen der »68er Generation« weiter voranschreitet und Mitte der 1970er Jahre als abgeschlossen gilt.[3] Genauso, wie das von Aicher geschaffene Zeichensystem stets durch Aktualisierung erweitert wurde und wird, wenn es um neue Entwicklungen geht – beispielsweise Aerobic in den 1980er Jahren oder zuletzt Symbole für Laptop und WLAN 2016 – ist das Piktogramm »Sex Shop« ein Zeichen seiner Zeit, das, so mag man fast froh sein, uns nicht bekannt ist, aber gesellschaftliche Entwicklung auf seine Art bezeugt.

[1] Laut Angaben der Bundeszentrale für politische Bildung gibt es »[w]eltweit [...] etwa 780 Millionen Analphabeten, fast zwei Drittel sind Frauen. Die meisten von ihnen leben in Asien, Afrika und Südamerika. Und in Deutschland sind es etwa 7,5 Millionen Menschen, die auch nach der Schule nur wenig oder gar nicht lesen oder schreiben können.« Zitiert nach: Gerd Schneider / Christiane Toyka-Seid: Das junge Politik-Lexikon von www.hanisauland.de, Bonn: Bundeszentrale für politische Bildung 2019, abrufbar unter: http://www.bpb.de/nachschlagen/lexika/das-junge-politik-lexikon/160810/analphabet, zul. abgerufen am 05.10.2019.
[2] AiAZ. 1027 gibt eine Übersicht zu der Entstehung der Piktogramme nach Jahren. Aus den Akten geht nicht hervor, wer das Piktogramm entworfen hat, jedenfalls wurde es aber in die Übersicht »Branchen und Gewerbe« aufgenommen, wie sowohl die Übersicht als auch die Plakate belegen.
[3] Vgl. hierfür u.a. Sarnow, Melanie. 2013. Sex im Alltag – Die Entwicklung des Umgangs mit Sexualität seit den 1960er Jahren in Deutschland und den USA, S. 38; Pascal Eitler, »Das Stripteaselokal«. In Orte der Moderne – Erfahrungswelten des 19. und 20. Jahrhunderts, hrsg. v. Alexa Geisthövel und Habbo Knoch, S. 248–253.

that the intended readers of the sign are likely men. Hence, the pictogram triggers justified assumptions, which are primarily or only possible because the pictogram doesn't have a place in our everyday repertoire of symbols. Research in the archives of Otl Aicher's design office provided information that the pictogram was enhanced in 1975.[2] This is particularly telling given the fact that the first sex shops in West Germany were founded at the beginning of the 1960s by Beate Uhse – at that time under the illustrious name »specialty shop for marriage hygiene«. A beginning of the sexual liberation that advanced with the revolutions of the »68 generation« and was considered to be over by the mid-1970s.[3] Just like how Aicher's sign system was and is still being extended with updates whenever there were new developments – for example, aerobics in the 1980s or recent symbols for laptop and WLAN in 2016 – the »sex shop« pictogram is a sign of its time, which, and we can almost be happy, we are not familiar with, yet it attests to developments in society in its own way.

[1] *Information provided by the German Federal Agency for Civic Education states that there are approximately 780 million illiterate people worldwide, almost two-thirds are women. The majority of them live in Asia, Africa, and South America. And in Germany there are approximately 7.5 million people with insufficient or no reading and writing skills. Cf. Gerd Schneider and Christiane Toyka-Seid, »Das junge Politik-Lexikon von www.hanisauland.de,« Bonn: German Federal Agency for Civic Education, 2019, http://www.bpb.de/nachschlagen/lexika/das-junge-politik-lexikon/160810/analphabet.*
[2] *AiAZ. 1027 provides an overview of the chronological development of the pictograms. From the files it is unclear who designed the pictogram, in any case it was included in the section »Shops and Markets« as the list and the posters evidence.*
[3] *Cf. Melanie Sarnow, Sex im Alltag – Die Entwicklung des Umgangs mit Sexualität seit den 1960er Jahren in Deutschland und den USA (Hamburg: Bachelor + Master Publishing, 2013), p. 38; Pascal Eitler, »Das Stripteaselokal,« in Orte der Moderne – Erfahrungswelten des 19. und 20. Jahrhunderts, edited by Alexa Geisthövel and Habbo Knoch (Frankfurt a.M.: Campus, 2005), 248–253.*

3 **»Was ist Ihr Ding?«** / *»What's your thing?«* / DE 2019 / Von Ausstellungsbesucher*innen mit Aicher-Piktogrammen bestempelte Postkarten / *Postcards stamped with Aicher pictograms by exhibition visitors* / Stempelstation realisiert mit freundlicher Unterstützung von: / *Stamping station created with the kind support of:* www.otl-aicher-piktogramme.de

»Was ist Ihr Ding?« In der Ulmer Ausstellung konnten wir mit freundlicher Unterstützung von www.otl-aicher-piktogramme.de (attoma Berlin GmbH) nicht nur die thematischen Bereiche durch entsprechende Piktogramme gliedern, sondern auch eine Station realisieren, an der die Besucher*innen große Freude hatten: Unter der Frage »Was ist Ihr Ding?« durften Besucher*innen nicht andere, aber dafür Postkarten nach Herzenslust »abstempeln« und direkt zum Versand aus der Ausstellung in den Briefkasten einwerfen. Die Figur, die wie alle Stempel aus der Piktogramm-Welt des Aicher'schen Systems stammen, hat eine leichte Änderung erfahren. Sie ist eine Verschmelzung aus dem Piktogramm »Mann« und »Frau« und wirft zugleich die Frage auf, die auch immer wieder z. B. bei der Gestaltung von Straßenschildern mit figürlicher Abbildung diskutiert wird: Wie kann eine Figur aussehen, die möglichst alle repräsentiert? Bezüglich des Geschlechts ist die Einschreibung der weiblichen Figur mit Rock so stark gegenüber der männlich gelesenen Variante, die auch diejenige ist, die als »neutral« geltend die Norm repräsentiert – was zugleich Kern der Kritik ist. Haben sich Zeichen einmal in kulturelle Systeme mit einer Lesart eingeschrieben, ist es, ähnlich wie bei Farben, schwer diese anders zu besetzen.

»What's your thing?« With the kind support of www.otl-aicher-piktogramme.de (attoma Berlin GmbH), we could not only organise the thematic areas of the exhibition with corresponding pictograms, but also realise a station that visitors had a lot of fun with: Under the banner »What's your thing?« as opposed to labelling others, visitors could stamp postcards to their heart's desire and put them directly into the post box to be sent out into the world. The figure on the postcard, which originated from the pictogram world of Aicher's system like all of the stamps, underwent a slight modification. The figure is a fusion of the »man« and »woman« pictograms and as such raises a question that is discussed time and again, for example, in the design of street signs with depictions of persons: How should a figure look like so that it represents as many people as possible? With regard to gender, the ascription of the female figure in a dress is so strong in contrast to the reading of the male variant, which is also the one that is considered »neutral« for representing the norm – and that is also at the core of the critique. Once signs have entered into a cultural system with a certain reading, like colours, it is difficult to assign a different meaning to them.

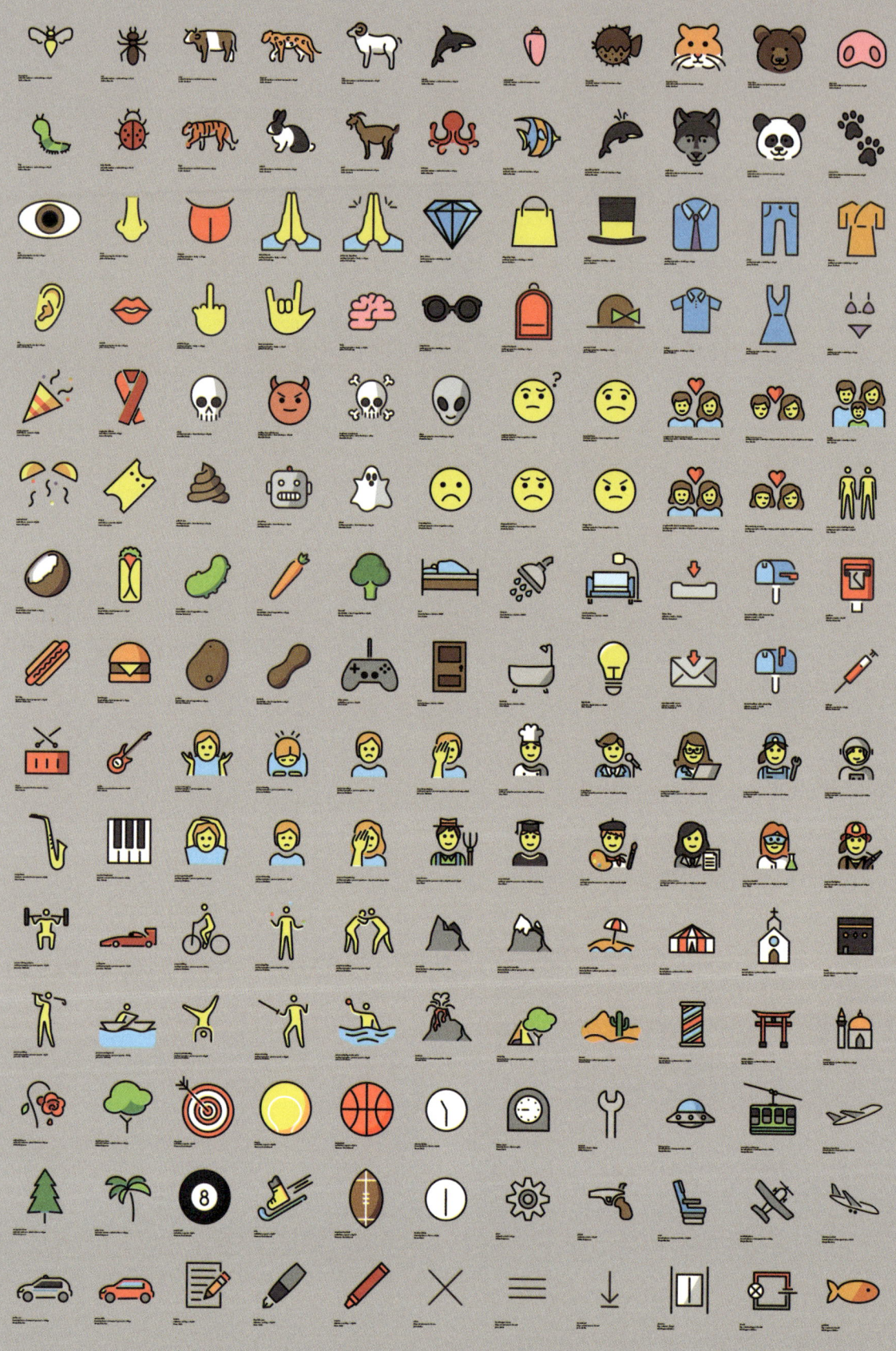

OpenMoji – Emojis für alle! Als Erweiterung des öffentlichen Raums kann der digitale inzwischen zweifelsfrei gelten. Dass die Kommunikation über diesen Kanal und die damit im Zusammenhang entstandenen sogenannten Emojis einen großen Stellenwert im Alltag einnehmen, ist nicht nur an der Einführung eines »World Emoji Days« (17. Juli) festzumachen. Doch wieso überlässt die Design-Community es den großen und etablierten Tech-Firmen wie Google, Apple und Co., diese zu gestalten? Das haben sich die Dozenten Daniel Utz und Benedikt Groß gefragt und an der Hochschule für Gestaltung Schwäbisch Gmünd im Wintersemester 2017/18 das Projekt »OpenMoji« mit Studierenden durchgeführt. Wie bei herkömmlichen Piktogrammen gilt es hierbei nicht nur Zeichen, sondern auch zugehörige Gestaltungsrichtlinien für ein stringentes System zu entwickeln. Ziel des Projekts war die Konzeption, Gestaltung und Veröffentlichung einer freien Icon Library – das Ergebnis »OpenMoji.org« ist das erste open-source und unabhängige Emoji-System. Die Datenbank zählt heute weit über 3.000 Emojis verschiedenster Kategorien. Während einzelne Studierende sich im Rahmen des Projekts mit Möglichkeiten der Diversifizierung von Emojis beschäftigten, veröffentlichten Apple und Google 2019 umfangreiche, neue Sets, die erstmals für die volle Bandbreite der menschenähnlichen Emojis nicht-binäre bzw. »geschlechtsneutrale« Versionen einschließen. Darstellungen, beispielsweise von Menschen mit Prothesen oder Rollstuhl sowie die Optionen, unterschiedliche Hautfarben oder diverse sexuelle Orientierungen auszuwählen, gehören inzwischen zu den Unicode-Sets. Besondere Neuerungen für 2020 (Emojipedia 13.0) sind u. a. das Transgender-Symbol und die Transgender-Flagge sowie Personen verschiedenen Geschlechts, die einen Säugling füttern.

OpenMoji – Emojis for all! Without doubt, the digital realm can nowadays be understood as an extension of public space. That digital communication and the so-called emojis developed for this purpose play an important role in our everyday can latest be seen in the declaration of »World Emoji Day« (July 17). But why has the design community left it to the big, established tech companies like Google, Apple, and co. to design them? That's what teachers Daniel Utz and Benedikt Groß at Schwäbisch Gmünd University of Design asked, when they initiated the project »OpenMoji« with students in the 2017/18 winter semester. As with conventional pictograms, it is not only about developing signs but also the corresponding design guidelines for a stringent system. The objective of the project was to conceive, design, and publish a free icon library – the result »OpenMoji.org« is the first open source, independent emoji system. Today, the databank comprises more than 3000 emojis in a diverse array of categories. While individual students explored ways to diversify emojis within the project, Apple and Google released extensive new sets in 2019, including non-binary or »gender-neutral« versions for the full range of human-like emojis for the first time. Representations for example of people with prostheses or wheelchairs and options of different skin colors or as well as various sexual orientations are today part of the Unicode sets. Latest releases for the 2020 emoji list (Emojipedia 13.0) include i.e. the Transgender Symbol and Flag as well as binary and non-binary bottle-feeding persons.

OpenMoji / DE 2017/18 / Open-Source Icon Library openmoji.org / Projektentwicklung: / *Project development:* Daniel Utz, Benedikt Groß / Abt. Interaktions- und Kommunikationsgestaltung / *Dept. Interaction and Communication Design* / HfG Schwäbisch Gmünd / Studierende: / *Students:* Sofie Ascherl, Jose Avila, Selina Bauder, Ronja Bäurlen, Vanessa Boutzikoudi, Rana Cakir, Baris Camli, Julian Grüneberg, Laura Humpfer, Emiliy Jäger, Hilda Kalyoncu, Kai Magnus Müller, Jonas Roßner, Marius Schnabel, Lisa Schulz, Sina Schulz, Mariella Steeb, Lisa Thiel, Miriam Vollmeier, Kai Wanschura, Martin Wehl, Johanna Wellnitz

Lounge-Möbel ⁄ DE 2014 ⁄ 2015 ⁄ Sitzelemente für den öffentlichen Raum ⁄ *Seating elements for public space* ⁄ Bingyan Liu ⁄ Masterarbeit, Abt. Produktdesign an der HBK Saar betreut von ⁄ *Master's thesis in product design at HBK Saar supervised by* ⁄ Prof. A. Brandolini und Prof. R. Sachsse

Lounge-Möbel Die Produktdesignerin Bingyan Liu beschäftigte sich in ihrer Masterarbeit an der Hochschule der Bildenden Künste Saar mit Geschlecht und Gestaltung. Dafür analysierte sie Prinzipien gendersensiblen Designs, um sie auf ein zu kreierendes Produkt zu übertragen. Entstanden ist eine Serie von geometrischen Lounge-Möbeln, die als unterschiedliche Kombinationen in Wartezimmern, Foyers und anderen öffentlichen Räumen stehen können. Die Serie besteht aus insgesamt sechs Sitzelementen sowie einem Beistelltisch, der als Zwischenelement fungieren kann.

Lounge Furniture Bingyan Liu addressed gender and design in her master's thesis at HBKsaar. She analysed the principles of gender-sensitive design in order to arrive at a corresponding product design. The result was a series of geometrical lounge elements, which can be arranged in various combinations to furnish waiting rooms, foyers, and other public spaces. The series consists of six different seating elements and a table that serves as a connecting element.

Stillen in der Öffentlichkeit? Mit »heer« hat das Prager Designteam 52hours eine Bank entworfen, die schon durch ihren doppelsinnigen Namen (bestehend aus »her«, zu Deutsch: »ihr«, und »here«, zu Deutsch: »hier«) andeutet, eine Antwort zu geben. Die raumgreifende Bank macht das Thema des Stillens im öffentlichen Raum an sich und damit ein noch immer gesellschaftliches Tabu sichtbar – es wird buchstäblich in die Öffentlichkeit getragen. Anlass für diesen bereits zweifach ausgezeichneten Entwurf war die Erkenntnis von Ivana Preiss und Filip Vasić, dass Mütter keine adäquaten, sondern oft unhygienische und isolierende Orte vorfinden, wenn sie ihr Baby unterwegs stillen möchten. »heer« soll laut Angaben des Studios ein kleiner Ort der Ruhe inmitten der geschäftigen Städtelandschaft sein – nicht ausschließlich zum Stillen, sondern auch zum Erholen. Der Sitz ermöglicht ein Wippen und Schaukeln und lässt sich rotieren. Dadurch und dank der halbhohen, nicht geschlossenen Flügel wird die Nutzerin nicht völlig isoliert, kann sich aber auch wegdrehen. Design wie dieses ist weit mehr als der Versuch, den Alltag zu verändern: Es erlaubt, gesellschaftliche Debatten nicht bloß abstrakt zu führen, sondern ist Diskussionsanlass und Lösungsvorschlag zugleich. Auf einer digitalen Karte über die Webseite inviteheer.com können Städte markiert werden, um den Stillbank-Prototypen in die eigene Stadt einzuladen. Denn was wäre eine solche Bank für den öffentlichen Raum, wenn sie sich nicht im Alltag beweisen sollte?

Breastfeeding in public? The Prague-based design team 52hours has designed a bench, whose ambiguous name »heer« (a combination of »her« and »here«) already suggests that there is an answer. The capacious bench design draws attention to the topic of breastfeeding in public, which is still a social taboo – and literally takes it to the streets. The design, which has already won two awards, was triggered by Ivana Preiss and Filip Vasić's realisation that there are no adequate provisions for mothers who want to nurture their babies when they are on the go, rather they have to resort to often unhygienic, isolated places. According to the designers, »heer« should offer a small oasis of peace in the hectic urban surroundings – and not just to breastfeed, also to relax. The seat rocks, swings, and can rotate. Thanks to half-height, semi-enclosed wings, the user is not totally isolated, but also has the option to turn away. Designs like these are far more than an attempt to change daily life: They turn abstract social debates into concrete discussions and propose solutions. On a digital map on the website inviteheer.com cities can be marked to invite a breastfeeding bench prototype. For what would such a bench be if it is not put to the test in public space?

heer / CZ 2018 / Prototyp einer Stillbank für den öffentlichen Raum / *Prototype of a breastfeeding bench for public spaces* / Design Studio 52hours, Ivana Preiss, Filip Vasić, Nikola Knežević

»Gender – Space – Architecture« Die PUTTE stellte fotografische Arbeiten von Juliane Peil aus, die Perspektiven auf die Beziehungen zwischen Gender und öffentlichem Raum wiedergeben. Auf ihren Streifzügen durch die urbanen Räume der »Zweilandstadt« Ulm ∕ Neu-Ulm erkundete Juliane Peil u. a. Darstellungen stereotyper Rollenbilder, die uns im Alltag begegnen.

    Gleichzeitig setzte sie sich mit der Gestaltung des Stadtbildes auseinander und fragte darüber implizit, inwieweit damit das Verhalten und Wohlbefinden aller Bewohner*innen beeinflusst wird – bewusst oder unterbewusst, positiv oder negativ. Wer eignet sich öffentlichen Raum wie an? Wie wird er von uns mitgestaltet?

    »Gender – Space – Architecture« erweiterte als Schaufenster im städtischen Raum die Ausstellung »Nicht mein Ding – Gender im Design« und war damit Teil einer erstmaligen Kooperation der PUTTE (Neu-Ulm) und dem HfG-Archiv (Ulm) über die natürliche Landesgrenze der Donau zwischen Baden-Württemberg und Bayern hinweg.

Gender – Space – Architecture ∕ DE 2019 ∕ Ausstellung mit Fotografien von ∕ *Exhibition with photographs by* Juliane Peil ∕ PUTTE, Neu-Ulm ∕ Leitung: ∕ *Head:* Axel Städter ∕ Laufzeit: ∕ *Duration:* 13.04. – 05.05.2019

»Gender – Space – Architecture« PUTTE presented an exhibition of the photographic works of Juliane Peil, which capture perspectives on the relationships between gender and public space. On her forays through the urban spaces of the twin city Ulm/Neu-Ulm, Juliane Peil investigated representations of stereotypical gender roles, which we are confronted with on a daily basis.

Parallel, she examined the design of the cityscape and posed implicit questions about the extent to which the behaviour and well-being of all inhabitants are being influenced – consciously or subconsciously, positively or negatively. Who appropriates public space and how? How do we participate in its design?

»Gender – Space – Architecture« expanded the exhibition »Not My Thing – Gender in Design« as a display window in urban space and thus formed a part of the first collaboration between PUTTE (Neu-Ulm) and the HfG-Archiv (Ulm), which transcended the natural state border, the Danube river, between Baden-Württemberg and Bavaria.

Machtsymbol Geld: das Projekt »Womoney«
Münzen und Banknoten als Machtsymbol zu modifizieren, ist die Intention des Projekts »Womoney«. Einflussreiche Frauen aus Geschichte und Gegenwart ersetzen die männlichen Präsidenten, deren Konterfei ansonsten auf der US-Währung »Dollar« prangt – eine der mächtigsten Währungen auf dem globalen Markt. Alicia Shao, Paul Guddat und Matthias Grund eröffnen so eine neue Perspektive auf das männlich konnotierte Machtsymbol.

Power Symbol Money: The »Womoney« Project
The intention of the project »Womoney« was to modify the symbolic power of US American coins and banknotes. Influential women in history and from the present day replace the male presidents, whose likeness is otherwise flaunted on the US dollar – one of the most powerful currencies on the global market. Alicia Shao, Paul Guddat, and Matthias Grund present a new perspective on the male connoted power symbol.

Womoney / DE 2015 / Projekt bestehend aus Banknoten und Münzen mit weiblichen Porträts / *Project consisting of banknotes and coins with female portraits* / Paul Guddat, Matthias Grund, Alicia Shao

Von links nach rechts / *left to right:* **50 Dollar:** Facebook Co-Geschäftsführerin / *chief operating officer (COO)* Sheryl Sandberg (statt / *replacing* Ulysses S. Grant, 18. Präsident der Vereinigten Staaten / *18th President of the United States*) / **10 Dollar:** Talkshow-Moderatorin und Unternehmerin / *Talk show host and entrepreneur* Oprah Winfrey (statt / *replacing* Alexander Hamilton, Gründervater der Vereinigten Staaten / *Founding Father of the United States*) / **1 Dollar:** Zweifache Nobelpreisträgerin / *Two-time Nobel Prize winner* Marie Curie (statt / *replacing* George Washington, erster Präsident der Vereinigten Staaten / *1st President of the United States*) / **100 Dollar:** Deutsche Bundeskanzlerin / *German Chancellor* Angela Merkel (statt / *replacing* Benjamin Franklin, Gründervater der Vereinigten Staaten / *Founding Father of the United States*) / **5 Dollar:** Erste DC Comic Superheldin / *First DC super heroine* Wonder Woman (statt / *replacing* Abraham Lincoln, 16. Präsident der Vereinigten Staaten / *16th President of the United States*)

Ein Hijab für den Leistungssport? Der Nike Pro Hijab wird nach dem Produktlaunch im Jahr 2017 als eine Innovation gefeiert – wenngleich nicht völlig kritiklos, da Sport-Hijabs bereits zuvor entwickelt worden waren, die nicht dieselbe öffentliche Aufmerksamkeit generierten und nun, so die Befürchtung, vom Global Player Nike verdrängt würden. Für die große Resonanz ist die Vermarktung durch einen derart populären Hersteller ein erheblicher Faktor. Nike initiierte zu diesem Zweck eine Kampagne mit erfolgreichen muslimischen Athletinnen, wie der Boxerin Zeina Nassar, Deutsche Meisterin im Federgewicht (2018). Die Berlinerin erkämpfte 2013 gemeinsam mit ihrer damaligen Trainerin Linos Bitterling, der ersten Ringrichterin Deutschlands, bei dem Deutschen Boxsport-Verband die Erlaubnis, mit Hijab und Ganzkörperbekleidung in den Boxring steigen zu dürfen. Nassars Nominierung des Deutschen Boxsport-Verbands für die U22 Europameisterschaften in Russland lehnte man hingegen ab, da die Verbotsregel auf internationaler Ebene weiter bis Februar 2019 galt. Mittlerweile ist die Teilnahme an internationalen Meisterschaften und den Olympischen Spielen möglich geworden – und damit das nächste Ziel der jungen Boxsportlerin. Es zeigt sich, dass Zeina Nassar Neuland in einer Männerdomäne erkämpft hat und obendrein für ihre Glaubensfreiheit als Muslimin einsteht. Der Hijab war und ist dabei ein feministisch, politisch und religiös-kulturell umstrittenes, dingliches Zeichen. Die Marke Nike agiert als Botschafterin dieser neuesten Entwicklungen und beweist zugleich als Konzern, wie gesellschaftliche Trends kombiniert mit wirtschaftlichem Profit als Markt erschlossen werden können.

A Hijab for Competitive Sports? Following the product launch in 2017, the Nike »Pro Hijab« was celebrated as an innovation – albeit not without critique: Sport hijabs have already been developed previously, which didn't attract the same public attention, and there was fear of being driven out by global player Nike. The marketing capacities of such a popular manufacturer were a significant factor behind the enormous response. To this end, Nike initiated a campaign with successful Muslim female athletes, like Zeina Nassar, the German featherweight boxing champion (2018). In 2013 the Berlin-based boxer and her trainer at the time Linos Bitterling, the first female ring referee in Germany, fought with the German Boxing Federation for permission to step into the ring wearing a hijab and full-body clothing. However, the German Boxing Federation's nomination of Nassar for the U-22 European Boxing Championships in Russia was rejected as the prohibition rule was still in force on an international level until February 2019. In the meanwhile, participation in international championships and the Olympic Games is possible – and thus the next goal of the young athlete. It is clear to see that Zeina Nassar has achieved new grounds in a domain dominated by men and, for good measure, also stands up for her freedom of religion as a Muslima. The hijab was and is a material symbol contested in feminist, political, and religious-cultural circles. The brand Nike acts as an ambassador of these latest developments and demonstrates, at the same time, how a corporation can combine societal trends and economic profit into a market.

Nike Pro Hijab / US 2017 / Werbekampagne: / *Advertising campaign:* Zeina Nassar Running / Nike

1

Zeig' mir wie du isst und ich sag' dir wer du bist.
Was sagt es über uns aus, wie wir essen und womit?
Abgesehen davon, dass es auf der Welt verschiedene
Tischkulturen gibt, ist das Essen eine Tätigkeit, bei
der wir soziale, insbesondere aber auch Geschlechter-
rollen ausüben.

Inspiriert vom täglichen Mittagessen in der
HfG-Mensa und aus einer feministisch-kritischen
Perspektive studierte Olivia Daigneault Deschênes
Fotobestände, Diplomarbeiten und andere Archivalien
der ehemaligen HfG-Ulm in Bezug auf die Themen
Sitzen und Besteck-Design, sowie die Ausstattung
und Architektur der Mensa (entworfen von Max Bill).
Die Ergebnisse ihrer Untersuchungen sind Studien,
Performances, Entwürfe und Modelle einer angewand-
ten Designforschung, keine funktionalen Gestaltungs-
vorschläge. In Bezug auf geschlechtsspezifisches
Rollenverhalten legen sie offen, spitzen zu, bis hin zu
einem Karikieren stereotyper Erwartungshaltungen.

Die Designerin Olivia Daigneault Deschênes
(Vancouver ⁄ Montreal) war die erste Stipendiatin
des 2018 initiierten Designer in Residence-
Programms im HfG-Archiv. Von einer Jury aus einer
Vielfalt inter-⁄nationaler Bewerber*innen ausge-
wählt, arbeitete sie für drei Monate unter dem Fokus
»Gender Design« mit den Beständen des Archivs
der ehemaligen HfG Ulm. Durch freundliche Unter-
stützung der Stiftung Hochschule für Gestaltung
HfG Ulm bewohnte sie auf dem Campus ein Apparte-
ment in der Nähe der sogenannten Dozentenhäuser.
Themenspezifisches Jurymitglied dieser von Katharina
Kurz neu konzipierten Residence-Reihe war Uta
Brandes, die die erste Professur für Gender Design
an der Köln International School of Design (KISD)
von 1995 bis 2015 innehatte.

1 Zeig' mir wie du isst und ich sag' dir wer du bist ⁄ *Show me how you eat, I will tell you who you are* ⁄ DE 2018 ⁄ Videostills ⁄ Olivia Daigneault Deschênes ⁄ Sign. DiR 2018.45.02 ⁄ HfG-Archiv ⁄ Museum Ulm

2 Besteck als Binarität, Modell A: Schöpfen; Modell B: Schaufeln, Stochern, Hacken ⁄ *Cutlery as Binary, Model A: Scoop; Model B: Shovel, Poke, Chop* ⁄ DE 2018 ⁄ Olivia Daigneault Deschênes ⁄ Sign. DiR 2018.02, DiR 2018.05-07 ⁄ HfG-Archiv ⁄ Museum Ulm

→ Teilprojekte Subprojects, S. / p. 178

Öffentlicher Raum / Public Space

36 / 37

Show me how you eat, I will tell you who you are. *What does it tell about us, how we eat and with what? Aside from the fact that there are different table cultures all around the world, eating is an activity in which we perform social and especially gender roles.*

Inspired by the daily lunches in the HfG canteen and taking a critical, feminist perspective, Olivia Daigneault Deschênes studied the photographic material, diploma theses, and other archive inventories from the former Ulm School of Design in their references to the topics of sitting and cutlery design, along with the equipment and architecture of the canteen designed by Max Bill. The results of her research are studies, performances, designs, and models of an applied design research, not functional design proposals. In the context of gender-specific role behaviour, they expose and exaggerate to the point of a caricature of stereotypical expectations.

Designer Olivia Daigneault Deschênes (Vancouver/Montreal) was the first scholar in the Designer in Residence programme of the HfG-Archiv, which was initiated in 2018. Selected by a jury from a diverse range of inter/national applicants, she worked for three months with the inventories of the archive of the former Ulm School of Design, focusing on »Gender Design«. With the kind support of the HfG Ulm Foundation, she lived on campus in an apartment nearby the so-called »lecturer houses«. A theme-specific jury member of the new residence series, conceived by Katharina Kurz, was Uta Brandes, the first professor for Gender Design at Köln International School of Design (KISD) from 1995 to 2015.

3 Collage zum Thema Essen, Körper und Bewusstsein basierend auf Fotografien aus dem Archiv / *Collage on Eating, Bodies and Memory based on Photography Findings at the Archive* / DE 2018 / Olivia Daigneault Deschênes / Sign. DiR 2018.54 / HfG-Archiv / Museum Ulm

4 Zusammengeführte Teilprojekte in fragmentarischem Architekturmodell der HfG-Mensa / *Merged Sub-projects in a Fragmentary Architectural Model of the HfG-Canteen* / DE 2018 / Olivia Daigneault Deschênes / Sign. DiR 2018.33 / HfG-Archiv / Museum Ulm

5 Sitzen auf Hockervariante 1 / *Sitting on Stool 1* / DE 2018 / Fotomontage / *Photomontage* / Olivia Daigneault Deschênes / Sign. DiR 2018.29 / HfG-Archiv / Museum Ulm

Spielen und Erziehung
/ *Play and Education*

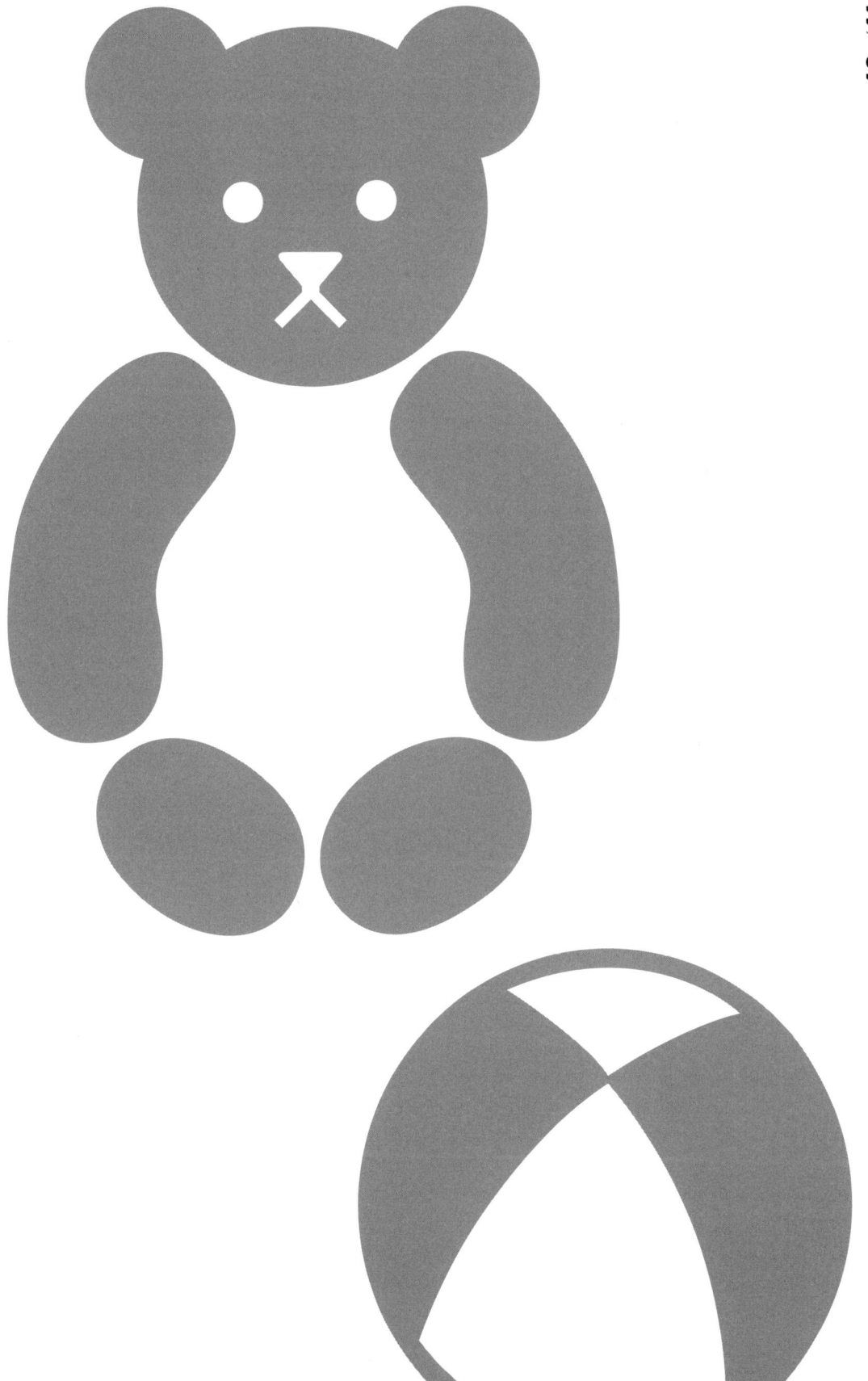

Jungensachen, Mädchenkram? Spielen ist etwas für Jung und Alt. Es vergnügt und vertreibt die Zeit. Beim Spielen können wir etwas lernen. Spielen ist ein wesentlicher Teil der Kindheit – einer Phase, in der Kinder einen eher unvoreingenommenen Blick haben und in der nahezu alles zum Spiel und Spielzeug werden kann. In dieser Zeit werden nicht nur Fähigkeiten wie Konzentration oder Feinmotorik geprägt, sondern auch Verhaltensmuster erkannt und durch Einübung angeeignet – sie geben Sicherheit, werden aber später im Erwachsenenalter kaum mehr hinterfragt.

Puzzles zählen zu den Spielzeugen, mit denen wir Form-, Raum- und Flächenkonstruktion zu verstehen lernen. Ein ähnliches Prinzip gilt für den Tierbaukasten, den der HfG-Student Hans von Klier 1958 entwarf. Andere erlernbare Muster betreffen die Sozialisation, die wir vor allem im Alltag oder durch Rollenspiele kennenlernen. Im Spiel können Muster erprobt, wiederholt und bestätigt werden, wie auch Klischees bzw. Stereotype: Jungen spielen mit Waffen oder Mädchen interessieren sich für die Hausarbeit. Geschlechterrollen im Allgemeinen haben sich seit den 1950er Jahren zwar (vermeintlich) stark gewandelt. Spielzeug, durch das die binären Geschlechter, also männlich und weiblich, auf ihre sozialen Rollen vorbereitet werden, gibt es dennoch heute wie damals. Mehr noch: Gegenwärtig sind blau und pink gegenderte Spielzeugwelten mit der global-kapitalistischen Vermarktungs- und Konsumwelt auf dem Höhepunkt der binären Geschlechtertrennung angekommen. Dass es dabei allzu oft nicht das Spielzeug selbst, sondern die rentable Vermarktungsstrategie ist, die sich wiederum in das Einteilen einer jeden Kaufhausabteilung überträgt, in der Spielzeug für Jungen und Mädchen sich offenbar konträr gegenübersteht, ist so augenfällig wie gleichzeitig unhinterfragt. Nicht selten setzt sie sich im Zuhause fort, wie das »Pink and Blue Project« (seit 2005) der Südkoreanerin JeongMee Yoon eindrücklich abbildet.

Warum all das u. a. seitens der Geschlechterforschung kritisiert wird? Weil es Kinder nicht dazu einlädt, sich auszuprobieren und ihre Identität – zu der zweifelsohne die geschlechtliche gehört – individuell zu entfalten. Es hält vielmehr dazu an, sich in vorgefertigte Rollen einzufügen, sich selbst und andere in Schubladen zu stecken, was unserer vielfältigen Gesellschaft entgegensteht. Ein bemerkenswerter filmischer Beitrag von Hollie McNish und Jake Dypka, »Pink or Blue« (2017), veranschaulicht dies auf poetische, berührende Weise. Um hierzu Aufklärungs- und Beratungsangebote anzubieten, haben sich Vereine gegründet, wie in Deutschland allen voran Pinkstinks Germany e.V., die sich als gemeinnützige Protest- und Bildungsorganisation u. a. für Geschlechtersensibilität und Persönlichkeitsentfaltung einsetzt. Sie formulieren in ihrer Broschüre »Rosa für alle?! Gendersensible Erziehung in der Kindertagesstätte und Zuhause« (2019): »Gegen gegenderte Produkte zu sein, heißt nicht, etwas gegen Prinzessinnen zu haben. Oder Piraten. Oder gegen Pink. Oder Blau. Sondern es heißt, dafür

Boys' things and girly stuff? Play is for young and old alike. It is a fun way to pass the time. People learn through play, and playing is an essential part of childhood – a time when children are still open-minded enough to turn almost anything into a game or a toy. During this phase, not only does a child's concentration improve and fine motor skills develop, but patterns of social behaviour are instilled, too – patterns that provide a secure roadmap to help navigate the world, but are rarely questioned later on in life.

Puzzles help us acquire the concepts of volume, space, and surface area; skills also nurtured by the wooden toy animal kit that Ulm School of Design student Hans von Klier designed in 1958. Other learned behaviours relate to socialisation, which are mainly picked up in everyday life and through role playing. Games allow behavioural patterns, clichés, and stereotypes to be tested, re-enacted, and embedded: boys play with guns, girls are interested in housework. Gender roles have (apparently) changed dramatically since the 1950s, but toys – through which the binary genders, i.e. males and females, are prepared for their respective social roles – have changed very little since then. If anything, they are more gendered than ever before, with today's global capitalist marketing and consumer culture increasingly segregating between pink and blue toy worlds. That this gendering is all too often about the profitability of the marketing strategy, rather than the toys themselves, is as obvious as it is left unquestioned – with the result that girls' toys and boys' toys seem to stand opposite of one another in the aisles of department stores. This segregation often carries over into the home, as Korean artist JeongMee Yoon's »Pink and Blue Project«, begun in 2005, so impressively illustrates.

Why is gender studies, among other disciplines, so critical of all this? Because it deters children from trying things out for themselves and developing their own personal identities – which undoubtedly includes gender. Instead, it encourages children to fit into ready-made roles and to pigeonhole themselves, and others, which is contrary to the diverse society we live in. Hollie McNish and Jake Dypka's remarkable short film Pink or Blue (2017) demonstrates this in a poetic, touching way. Non-profit campaigning and educational organisations such as Pinkstinks, originally founded in the UK and later in Germany, offer advice, advocate for gender sensitivity, and promote personality development. Pinkstinks Germany's brochure »Rosa für alle?! Gendersensible Erziehung in der Kindertagesstätte und Zuhause» [Pink for Everyone?! Gender-Sensitive Education in Nursery Schools and at Home] (2019) states: «To be against gendered products does not mean to be against princesses, or pirates, or the colours pink or blue. What it does mean, however, is that we believe all children should be allowed to play and be anything they want.« In Germany a board of experts for the

zu sein, dass alle Kinder spielen können. Oder alles sein.« Schon in der frühen deutschen Nachkriegsgeschichte entstand ein Gegenpol zu beschriebenen Entwicklungen: 1954 wurde der bis heute existente Arbeitsausschuss »spiel gut Kinderspiel + Spielzeug e.V.« in Ulm gegründet. Im damals genannten »Museum der Stadt Ulm«, heutiges Museum Ulm, zeigte man in der ersten »spiel gut« Ausstellung zertifizierte Spielzeuge, wie das modulare Kinderspielmöbel von Hans Gugelot und gab die Broschüre »Gutes Spielzeug« mit Fotografien von Sigrid von Schweinitz-Maldonado auf Deutsch und Englisch heraus.

evaluation of toys was founded in Ulm as early as 1954, the »spiel gut Kinderspiel + Spielzeug e.V.« [play well, children's play and toy association], which offers a counterpoint to the developments described above. Still today, the organisation awards toys with their distinctive orange-coloured »spiel gut« quality label. In the first »spiel gut« exhibition today's Museum Ulm showed certified toys such as Hans Gugelot's modular children's play furniture and published a catalogue entitled Gutes Spielzeug [Good Toys], in both German and English, with photographs by Sigrid von Schweinitz-Maldonado.

1

The Pink and Blue Project Seit 2005 lichtet die Künstlerin und Fotografin JeongMee Yoon mit ihrer Mittelformatkamera Kinder aus Südkorea und den Vereinigten Staaten in ihren Zimmern ab. Die Inszenierungsstrategie dafür ist alles andere als subtil und schnell erfasst: Inmitten ihres Spielzeugs, ihrer Kleidung, ihrer zahlreichen Besitztümer hocken, liegen, posieren die Kinder allein oder mit Geschwisterkind. Das Ergebnis jedes einzelnen Fotos ist in doppeltem Sinne unheimlich einprägsam. Es sind Momentaufnahmen zweier dichotomer, bizarrer Welten in Pink und Blau, die sich scheinbar gegenüberstehen und doch ähnlich sind – ob in Seoul oder New York City. In diesem Sinne werden nicht nur die Kinder einer Taxonomie von männlichen und weiblichen Stereotypen zugeordnet, sondern ebenso ihre Besitztümer: Bei genauerem Hinsehen erschließt sich neben den codierten Farbwelten, dass in Anteilen auch die Art der Spielzeuge, die in den jeweiligen Zimmern auftauchen, den binären Rollenklischees entsprechen. Ein massiver Spiegel unserer globalen Konsumkultur ist zudem die Masse der Dinge, über die die Kinder teilweise zu »herrschen«, teilweise darin unterzugehen scheinen.

The Pink and Blue Project Since 2005 artist and photographer JeongMee Yoon has photographed children from South Korea and the United States in their bedrooms with a medium format camera. Her approach to the staging of these images is anything but subtle and far from the snapshot: The children pose, crouched or lying, alone or with their siblings, in the middle of their toys, their clothes, their numerous possessions. Each resulting image is eerily memorable in two ways: Whether in Seoul or New York City, the photographs present us with images of two bizarre and dichotomous pink and blue worlds that seem to both oppose and resemble each other. In this sense, it is not only the children who are assigned to a taxonomy of (male and female) gender stereotypes, but also their possessions: Upon closer inspection, it becomes clear that, in addition to the coded colour worlds, the types of toys that appear in the girls' and the boys' rooms also correspond to clichés associated with their respective binary roles. Furthermore, the mass of things over which the children partly »rule« – and almost seem to drown in – is like a huge mirror reflecting our global consumer culture.

1 **The Blue Project** / Sunjae & Seungjae and Their Blue Things / Seoul, KR 2008 / JeongMee Yoon

2 **The Pink Project** / Songmi & Gayoung and Their Pink Things / Seoul, KR 2007 / JeongMee Yoon

3 **The Pink Project I** / Jiwoo and Her Pink Things / Seoul, KR 2007 / JeongMee Yoon

4 **The Pink Project** / Emily and Her Pink Things / New York, US 2005 / JeongMee Yoon

5 **The Blue Project I** / Cole and His Blue Things / New York, US 2006 / JeongMee Yoon

6 **The Blue Project I** / Jake (Jaewook) and His Blue Things / New York, US 2006 / JeongMee Yoon

7 **The Blue Project I** / Jeonghoon and His Blue Things / Gyeonggi-do, KR 2007 / JeongMee Yoon

1 gutes spielzeug – ausstellung im museum der stadt ulm / *Good Toys – Museum of the City of Ulm exhibition* / 28.11.1954 – 09.01.1955 / DE 1954 / Ausstellungsplakat / *Exhibition poster* / HfG Ulm / Abt. Visuelle Kommunikation / *Dept. Visual Communication* / Dozent: *Lecturer:* Otl Aicher / Student: Martin Krampen / Sign. 2.1127 / HfG-Archiv / Museum Ulm

2 Junge mit Teddybär / *Boy with teddy bear* / DE ca. 1954–1955 / Fotografie / *Photography* / Sigrid von Schweinitz-Maldonado / Sign. Schw. 2.082 / HfG-Archiv / Museum Ulm

»spiel gut« – Gutes Spielzeug Der in Ulm 1954 gegründete Arbeitsausschuss »spiel gut e.V.« besteht bis heute und gibt den Ratgeber »Vom Spielzeug und vom Spielen« seit Jahren in stets aktualisierter Auflage heraus. Er empfiehlt zudem durch die Auszeichnung mit seinem orangefarbenen, kreisrunden Siegel von Gutachter*innen befürwortetes und von Kindern getestetes Spielzeug für die Altersklassen 0 bis 14 Jahre. Kriterien sind, neben materiellen Eigenschaften wie Umweltverträglichkeit und Haltbarkeit, die Anregung der Fantasie sowie vielfältige und fortwährende Spielmöglichkeiten. Laut eigenen Angaben sei das Ziel der Gründung, Ideen würden für die Spielzeugherstellung aufgegriffen, eine Illusion gewesen, weshalb man sich darauf besonnen habe, sich mit Ausstellungen, Vorträgen und Interviews direkt an Eltern zu wenden, um die Nachfrage nach gutem Spielzeug zu erhöhen.[1] Im selben Jahr wurde die von Lieselotte Pée kuratierte Wanderausstellung »gutes spielzeug« (1954) im Ulmer Museum gezeigt. Die Plakatgestaltung übernahmen Otl Aicher und Martin Krampen (s. Abb. 1). Aicher gestaltete auch Plakate für die sogenannten »Donnerstagvorträge« der vh ulm, geleitet von Inge Aicher-Scholl (s. Abb. 3–4). Ausgestellt wurde u. a. ein modulares Kinderspielmöbel-System (s. Abb. 5–6). Bestehend aus vier Elementen (offenen Kuben, zwei verschieden großen Brücken und einer Holztafel), bietet es verschiedenste Kombinationsmöglichkeiten, die leicht zusammenstellbar sind. Entworfen hatte es HfG-Dozent Hans Gugelot, der auch den Ulmer Hocker zusammen mit Max Bill und Paul Hildinger gestaltete. Außerdem wurde die erste Broschüre »Gutes Spielzeug. Kleines Handbuch für die richtige Wahl« (1954) vom Arbeitsausschuss publiziert, später auch auf Englisch (s. Abb. 7). Die Gestaltung lag unter der Leitung von Otl Aicher bei der Abteilung Visuelle Kommunikation der HfG Ulm, ebenso wie zeitgleich Ausgaben der Zeitschrift »Lebendige Erziehung« (s. Abb. 8). Sigrid von Schweinitz, die mit ihrem Mann und HfG-Dozent Tomás Maldonado nach Ulm gekommen war, fotografierte für diese Broschüre Kinder beim Spielen in der gleichen hochästhetischen Weise, wie sie auch das Leben rund um die Hochschule für Gestaltung visuell dokumentierte. Nicht nur wegen ihrer Schwarz-Weiß-Ästhetik sind diese zugleich Dokument einer Nachkriegsgesellschaft, die unserer heutigen Konsumkultur entgegensteht (s. Abb. 2; 7). Auch 65 Jahre nach der Gründung bemüht sich der Arbeitsausschuss »spiel gut« mit seiner gemeinnützigen Arbeit um pädagogisch wertvolles und Kinder erfreuendes Spielzeug – ein verlässlicher Fels außerhalb von wirtschaftlichen Interessen der globalisierten Massenkultur.

[1] Vgl. spiel gut e.V., Historie, o.D., https://www.spielgut.de/spielgut_historie.php, zul. abgerufen am 17.11.2019.

»spiel gut« – Good Toys The »spiel gut Arbeitsausschuss Kinderspiel + Spielzeug e.V.« [children's play and toy association] is a German independent association founded in Ulm in 1954. Still in existence today, it awards toys for ages 0 to 14, which have been endorsed by experts and tested by children, with its distinctive orange-coloured circular »spiel gut« [play well] quality label. The organisation recommends these toys in the guide On Toys and Play, which it has been publishing in updated editions for years. Besides the toys' material properties, such as their durability and level of environmentally friendliness, other criteria they are judged on include whether the toys stimulate the imagination or offer a variety of versatile or upgradable ways to play. By their own admission, it proved impossible to fulfil the foundation's original aim of influencing the production stage of toy manufacturing, so they decided to increase the demand for good toys by reaching out to parents directly through exhibitions, talks, and interviews.[1] That same year (1954), the »Good Toys« touring exhibition, curated by Lieselotte Pée, was presented at today's Museum Ulm. The show's poster was designed by Otl Aicher and Martin Krampen (fig. 1). Aicher also designed posters for the so-called »Donnerstagsvorträge« [Thursday Lectures] that took place at Ulm Adult Education Centre (vh ulm) and were led by Inge Aicher-Scholl (fig. 3–4). Items displayed in the exhibition included a modular children's play furniture system (fig. 5–6), designed by HfG lecturer Hans Gugelot (who also designed the Ulmer Hocker [Ulm stool] together with Max Bill and Paul Hildinger). The play furniture system consists of four separate elements – open cubes, two different sized bridges, and a wooden panel – than can be easily put together in countless combinations. 1954 also saw the publication of the »spiel gut« organisation's first brochure entitled Gutes Spielzeug: Kleines Handbuch für die richtige Wahl, which was later also produced in English as Good Toys: A short guide (fig. 7). The brochure's design was overseen by Otl Aicher at HfG Ulm's Visual Communication Department, who, at the time, was also in charge of designing a magazine entitled Lebendige Erziehung [Living Education] (fig. 8). Sigrid von Schweinitz, who had come to Ulm with her husband and HfG lecturer Tomás Maldonado, photographed children playing for this brochure in the same highly aesthetic manner as she documented life around the Ulm School of Design. Besides their black-and-white aesthetic, the photographs document a post-war society so at odds with today's consumer culture (fig. 2; 7). Even some 65 years after the founding of the »spiel gut« non-profit organisation, it remains dedicated to promoting educationally valuable and child-centred toys – a reliable bulwark against the economic interests of globalised mass culture.

[1] *Cf. spiel gut e.V., Historie [History], n.d., https://www.spielgut.de/spielgut_historie.php.*

3

4

3 **Das spielende Kind – Donnerstagvorträge im Dezember** ⁄ *The Playing Child – Thursday Lectures in December* ⁄ DE 1954 ⁄ Plakat ⁄ Poster ⁄ vh ulm ⁄ Entwurf: *Design:* Otl Aicher ⁄ Sign. Ai.G.88 ⁄ HfG-Archiv ⁄ Museum Ulm

4 **Umgang mit Kindern – Vorträge von Dr. Hans Zulliger** ⁄ *Handling Children – Lectures by Dr. Hans Zulliger* ⁄ DE 1955 ⁄ Plakat ⁄ Poster ⁄ vh ulm ⁄ Entwurf: *Design:* Otl Aicher ⁄ Sign. Ai.G.97 ⁄ HfG-Archiv ⁄ Museum Ulm

5

5 **Kinderspiel-Möbel** / *Children's play furniture* / DE 1954 / Ansichten des Spielmöbelsystems von Hans Gugelot / *Photos of Hans Gugelot's play furniture system* / Sign. Ai.F.1517 (03), F-Ki.4.042 / HfG-Archiv / Museum Ulm

6 **Grünzig Kinderspiel-Möbel** / *Grünzig children's play furniture* / DE 1954 / Prospekt zum Spielmöbelsystem von Hans Gugelot / *Brochure for Hans Gugelot's play furniture system* / Herausgabe und Herstellung: *Publisher and manufacturer:* Albin Grünzig und Co. Eystrup / Sign. Ai.Br.607 / HfG-Archiv / Museum Ulm

6

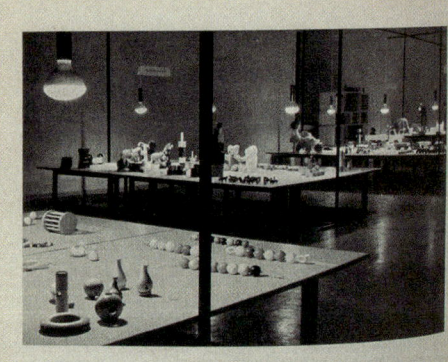

Blick in die Wanderausstellung „Gutes Spielzeug", Museum Ulm, Weihnachten 1954

7 Gutes Spielzeug: Kleines Handbuch für die richtige Wahl / *Good Toys. A short guide* / DE 1954, 1956, 1960 / Handbuch / *Guide book* / Herausgabe: / *Editor:* spiel gut Arbeitsausschuss Gutes Spielzeug e.V. Ulm / Verlag: / *Publisher:* Otto Maier, Ravensburg / Typographie: / *Typography:* HfG Ulm / Entwicklungsgruppe 5 / *Development Group 5* / Sign. HfG Bib. 372.211 Spi, Ai.Br. 600, Ai.Br. 608 / HfG-Archiv / Museum Ulm

8

8 **Lebendige Erziehung** ╱ DE 1954╱55 ╱ Zeitschrift ╱ *Magazine* ╱ Vier Ausgaben der Monatsschrift der Deutschen Gesellschaft für Erziehung ╱ *Four issues of the monthly Deutsche Gesellschaft für Erziehung magazine* ╱ Verlag: ╱ *Publisher:* Urban & Schwarzenberg, München ╱ Umschlag und Typographie: ╱ *Cover design and typography:* HfG Ulm, Otl Aicher, Fritz Querengässer ╱ Sign. Ai.Br.601.01-.04 ╱ HfG-Archiv ╱ Museum Ulm

LEGO gestern und heute Ähnlich wie schon Jahre zuvor Hilary Fisher Page für ihr Unternehmen »Kiddicraft« entwickelte der dänische Tischler Ole Kirk Christiansen 1949 ein Spielsteinsystem – auch bekannt als »LEGO« (dän. leg godt = spiel gut). Die Steine des gleichnamigen und erfolgreichsten Spielwarenherstellers der Welt sind ein Systemprodukt, das sich bis heute altersübergreifend hoher Beliebtheit erfreut und dessen Baustein-Design charakteristisch, ja markenbildend für ein ganzes Spielzeug-Imperium wirkt, das für Fantasie und Kreativität steht. Geht es um die Produktpalette hat sich diese seit Markterscheinen durchaus verändert: Über die Jahre hat das Unternehmen immer wieder Produktlinien oder Zusatzsets entwickelt, erweitert oder auch eingestellt. Interessanterweise ist hierbei zu beobachten, dass diese meist nicht nur eine technische o. ä. geartete Differenzierung der Spielwelt bedeuten – vielmehr geht und ging mit ihr eine Ausrichtung an entweder Jungen oder Mädchen und damit spezifischen Vorstellungen einher. Der Spielwarenhersteller scheint im Laufe der Zeit unentschieden zwischen der ursprünglichen Intention, ein Spielzeug für alle zu vertreiben, und der geschlechterspezifischen Ausrichtung zu wanken. Während in den 1970er Jahren zum ersten Mal mit einer Art Puppenhaus-Set (»LEGO Homemaker« 1972) und einem Schmuckset (»LEGO Scala« 1979) zwei Produktlinien erscheinen, die sich der Art und Werbung nach an Mädchen richteten, kehrte man in den 1980er Jahren zu einer anderen Werbestrategie zurück, die weitaus weniger genderspezifisch daherkam.

Von heutiger Perspektive aus nahm sich die feministische Medienkritikerin und Videobloggerin Anita Sarkeesian der Thematik und einer LEGO-Evolution aus genderkritischer Perspektive an und traf damit offenbar einen Nerv. Ihre zweiteilige Videobesprechung »LEGO & Gender« (2012) wurde zusammen über eine Million Mal angesehen (s. Abb. 3). Ihre Hauptkritik an den noch heute existenten Produktsets der Reihe »LEGO Friends« und »LEGO TECHNIC« ist die völlige Trennung zweier Produkt- und Farbwelten: nämlich »Heartlake City«, wo es nicht mehr um das Konstruieren geht, sondern eine abgerundete Pastellwelt aus Freundinnen und Milchshakes. Gleichzeitig liegt sie fernab von »LEGO City«, der eigentlichen und vergleichsweise düsteren Hauptwelt. Sie richtet sich thematisch und durch die Darstellung stereotyper Spielszenarien, hauptsächlich Kampfsituationen, an Jungen und Väter bzw. Männer – »No Girls Allowed«.

Wieso dieses so gängige Prinzip nicht aufgreifen und via »Gender-Swap« mal umkehren? Was dabei entstehen kann, zeigt ein Ergebnis aus dem kooperativen Forschungsprojekt »Gender Codes im Design« der Hochschule Hannover und der Hochschule für Technik und Wirtschaft Berlin, geleitet von Birgit Weller und Katharina Krämer. Während die Spielzeugverpackung der »LEGO TECHNIC«-Serie (s. Abb. 1) längst keine Überraschung mehr hinsichtlich der grafischen Aufmachung ist, ist der Kniff der fiktiven Marke »OGEL« raffiniert: Während auf den ersten Blick die

LEGO: Past and Present Using a similar concept to the self-locking building bricks Hilary Fisher Page had invented years earlier for his Kiddicraft company, Danish carpenter Ole Kirk Christiansen developed his own version of the bricks in 1949 that he called »LEGO« (from the Danish Leg godt meaning »play well«) – which was to become the most successful toy manufacturer in the world. LEGO bricks remain incredibly popular across all age groups and their building-block design is representative – brand building even – of an entire toy empire that stands for imagination and creativity. But there is no doubt that the product range has evolved since LEGO toys first appeared on the market: Over the years, the company has developed, expanded, or discontinued many product lines and additional sets. Interestingly, these changes have not just involved technical differentiations in the toy world, rather, they have tended to be – and continue to be – about differentiating between boys and girls and, therefore, the gendered images that these new toy ranges project. Over time, the toy manufacturer seems to have swerved indecisively between their original intention to manufacture and sell toys made for all and those that are gender specific. While in the 1970s, two product lines were launched that were, for the first time, specifically aimed at girls, both in terms of its advertising approach and product type – the »LEGO Homemaker« dollhouse set (1972) and the »LEGO Scala« jewellery set (1979) – in the 1980s LEGO reverted to an advertising strategy that was much less gender specific.

Feminist media critic and video blogger Anita Sarkeesian recently tackled the subject of gendered toys and the evolution of LEGO products from a gender-critical perspective – it clearly hit a nerve, since her two-part video Lego & Gender (2012) was viewed over a million times (fig. 3). In the videos she criticises the »LEGO Friends« and »LEGO Technic« product lines – which are still available to buy today – for offering two completely separate product and colour worlds: »Heartlake City«, the backdrop for the »LEGO Friends« world, depicts a fluffy, pastel-coloured world of friends and milkshakes, far removed from the more construction-focused »LEGO City« theme, one of the company's original sets, that is based on altogether more mundane real-world locations. This latter world is, thematically and through stereotyped game scenarios (mainly fighting situations), aimed at boys and fathers, in other words: men – »No girls allowed«.

The findings of the research project »Gender Codes in Design«, jointly carried out by the Leibniz University Hanover and the HTW Berlin University of Technology and Economics and led by Birgit Weller and Katharina Krämer, show what happens when a Gender Swap Approach is applied to the above situation. While the packaging design for the »LEGO Technic« series (fig. 1) meets all current expectations of what it should look like for a toy of that kind, fictional brand OGEL has used it to manage a clever trick: At first glance, the visual language

typische Bildsprache signalisiert, es handle sich um einen Bausatz aus genannter Reihe, sorgt ein zweiter Blick für Irritation – es ist kein Rennauto oder sonstwie motorisiertes Mobil, sondern ein Kinderwagen abgebildet (s. Abb. 2). Dieser irritierende, bisweilen amüsierende Effekt zeigt, dass die Codes bekannt bzw. erlernt sind und wie wenig realistisch uns ein solches Produkt in einem der bekannten »Jungs-Regale«, noch die grafische Verpackungsgestaltung eines Kinderwagens in der »Mädchenabteilung« erscheint, die wir in Kaufhäusern vorfinden.

of the OGEL packaging tells us it belongs to the »LEGO Technic« range. Upon closer inspection, however, the viewer feels a pang of irritation: What is being presented here is no racing car, or any other motorised vehicle, but a pram (fig. 2). This irritating, and occasionally amusing, effect shows how learned and ingrained these visual codes are: It jars to see such a product in the »boys' aisle«, just as that kind of packaging design would never appear in the »girls' aisle« of any store.

1

2

1 LEGO Technic Go-Kart (Mod. 8256) / DE 2011 / Verpackung und Bausatz Go-Kart / *Toy packaging and construction kit Go-Kart* / Hergestellt von: / *Manufactured by:* LEGO GmbH / Sammlung Forschungsprojekt »Gender Codes im Design« der / *Collection research project »Gender Codes in Design« of the* / Leibniz Universität Hannover, HTW Berlin / Hinz, Weller, Krämer, Rajabi

2 OGEL Hybrid Puppenwagen / *Hybrid doll's pram* / DE 2011 / Renderings: Simon Hellwig / Forschungsprojekt »Gender Codes im Design« der / *Research project »Gender Codes in Design« of the* / Leibniz Universität Hannover, HTW Berlin / Hinz, Weller, Krämer, Rajabi

LEGO & Gender Part 1: Anita Sarkeesian zeichnet die Entwicklung der LEGO Produkte seit den 1970er Jahren nach und kritisiert, dass der Launch von »LEGO Friends« und dem »Heartlake City«-Universum keine gendersensible Spielvariante für Mädchen ist, sondern zur Verfestigung geschlechterstereotyper Vorstellungen beiträgt.
    Part 2: Während LEGO ursprünglich eine eher genderneutrale und spielerische Konstruktionserfahrung ermöglicht habe, habe sich dies seit den 1980er Jahren hin zu einer männlich dominierten und orientierten Perspektive stark verändert, so Sarkeesian. Sie wartet für die Entgrenzung einer starken Geschlechtertrennung mit Vorschlägen für LEGO auf.

LEGO & Gender Part 1: Anita Sarkeesian traces the development of LEGO products from the 1970s on and criticises the new »LEGO Friends« set and its »Heartlake City« universe for not being a gender-sensitive game choice for girls, but one that entrenches stereotypically gendered ideas.
    Part 2: Sarkeesian tells us that while LEGO originally provided more gender-neutral and playful designs, since the late 1970s, the company moved significantly towards a more male-dominated and male-oriented perspective. She suggests ways LEGO could abandon the strong gender segregation of its toys.

3

3 **LEGO & Gender** ⁄ US 2012 ⁄ Frames einer zweiteiligen Webserien-Episode ⁄ *Frames from a two-part web series episode* ⁄ LEGO Friends (1), The LEGO Boy's Club (2) ⁄ 24 Min. ⁄ Anita Sarkeesian ⁄ feminist frequency

Vom Frisieren und Schießen Die Imitation echter Waffen war bereits im frühen 19. Jahrhundert üblich und als militärisches Spielzeug besonders bei Jungen beliebt. Die anhaltende Kontroverse über das Spiel mit Waffen und der Gewaltbereitschaft von Kindern und Jugendlichen sowie die Tatsache, dass Spielzeug ein prägendes Element in der frühkindlichen Entwicklung ist, waren Ansätze für Anne-Sophie A. und Tabea Wegelin, ehemalige Kollegiatinnen des Aicher-Scholl-Kollegs. Sie bearbeiteten im Kurs unter der Leitung von Designer Uli Häussler drei Modelle von Spielzeugwaffen mit gestalterischen Mitteln, um durch Überzeichnung Stereotype zu kommentieren (s. Abb. 3). Gleichzeitig stellte sich die Frage: Ist eine rein weiße Waffe »neutral«?

Das Thema der Spielzeugwaffe taucht auch in der Diplomarbeit »Gender Calling« (2011) von Dominique Gehrke auf, zu der u. a. zwei Fotoarbeiten gehören. Zum einen ist da ein blondes Mädchen im rosa Kleid mit einem weißen, mit Blümchen verzierten Softair-Gewehr in der Hand zu sehen (s. Abb. 1). Das Pendant zeigt einen kleinen Jungen, den blonden Schopf einer Thor-Büste frisierend. Gehrke erzielt durch ihre Motive schnell zu erfassende und mehrdeutige Effekte: Einerseits überträgt sie jeweils ein klischeehaftes »Mädchen-« bzw. »Jungenspielzeug« in den jeweils anderen Zusammenhang

On Shooting Guns and Styling Hair Even by the early 19th century, replica weapons were a common and particularly popular military toy amongst boys. The ongoing debate about whether playing with toy guns encourages violent behaviour amongst young children and adolescents, and the fact that toys are a crucial part of a child's early development, were the starting points for a project by Anne-Sophie A. and Tabea Wegelin, both former Aicher-Scholl-Kolleg students. In a course led by designer Uli Häussler, they elaborated three models of toy weapons using creative means to comment on stereotypes through exaggeration (fig. 3). During this process, they asked themselves: Would spraying a weapon pure white make it »neutral«?

Artist Dominique Gehrke's diploma thesis *Gender Calling* (2011) also deals with the issue of toy weapons. It includes two photographic works: In one, a blonde girl who wears a pink dress is seen holding a white airsoft rifle decorated with flowers (fig. 1); in the other, a little boy is seen styling the blonde hair on a bust of action figure Thor. Gehrke's images are easy to »read« yet they produce multiple meanings: On the one hand, she puts the cliché of a »boy's toy« into the hands of a girl, and the cliché of a »girl's toy« into the hands of a boy, all while retaining the formal language typically associated with each context. Seeing a girl with a gun seems somewhat less incongruous than seeing a boy hairdressing a comic

1

und stülpt ihnen andererseits die Formensprache des typischen Kontexts über. Dabei scheint das Motiv einer Waffe für Mädchen durch das Einverleiben eher bekannter Praktiken etwas weniger atypisch, als das Frisieren eines aus nordischer Mythologie entlehnten Comic-Helden, gepaart mit der sonst kaum bedienten Eigenschaft des Sich-Kümmerns und Schönmachens in Bezug auf Jungen. Frisier- und Schminkpuppen sind ansonsten eher marktüblich als weibliche, weiße und Barbie-ähnliche Büsten, die keinesfalls im Gewand des Jungen-Spielzeugs daherkommen. In anderem Kleid zeigt sich der »Fuzzy Pumper Barber & Beauty Shop« (1977) der Spielzeugknete »Play-Doh« (s. Abb. 2). In modernisierter Aufmachung ist dieses Set nach wie vor erhältlich, ungeachtet der Tatsache, dass generell bei der Verpackung und Vermarktung stets das Produkt, oft in Ergänzung um ein spielendes, gemischtes Kinder-Duo, und dessen farbenfrohes Corporate Design im Vordergrund stehen. Hinzugesellt haben sich inzwischen allerdings durch Franchises u. a. auch ein »Rapunzel-Haarsalon« sowie weitere Disney-Motive und die Sparte »DohVinci«, deren Zielgruppe eher geschlechtsspezifisch zu sein scheint.

hero borrowed from Norse mythology because it is so very rare to see the care and beautification of boys shown in this way. Makeup and hairdressing dolls are typically white, female Barbie-like busts – such dolls would never be marketed as a boy's toy. The »Fuzzy Pumper Barber & Beauty Shop« (1977), produced by modelling clay company Play-Doh, is the hairdressing bust in another guise (fig. 2). The set can still be purchased in a more contemporary updated version, however the marketing and packaging were always generally centred around the product and its colourful corporate design, often complemented with a mixed duo of playing children. Play-Doh has since brought out other more recent product lines in franchise partnerships, including the Disney Princess »Rapunzel Hair Salon« and the »DohVinci« sets, whose target markets tend to be more gender specific.

1 **Gender Calling** ／ Softair-Gewehr für Mädchen ／ *Airsoft gun for girls* ／ DE 2011 ／ Dominique Gehrke

2 **Play-Doh Frisier-Salon** ／ *Hairdressing salon (the original Fuzzy Pumper Barber and Beauty Shop)* ／ ca. 1977 ／ Knet-Spielzeug und Verpackung ／ *Clay and toy packaging* ／ Hergestellt von: ／ *Manufactured by:* Play-Doh (by Hasbro) ／ Sammlung ／ *Collection* Herr Zopfs Friseurmuseum

3 **Killing Boys, Killing Girls** ⁄ DE 2018 ⁄ drei Versionen einer Spielzeugpistole ⁄ *three variations of a toy gun* ⁄ Aicher-Scholl-Kolleg ⁄ Produktdesignkurs ⁄ *Product design course* ⁄ Dozent: ⁄ *Lecturer:* Uli Häussler ⁄ Idee und Umsetzung: ⁄ *Idea and realisation:* Anne-Sophie A., Tabea Wegelin

Puzzles für Kindergartenkinder / *Jigsaw puzzle designed for nursery school children* / DE 2018 / Schulprojekt mit einer 9. Klasse der Realschule Dornstadt / *School project with 9th grade pupils from Realschule Dornstadt* / Konzeption und Durchführung: / *Concept and realisation:* Susanne Umscheid (Produktdesignerin / *product designer*) / Fabian Karrer (Grafikdesigner / *graphic designer*)

1 **Plan A** / Entwurf: / *Design:* Damian, Felix, Laura, Sina

2 **New York 42** / Entwurf: / *Design:* Lauri, Lukas, Robin, Vanessa

3 **Diversum** / Entwurf: / *Design:* Ella, Meike S., Meike Z., Moritz

4 **Wurm dich durch** / *Worm your way through* / Entwurf: / *Design:* Benjamin, Hanna, Samuel

5 **Ein Tag bei der Feuerwehr** / *One day with the fire brigade* / Entwurf: / *Design:* Damian, Felix, Laura, Sina

Puzzlen leicht gemacht? Puzzles zählen zu den Spielzeugen, mit denen wir Form-, Raum- und Flächenkonstruktion erlernen und für dessen Verstehen Geduld und Beobachtung erforderlich sind. Ein ähnliches Prinzip gilt für den Tierbaukasten aus Holz, den der HfG-Student Hans von Klier 1958 nach katametrischem System entwarf. Der Baukasten war zugleich Ausgangspunkt für eine der Aufgabenstellungen an die Schüler*innen der Realschule Dornstadt während der Projektwoche: Wie könnte ein Spielzeug mit ähnlichem Prinzip für ein ca. dreijähriges Kindergartenkind gestaltet sein? Dabei wurde das Geschlecht nicht vorgegeben und in Kleingruppen gearbeitet. Während für die einen das Prinzip des Puzzelns und die damit verbundene logische Flächen- und Raumkonstruktion im Mittelpunkt ihrer Überlegungen standen, war für andere eine Motivik zentral, die möglichst viele anspricht, wie z. B. das farbenfrohe Puzzle »Ein Tag bei der Feuerwehr«. Die dreidimensionalen Varianten »Diversum« und »Plan A« haben verschieden gestaltete Oberflächen: eine Seite mit Pferden, eine andere mit glitzernden Quadraten und eine mit Autos.

Jigsaw puzzles made easy? Puzzles require observation and patience, and help us acquire the concepts of volume, space, and surface area; skills also nurtured by the wooden toy animal kit that Ulm School of Design student Hans von Klier designed in 1958 applying a catametric system. Klier's modular kit was also the starting point for one of the tasks given to Realschule Dornstadt pupils as part of the Project Week, which asked them to design a similar toy for a three-year-old child. For this assignment, students worked in small groups without sex or gender being specified with regard to the finished product. While some students focused on the principle of jigsaw puzzles as logical constructions that play with surface and space, others focused on finding motifs that appeal to as many children as possible – the colourful puzzle »One day with the fire brigade« being one example. The three-dimensional puzzles entitled »Diversum« and »Plan A« have different designs on each surface: One side features horses, another side features glittering squares, and a third side has images of cars.

Tierbaukasten / *Animal construction kit* / DE 1958 / Kasten mit abstrakten Tierfiguren nach katametrischem System / *Box of animal-shaped bricks based on catametric principle* / HfG Ulm / Student: Hans von Klier / Sign. 61.0153, 1.0565 / HfG-Archiv / Museum Ulm

Wer ist es? Das Ratespiel »Wer ist es?« erschien 1988 in Deutschland, zuvor kam es 1979 unter dem Titel »Guess Who?« in Großbritannien auf den Markt. Ziel des Spiels ist es, den jeweiligen vorher gezogenen Charakter des Gegenübers per Ausschlussprinzip durch Ja ∕ Nein-Fragen wie »Trägt die gesuchte Person eine Brille?« zu erraten. Gesichter der Personen, die ausgeschlossen werden können, werden heruntergeklappt.

Die Gestaltung der Charaktere spielt für das Funktionieren des Spielprinzips eine wichtige Rolle: Von den insgesamt 24 Personenabbildungen haben jeweils mehrere ein übereinstimmendes Merkmal, wie z.B. »Brille tragen«, welches die anderen nicht haben. Das kurzweilige Zweipersonen-Deduktionsspiel erfreut sich in all seinen stets aktualisierten Versionen bis heute großer Beliebtheit, obschon immer wieder Kritik an dem Spiel geäußert wird, die auf das beschriebene Ausschlussprinzip abzielt: Mit ursprünglich fünf und heute acht abgebildeten weiblichen Figuren, wird »Frausein« als »Nicht-Männlichsein« bzw. als ein besonderes Merkmal dargestellt. Ebenso kritisiert wird das überwiegend europäische Aussehen bzw. die stereotype Darstellung von Äußerlichkeiten.

Wer ist es? [Guess who?] The two-player guessing game »Guess Who?« was first released in the UK in 1979; it came out in Germany in 1988 under the name »Wer ist es?« The aim of the game is to guess which one of the 24 Guess Who characters your opponent has drawn by asking yes or no questions about that character: »Do they wear glasses?«, for example. The faces of those characters that can be excluded are folded down on the Guess Who board.

The characters' visual appearance plays an important role in the functioning of the game: Of all 24 portraits, several have a matching characteristic (e.g. wearing glasses) that are not shared by the other characters. This entertaining game of deduction continues to be very popular in all its updated versions, despite repeated criticism of the way physical features are used as a basis for how the game works: With originally five and now eight women included in the game, »to be female« is represented as »not being male« or as being some kind of special feature. Likewise, the predominantly European appearance and stereotypical representation of the physical features have also been criticised.

Wer ist es? *[original: Guess who?]* ∕ Edition 2004 ∕ Tabletop Deduktionsspiel ∕ *Guessing board game* ∕ Hersteller: ∕ *Manufactured by:* Milton Bradley Company (MB), Hasbro Deutschland GmbH

Who's She? / PL 2018 / Tabletop Deduktionsspiel / *Guessing board game* / Hersteller: / *Manufactured by:* Playeress / Erhältlich in sechs Sprachen / *Available in six languages* / Entwurf: / *Design:* Zuzanna Kozerska-Girard / Illustrationen: / *Illustrations:* Daria Gołąb

Who's She? (dt.: Wer ist sie?) ist ein Ratespiel, das Playeress-Gründerin und Designerin Zuzanna Kozerska-Girard in Anlehnung an den Spieleklassiker »Wer ist es?« (»Guess who?«) entwickelt hat. Allerdings mit 28 ausschließlich weiblichen Charakteren, wie z. B. Amelia Earhart, Frida Kahlo oder Malala Yousafzai. »Couragierte Frauen, die die Welt veränderten«, heißt es bei Playeress. Mit dieser programmatischen Setzung macht das Spiel auch darauf aufmerksam, dass Frauen und ihre Leistungen in (Schul-)Geschichtsbüchern unterrepräsentiert sind. Im Gegensatz zu dem Prinzip des Originals fragt man nach den Lebensleistungen und -läufen wie »Hat sie einen Nobelpreis gewonnen?« oder »Hat sie etwas erfunden?«, statt nach äußeren Erscheinungsmerkmalen, um zu gewinnen. Deshalb gibt es bei »Who's She?« zu jedem Charakter eine Karte, die Fakten und Anekdoten zur Biografie bereithält, wodurch neben der Inspiration von einer Vielfalt an Berufen, Altersgruppen und Nationalitäten wiederum ein zusätzlicher Lerneffekt entsteht. Kozerska-Girard launchte im Dezember 2018 eine Kampagne zur Finanzierung auf der Crowdfunding-Plattform Kickstarter, die sie mit überragender Überfinanzierung von 3300 Prozent zur erfolgreichen Umsetzung des Projekts brachte.

Who's She? is a guessing game that Playeress company founder and designer Zuzanna Kozerska-Girard developed based on the classic game »Guess who?« – the major difference being that it features 28 exclusively female characters, such as Amelia Earhart, Frida Kahlo and Malala Yousafzai. »Courageous women who changed the world«, in Playeress' own words. The very basis of the game highlights the fact that women and their achievements are rarely mentioned in history or school books. Rather than focusing on physical appearances, as in the original game, »Who's She?« players ask about a character's achievements and biographical details, questions like »Is she a Nobel Prize winner?« or »Did she invent something?« »Who's She?« includes a card for each character that contains facts and information about that individual's life story which, besides providing inspiration given the range of professions, age groups, and nationalities, adds to the learning experience. In December 2018 Kozerska-Girard launched a crowdfunding campaign on Kickstarter, which led to the project being realised after exceeding its funding target by an incredible 3300 percent.

Pink oder Blau, Entweder-oder Es mutet heute selbstverständlich an, dass die Farben Pink bzw. Rosa und Blau das binäre Geschlechtersystem der westeuropäischen Kultur aus männlich und weiblich repräsentieren. Dass es sich dabei vor allem um soziokulturelle Festschreibungen handelt, wird an keinem vergleichbaren Thema derart ersichtlich und diskutiert. Während es weiterhin einerseits Bereiche gibt, in denen »Degendering«, also das Auflösen von Geschlechtszuschreibungen, z. B. in Verbindung mit Haushaltstätigkeiten erstrebenswert scheint, ist in anderen Fällen ein »Regendering«, z. B. in der medizinischen Forschung für Berücksichtigung von Geschlechterunterschieden erkannt worden (s. Kap. 3 Medizin und Gesundheit). Letzteres ist aber vor allem ein taxiertes Prinzip der Wirtschaft und tritt deutlich auf dem Spielzeugmarkt zutage.

Dass die Trennung zwischen den Geschlechtern heute teilweise so vehement erscheint, mag auch der Grund für das oder im Titel des anregenden Kurzfilms »Pink or Blue« (2017) als eine Kollaboration zwischen Dichterin und Autorin Hollie McNish und Regisseur Jake Dypka sein: Entweder-oder, ein Dazwischen scheint schwer (s. Abb. 2). Die Videoarbeit wurde zur Eröffnung des »Saatchi & Saatchi New Directors' Showcase« in Cannes gezeigt und erlaubt im Original mittels 3D-Technologie einen Perspektivwechsel zwischen der männlichen und weiblichen Sicht einzunehmen, während dasselbe Gedicht zu hören ist. Eine ähnliche Narration greift die Kollegiatin Anna-Lotta Dechow entsprechend persönlicher Wahrnehmung auf und setzt sie in einem Comic »Das pinke Rennauto« (2018) um: Ein Zwillingspaar, Mädchen und Junge, kommt zur Welt und beide erfahren in verschiedenen Lebenssituationen unterschiedliche Reaktionen auf ihr Verhalten, ihre Wünsche und Vorlieben – Junge oder Mädchen, Entweder-oder (s. Abb. 1).

Pink or blue, either-or It is taken for granted these days that the colours blue and pink represent the Western binary gender system of male and female. Indeed, no other topic reveals or explores to the same degree the fact that these are primarily sociocultural designations. While some areas of life, household chores for example, would benefit from a »de-gendering«, i.e. no longer being associated with a particular gender, in other areas of life, medical research for instance, a »re-gendering« has been recognised for the consideration of gender differences (s. Chap. 3 Medicine and Health). Still, we live in an economic system that places great value on the existence of gendered worlds, as is very clear in the toy market.

That everything these days seems to be gendered to such an extreme may be the reason for the »or« in the title of the stimulating short film *Pink or Blue* (2017), a collaboration between poet and author Hollie McNish and director Jake Dypka: it is either-or, no »in between« seems possible (fig. 2). The video work was presented at the opening of the »Saatchi & Saatchi New Directors' Showcase« in Cannes and, using 3D technology, it allowed viewers to switch between male and female perspectives while listening to the same poem. In her comic »The Pink Racing Car« (2018) college student Anna-Lotta Dechow addresses a similar theme based on personal experience. The book describes how a pair of twins, a girl and a boy, experience different reactions to their behaviour, their desires, their likes and dislikes in various situations throughout their lives – boy or girl, either-or (fig. 1).

1

1 Das pinke Rennauto / *The Pink Racing Car* / DE 2018 / Comic / Aicher-Scholl-Kolleg / Produktdesignkurs / *Product design course* / Entwurf und Umsetzung: / *Design and realisation:* Anna-Lotta Dechow

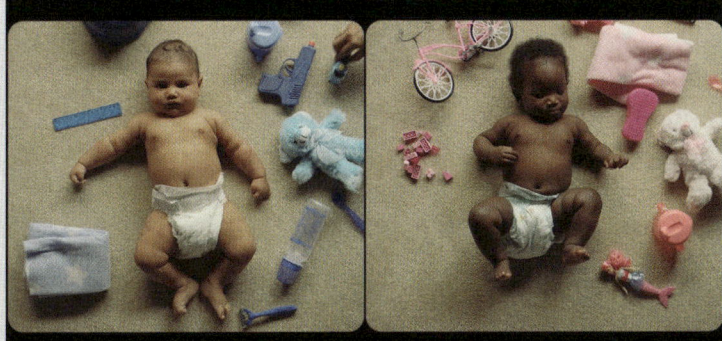

2 Pink or Blue / GB 2017 / Video stills / Text und Performance: / *Text and performance:* Hollie McNish / Produktion: / *Production:* Jake Dypka / 3:08 Min.

Medizin und Gesundheit
/Medicine and Health

»Mothers: Buy Flavored Bayer Children's Aspirin!« Insbesondere im Vergleich zum biologischen Geschlecht (engl. »sex«) wird deutlich, dass das deutsche Wort »Geschlecht« nicht ausreichend benennt, was das englische Wort »Gender« als soziokulturell geprägtes Geschlecht definiert. Während Verpackungen kosmetischer Produkte stark gegendert sind, um Zielgruppen zum Kauf zu animieren, sind Medikamentenverpackungen weitgehend frei davon. In den 1950er Jahren warb der Pharmaziekonzern Bayer für sein Produkt »Aspirin« allerdings mit starkem Bezug zu sozialen Geschlechterrollen: An die sich kümmernde und besorgte Mutter wird in der Print- und Fernsehwerbung sowie über die Verpackung appelliert, für ihre Kinder und die Familie Aspirin zu kaufen. Im Hinblick auf den medizinischen Bereich bedeutet das allerdings nicht, dass eine biologische Unterscheidung der Geschlechter unbedeutend wäre. Geht es um Erkrankungen oder beispielsweise das Ereignis des Herzinfarkts, wird immer häufiger bemängelt, dass die verschiedenen körperlichen Reaktionen, aber auch die Erforschung, Therapie und medikamentöse Behandlung nicht ausreichend geschlechtsdifferenziert betrachtet werden – was ernsthafte gesundheitliche Folgen haben kann.

Auch was den Alltag anbelangt, können Design-Innovationen durchaus zu kleinen Revolutionen führen: So entlastet der Fahrradsattel »600 Active« von SQlab die Prostata, das empfindlichste männliche Organ, zu 100 Prozent. Mit einer kabellosen, über das Smartphone steuerbaren Milchpumpe entwickelt die britische Firma Elvie ein Produkt, das nicht nur zukunftsgerichtet »smart« ist, sondern auch zur Mobilität von Frauen beitragen möchte. Wenn es um weibliche Hygieneprodukte geht, gehört in Deutschland seit dem 01.01.2020 die sogenannte »Tampon-Steuer«, die Waren der Monatshygiene wie Tampons, Binden und Menstruationstassen bislang mit dem höchsten Mehrwertsteuersatz von 19 Prozent besteuerte, der Vergangenheit an. Wie bereits in Indien, Irland, Kanada oder Australien sorgten Proteste, Petitionen und die Aktion »The Tampon Book« des Stuttgarter Unternehmens The Female Company für eine politische Wende.

»Mothers: Buy Flavored Bayer Children's Aspirin!« Unlike some languages, English distinguishes between a person's biological »sex«, as largely determined by the anatomy of an individual's reproductive system, and »gender« as a sociocultural construct. In German, »sex« and »gender« are covered by the single term Geschlecht, a word that does not fully convey the sociocultural aspect. And while cosmetics packaging is highly gendered to persuade certain target groups to buy them, this is rarely the case for medical packaging. Having said that, in the 1950s, the pharmaceutical company Bayer used very pronounced social gender roles to advertise its »Aspirin« product: print ads, TV commercials, and packaging designs encouraged concerned and caring mothers to buy the medication for their kids and family. Still, this does not mean that a biological distinction between the sexes is irrelevant to the medical field. Indeed, there is growing criticism that individual physical reactions to illnesses, such as heart attacks for example, as well as the research, therapies, and drug treatments developed for such conditions, are not sufficiently considered in terms of sex-based differences, which can have serious health consequences.

As far as everyday life is concerned, design innovations can lead to small revolutions, too: the SQlab-designed »600 Active« bike saddle, for example, ensures that the perineal area, and thus the very sensitive male prostate gland, is completely free of any saddle contact; while British company Elvie has developed a wireless breast pump that can be controlled via smartphone – pioneering »smart« technology that also increases women's mobility. When it comes to feminine hygiene products, in Germany the so-called »tampon tax« was consigned to history on January 1, 2020. Previous to that, feminine care products, such as tampons, sanitary towels, and menstrual cups, were taxed at the top valued added rate of 19 percent. Following the lead of countries such as India, Ireland, Canada, and Australia, a wave of protests, petitions, and the so-called »Tampon Book« campaign, led by the Stuttgart-based startup The Female Company, have succeeded in bringing about this change in policy.

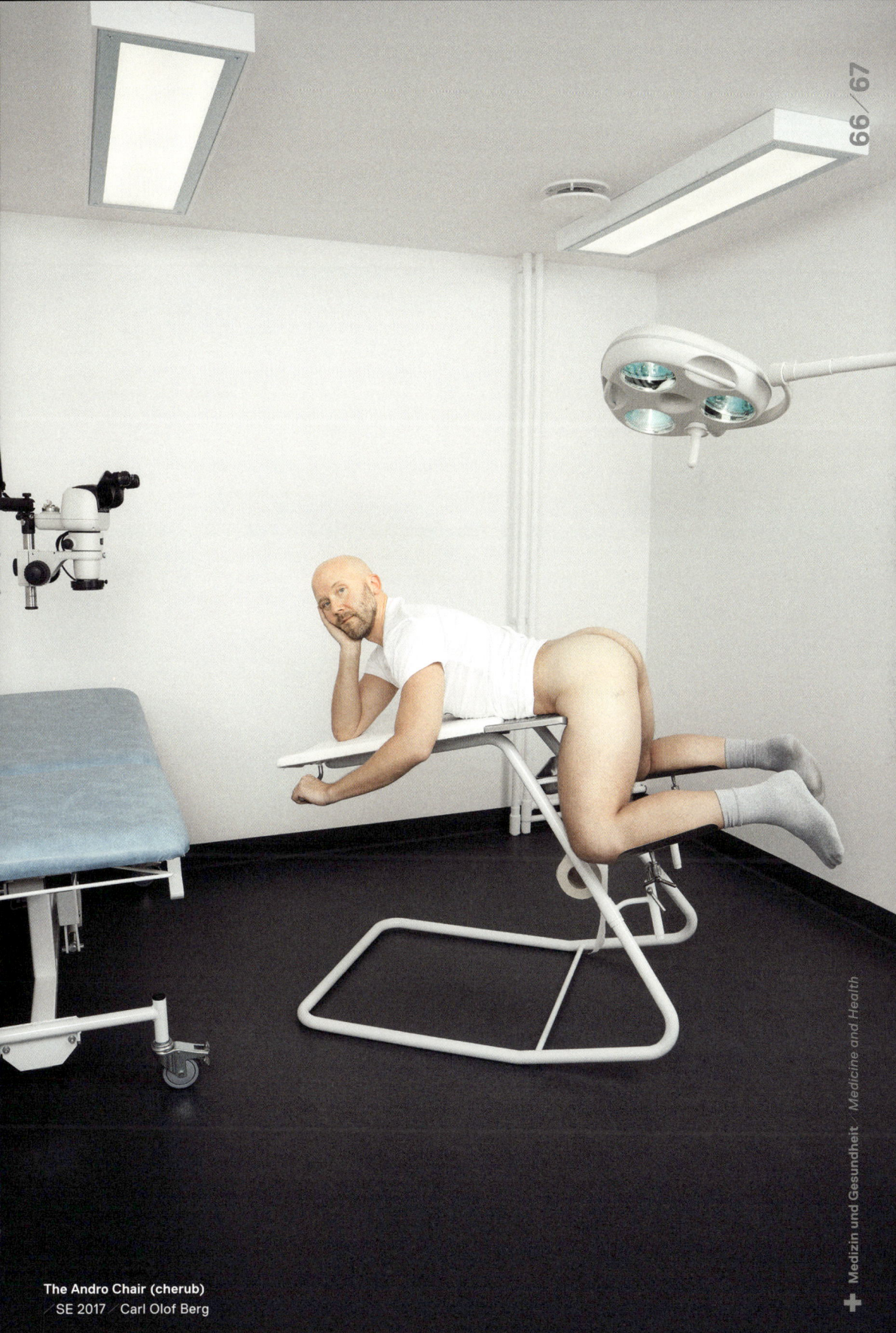

The Andro Chair (cherub)
SE 2017 / Carl Olof Berg

Das Undenkbare gestalten: The Andro Chair

Unter einer unangenehmen ärztlichen Untersuchungssituation stellen sich viele Frauen den Gynäkologiestuhl vor, der für sie Unbehagen und Schamgefühl auslöst. Auf diesen Erkenntnissen aufbauend, haben Emma Börjesson, Karin Ehrnberger, Anne-Christine Hertz und Cristine Sundbom »das Undenkbare« gestaltet: den Andro Chair, einen Andrologie-Stuhl für Männer, dessen Design-Konzept auf den Erfahrungen einer gynäkologischen Untersuchung von Frauen basiert. Die Gruppe führte dafür Interviews mit Frauen, die ihre Erfahrungen als »kalt«, »hart« bis hin zur »Tortur« beschrieben. Die Gestaltung des Andro Chairs ist deshalb keine Lösung im funktionalen Sinne, sondern eine Anknüpfung an den existierenden Gynäkologiestuhl und ein Versuch, über Gestaltung die geschilderten Erfahrungen kritisch sichtbar zu machen. Erklärtes Ziel des Projekts ist das Aufdecken verschleierter Gendernormen durch das Anwenden des »Gender-Swap«, also einer Umkehrung. Damit war einerseits deren Bedeutung für Frauen im benannten Problemfeld Untersuchungsgegenstand, wie auch die Frage danach, ob eine gleiche Situation – angewandt auf Männer – akzeptiert würde. Um dies zur Debatte zu stellen und inspiriert von der Sichtweise der gynäkologischen Untersuchung als einer Performance, wurde der Andro Chair als Requisite und Diskussionsobjekt während eines öffentlichen Seminars auf eine Bühne gestellt. Er ermöglichte sowohl kritische als auch mehrfache Lesarten des Gynäkologiestuhls und damit der gynäkologischen Untersuchung insgesamt. Darüber hinaus sei eine Diskussion über alternative Ideen angeregt worden, um eine positivere Erfahrung zu machen.

Gewissermaßen weitererzählt wird der Andro Chair und dessen performativer Charakter von Künstler und Choreograf Carl Olof Berg, der Karin Ehrnberger im Zusammenhang mit ihrer Dissertation kennenlernte. In Berlin öffnete er in Kollaboration mit ROCKELMANN& seinen »Andrology Showroom« (Juni 2017), wo er neben Performances auch Installationen als Gesamt-Kunstprojekt präsentierte. So bot Berg die Performance »A guided tour of the men's club« an – laut Berg eine Geschichte darüber, wie Architektur und Design unseren Körper formen, und wie er das Gefühl habe, dass Männlichkeit selbst wie ein Männer-Club sei, zu dem man Zugang haben müsse.[1] Ebenfalls dazu zählt die fotografische Arbeit, in der Berg auf dem Andro Chair, mit entblößtem Hinterteil und auf die Betrachtenden gerichtetem Blick, posiert. Somit schafft er es, dass selbst in der Fotografie die Zuschauenden sowie deren Blick auf seinen Körper der Fokus seiner Forschung und künstlerischen Praxis sind. Mit seiner Performance-Kunst spannt er einen Bogen zwischen der Konstruktion von Geschlechtsidentitäten, Geschlechternormalitäten, queerem Aktivismus und feministischer Theorie.

[1] Carl Olof Berg. o.D., vgl. http://cargocollective.com/carlolofberg/androstolen, zul. abgerufen am 18.11.2019.

Designing the Unthinkable: The Andro Chair

Many women associate the gynaecology chair with uncomfortable and embarrassing medical examinations. Emma Börjesson, Karin Ehrnberger, Anne-Christine Hertz, and Cristine Sundbom used this knowledge, together with the results of interviews conducted with a number of women who described their experiences of the gynaecological examination as »cold«, »harsh«, and even »torture, to design »the unthinkable«: the Andro Chair, an andrology chair for men. The Andro Chair does not provide a strictly functional solution to a given problem, rather it is a conceptual male equivalent to the gynaecology chair currently used in female examinations that attempts to make women's experiences of such examinations critically visible through design. The declared aim of the project is to uncover veiled gender norms using a so-called Gender Swapping Approach, or reversal. Thus, the study explores both what these gender norms mean to women in relation to this problem area, but also how acceptable an identical situation might be if it were applied to men. To debate this, and inspired by the idea of the gynaecological examination as performance, the Andro Chair was placed on stage and used as an object of discussion during a public seminar. This enabled both critical and multiple readings to be made about the gynaecology chair, and gynaecological examinations more generally, and also generated discussion and ideas about how to create more positive experiences in this area.

In a sense, artist and choreographer Carl Olof Berg, who met Karin Ehrnberger while she was working on her dissertation, extends the conversation about the Andro Chair and its performative character. Collaborating with ROCKELMANN& gallery, Berg opened his »Andrology Showroom« in Berlin in June 2017, which saw him present performances and installations as a »total art project«. Berg's performance entitled »A guided tour of the men's club« explained how architecture and design shape our bodies and how he feels masculinity itself is like a men's club one must gain access to.[1] The project included photographs of Berg posing on the Andro Chair with his naked buttocks exposed as he looks directly at the viewer. In this way, Berg ensures that, even in photography, the viewer and the viewer's gaze on him and his body are the focus of his research and artistic practice. His performance art bridges the gap between the construction of gender identities, gender norms, queer activism, and feminist theory.

[1] *Carl Olof Berg, n.d., cf. http://cargocollective.com/carlolofberg/androstolen.*

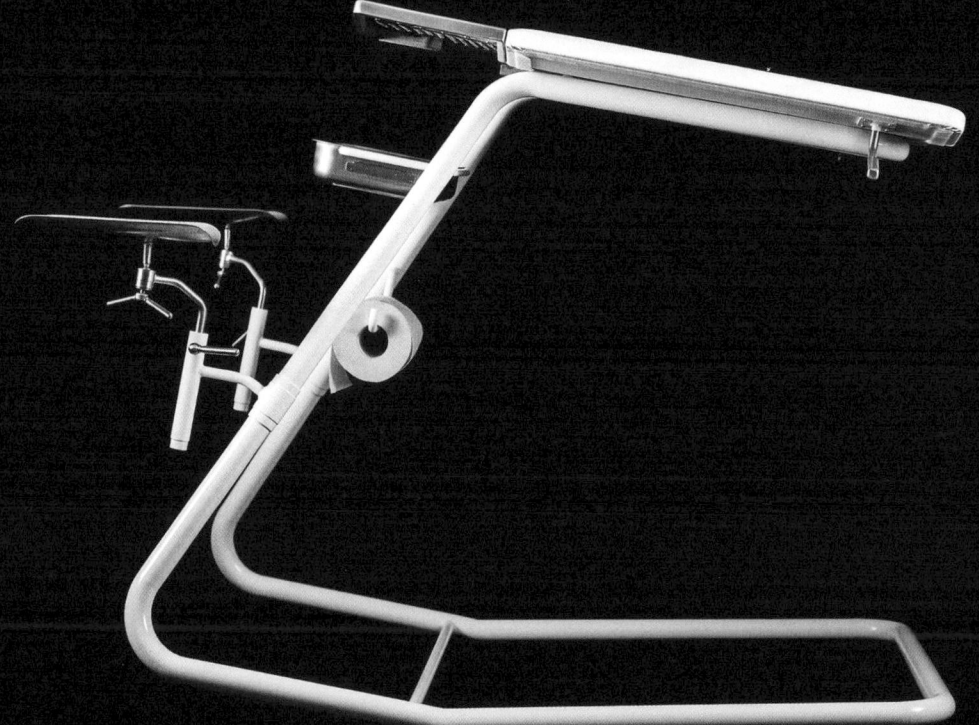

The Andro Chair. Designing the Unthinkable: Men's Right to Women's Experience in Gynaecology
SE 2013 / Angewandte Designforschung von: / *Applied design research by:*
Cristine Sundbom, Anne-Christine Hertz, Karin Ehrnberger, Emma Börjesson

»Warum ist Menstruation Luxus, aber Kaviar nicht?« Diese Frage stellten sich 2019 die Gründerinnen Ann-Sophie Claus und Sinja Stadelmaier von »The Female Company«, einem Unternehmen, das Bio-Hygieneprodukte mit nachhaltigem und sozialem Gedanken verbindet – aber nicht nur sie. Während Länder wie Kanada, Irland, Indien, Kenia oder Australien bereits die Steuer für Monatshygieneartikel völlig abgeschafft haben, galt der erhöhte Mehrwertsteuersatz von 19 Prozent in Deutschland für solche Artikel bis ins Jahr 2019. Dann war der Druck auf die Politik, das zu ändern, offenbar ausreichend hoch. Durch Petitionen wie »Die Periode ist kein Luxus« und wirksame Kampagnen auf Social Media geriet das Thema immer mehr in den Fokus der öffentlichen Wahrnehmung. Das junge Start-Up »The Female Company« initiierte eine Aktion, der es nicht an Witz fehlte und die damit gleichzeitig über nationale Grenzen hinweg sehr wirkungsvoll auf den Missstand aufmerksam machte. Dass in Deutschland auf Grundnahrungsmittel und andere Dinge des täglichen Bedarfs wie z. B. Blumen, Nutztiere, Nahverkehr oder eben auch Bücher ein geringerer Umsatzsteuersatz von sieben Prozent gilt, machte sich das Unternehmen zunutze. Im Frühjahr 2019 wartete es mit »The Tampon Book – Das Buch gegen Steuerdiskriminierung«, konzipiert von Marketing-Agentur Scholz & Friends, auf: Ein auf den ersten Blick übliches Buch, das allerdings auf der Rückseite 15 Bio-Tampons versteckt hält. Damit umgeht das Unternehmen die sogenannte »Tampon-Steuer«. Außerdem enthält die Publikation Geschichten rund um das Thema Menstruation, illustriert von Ana Curbelo und Alica Läuger.

»Why is menstruation considered a luxury, but caviar not?« In 2019 Ann-Sophie Claus and Sinja Stadelmaier, founders of The Female Company, a startup venture that combines organic feminine hygiene products with ideas of social sustainability, asked themselves this question. And they were not alone: Countries such as Canada, Ireland, India, Kenya, and Australia had already abolished taxes for menstrual products; in Germany, however, the top VAT rate of 19 percent was still being applied to these items until enough pressure was generated to enforce a change in policy at the end of 2019. While petitions such as »periods are not a luxury« combined with effective social media campaigns increasingly brought the issue to the fore of public awareness, The Female Company launched a campaign that was both witty yet also succeeded in drawing international attention to this grievance. Taking advantage of the fact that in Germany a lower VAT rate of seven percent is applied to basic foodstuffs and other everyday items, including flowers, livestock, local transport, and books, the young startup launched The Tampon Book: A Book Against Tax Discrimination in the spring of 2019. Designed by advertising agency Scholz & Friends, 15 organic tampons are concealed inside what looks like a conventional book – the tampon tax is thus cleverly avoided. The book also includes stories about menstruation with illustrations by Ana Curbelo and Alica Läuger.

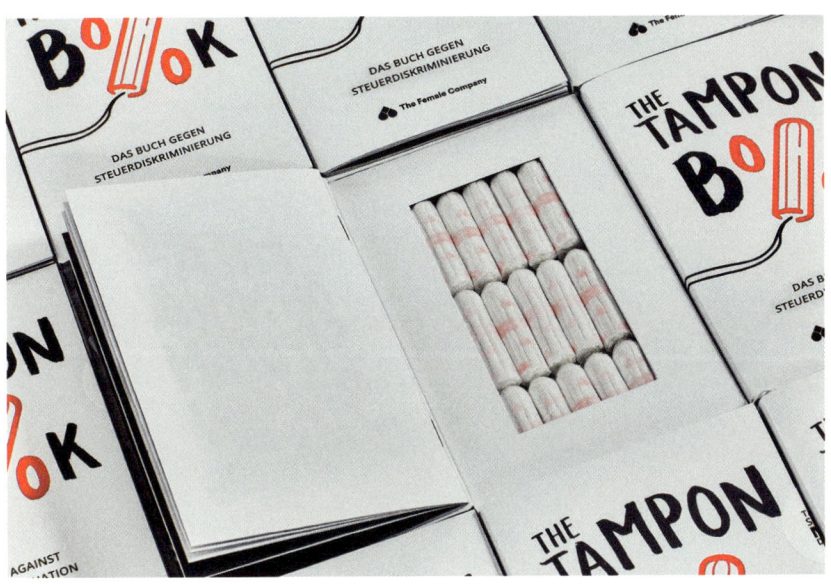

The Tampon Book / DE 2019 /
The Female Company GmbH mit
/ with Scholz & Friends Berlin
/ illustriert von: / illustrated by:
Ana Curbelo, Alica Läuger

SQlab 600 Active ⁄ medizinischer Fahrradsattel ⁄ *medical bike saddle* ⁄ DE 2014 ⁄
Hersteller: ⁄ *Manufactured by:* SQlab in
Zusammenarbeit mit ⁄ *in collaboration
with* Richard Hobson

Herrensattel, Damenrad – Fahrradfahren für alle Was den medizinischen Sattel »600 Active« der Firma SQlab[2] auszeichnet, ist die Entlastung der Prostata zu 100 Prozent sowie gleichzeitig eine Erleichterung für Bandscheiben und Lendenwirbel. Obwohl es sich nicht ausdrücklich um einen »Männer-Sattel« handelt, ist klar, dass die Prostata ein männliches, drüsenartiges Organ ist – und zwar ein hochempfindliches, welches beständig wächst und mit zunehmendem Alter Beschwerden verursachen kann. Rein zweckgerichtet kommt der Sattel als Lösung einem Problem nach, das geschlechtsspezifisch, also biologisch-anatomisch bedingt ist, und dient als medizinische Maßnahme. Kaum beachtet ist dagegen laut SQlab der anatomisch tiefer liegende Schambogen bei Frauen. Eine allgemein tiefer liegende Sattelnase ist für das Unternehmen Teil eines generellen Unisex-Sattelkonzepts, das aus Erkenntnissen eigener Untersuchungen sowie einer Studie der Sporthochschule Köln herrührt. Demnach sind Sitzknochenabstand und -position relevant für die angemessene Sattelwahl, die nicht maßgeblich geschlechtsspezifisch, sondern individuell verschieden ist.

Fahrradsättel sind Teil eines Alltagsgegenstands, der Menschen in variantenreicher Ausführung CO_2-frei mobil sein lässt und gleichzeitig ohne gewisse Grundelemente und deren bestimmter Anordnung nicht auskommt wie Räder, Pedalen, Lenker, etc. Wiederum die Unterscheidung von Herren- und Damenrad, wie sie sich bis heute vor allem durch eine Querstange bzw. einen tiefen Einstieg erhalten hat, ist bemerkenswert: Karl Drais' Erfindung der Laufmaschine »Draisine« (1817) beweist unvermittelt, dass die Vorgängerin des Fahrrads nicht vorsah, von Frauen benutzt zu werden, ohne gegen die gesellschaftliche Ordnung zu verstoßen. Einmal mehr wurde das Männliche als Norm bestärkt. Insofern war zunächst das Fahrrad eine technische und dann der tiefe Einstieg für Frauen eine soziokulturelle Errungenschaft. Ob letztlich der sogenannte »Diamant-« bzw. »Trapezrahmen« für das Herrenrad heute noch seine Berechtigung hat, stellen Debatten über das mit der hohen Querstange verbundene Sicherheitsrisiko infrage. Unabhängig davon wird der tiefe Einstieg noch immer mit Senior*innen und Frauen assoziiert, obschon er im Vergleich sichtbar niederschwellig »für alle« ist.

[2] Sowohl Logo und Name des Unternehmens SQlab sind symbolisch an den griechischen Gott der Heilkunst »Asklepios« (dt. Äskulap) angelehnt. Aus dem medizinischen Bereich ist das Symbol eines Schlangen umschlungenen Stabs sehr geläufig, das von der typischen Darstellung Asklepios' als bärtiger Mann, der sich auf einen Stab stützt, der wiederum von einer Schlange umschlungen wird, rührt. In abgewandelter Form – mit Sattel – ist es das Markenzeichen der Firma SQlab. Vgl. https://www.sq-lab.com/ueber-uns/meilensteine/, zul. abgerufen am 16.10.2019.

Men's Saddles and Women's Bikes – Cycling for All What distinguishes SQlab's[2] »600 Active« medical bike saddle from other models is that it ensures that the prostate gland is completely free of any saddle contact, while also relieving strain on the intervertebral discs and lumbar vertebrae. Although not explicitly marketed as a »men's saddle«, the prostate is, obviously, an exclusively male glandular organ – a highly sensitive one that continues to grow throughout a man's life and sometimes causes problems in older age. As such, the saddle provides a solution to a gender-specific problem – a biological and anatomical one – and serves a medical purpose. By contrast, according to SQlab, the pubic arch, which is anatomically lower in women than in men, is barely considered. SQlab's own research and a study by the Cologne Sport University both suggest that the most important thing to keep in mind when making the appropriate choice of saddle is the position of and distance between the sitting bones, which is not gender specific but differs from person to person. This insight led SQlab to design a unisex saddle with a lower-level nose that is suitable for all.

The saddle is just one of several elements that make up the bicycle, an everyday object that allows people – in all its varied forms – to travel with a zero-carbon footprint. But to be useful, saddles must be used in combination with a number of other pieces, such as wheels, pedals, handlebars, etc., that have been arranged together in a specific way. In turn, the difference between men's and women's bikes – still seen today with the horizontal crossbar for men and step-through frame for women – is striking: Karl Drais' invention of the »Draisienne« (1817) running machine proves that the predecessor of the bicycle was not intended to be used by women without violating the social order. Once again, masculinity as the norm was reinforced. In this respect, the bicycle was first a technical achievement but then also became a sociocultural one with the advent of the women's step-through frame. It is debatable whether the men's »diamond« or »trapezoidal« bike frame is still justified today given the safety hazards associated with the higher crossbar. Regardless, the step-through frame continues to be associated with older people and women, despite clearly being more equally accessible »to all« than men's frames.

[2] Both the SQlab name and logo are based on Asclepius, the Greek god of healing. A serpent-entwined rod is a very common symbol of medicine; it derives from depictions of Asclepius as a bearded man leaning on a staff with a snake coiled around it. SQlab's logo adapts this symbol by replacing the rod with a saddle. Cf. https://www.sq-lab.com/ueber-uns/meilensteine.

»Breast is best«? Stillen ist ein kontroverses, oft emotional aufgeladenes Thema. Dabei liegt es in der Biologie, dass es eine Fähigkeit ist, die Frauen zumindest theoretisch gegeben ist. Dennoch ist der Vorgang selbst nichts, was intuitiv beherrscht wird, sondern erfahren bzw. gelernt werden muss. Bei den vielen mit dem Stillen verbundenen Fragen – Dauer des Stillens, Zufüttern, Abpumpen, Stillen Zuhause oder in der Öffentlichkeit, ob berufstätig oder nicht – geht es immer auch um soziokulturelle Normen, die sich je nach Gesellschaftsform, Kultur und Zeitgeist unterscheiden. Aspekte von »Gender« und »sex« verschwimmen ineinander, sie sind nicht haarscharf trennbar.

Ein Beispiel für Tendenzen allgemeingesellschaftlicher Entwicklungen in Deutschland: Während in den 1960er und 1970er Jahren der Trend vom Stillen zur Flaschennahrung ging, ist heute das Stillen wieder höher angesehen und wird vom Mutterschutzgesetz (MuSchG) getragen. Seit 2018 regelt es auch den »Schutz des Stillens während der Erwerbstätigkeit«[3]. Gestützt von zahlreichen Studien wie u. a. der World Health Organisation (WHO) greifen außer dem Argument einer gesunden emotionalen Bindung zwischen Mutter und Kind insbesondere die Ergebnisse zu Risiken des Nicht-Stillens für beide Seiten. Diese praktisch institutionalisierte Still-Befürwortung bringt andererseits einen wohl eher unerwünschten psychologischen Nebeneffekt mit sich: Frauen, die aus verschiedenen Gründen gar nicht oder kürzer stillen als die empfohlenen 6 Monate, neigen durch den sozialen Druck dazu, sich ihrem Kind gegenüber und in ihrer Mutterrolle unzureichend zu fühlen. Unbestritten der dargelegten Tatsachen

»Breast is best«? Breastfeeding is a controversial and often emotionally charged topic. And although, theoretically at least, it is a biological ability that women have, the process itself is not mastered intuitively, but must be experienced or learned. The many questions that surround breastfeeding – how long to breastfeed, complementary feeding, pumping, breastfeeding at home or in public, being a working or stay-at-home mother – are also always about sociocultural norms, which differ between societies, cultures, and depend on the zeitgeist. Aspects of »gender« and »sex« blur into each other and are difficult to separate.

Indeed, the way German society views breastfeeding has shifted over time: While in the 1960s and 1970s there was a trend away from breastfeeding in favour of bottle feeding, today, breastfeeding is once again viewed more highly and is actively sanctioned in Germany by the Maternity Protection Act, which has also governed »the protection of breastfeeding women at work«[3] since 2018. Besides the argument that breastfeeding creates a healthy emotional bond between mother and child, what matters is that numerous studies, including those published by the World Health Organization (WHO), among others, show that not breastfeeding is associated with health risks for both mother and baby. However, this virtually institutionalised advocacy of breastfeeding has some adverse psychological effects: Women who, for whatever reason, do not breastfeed, or do not do so for as long as the recommended six months, tend to feel inadequate towards their children and as mothers because of social pressure.

melden sich deshalb vermehrt Forscher*innen und in Zeiten von Social Media auch Influencer*innen zu Wort, das Motto »Breast is best« als Mythos zu entlarven oder zumindest als Dogma aufzuweichen – ein Balanceakt zwischen »stillfreundlich« und »Stillzwang«.⁴

Während in Norwegen und Dänemark die Rate, ob ein Kind jemals bzw. überhaupt gestillt wurde, laut OECD bei nahezu einhundert Prozent liegt, ist sie in Frankreich und – weit unterdurchschnittlich – Irland am niedrigsten.⁵ Auch Großbritannien gehört zu den Ländern, in denen das Stillen insgesamt und weniger lang praktiziert wird. Ein bestehender Zusammenhang zwischen der Stilldauer und den sehr verschiedenen nationalen gesetzlichen Regelungen für Mutterschutz und Elternzeit liegt nahe, wie auch die damit einhergehende Nutzung und Akzeptanz von Milchpumpen. Die britische Firma Elvie gehört zu den aufstrebenden Unternehmen einer ganzen, sogenannten »Femtech«-Branche. Neben einem Beckenbodentrainer brachte das Unternehmen 2018 eigenen Angaben zu Folge die »welterste leise, tragbare Milchpumpe« auf den Markt.⁶ Das Produkt richtet sich dem modernen Bild einer Mutter und berufstätigen Frau entsprechend nach einem Bedürfnis aus, unabhängig und mobil sein zu können. Dafür kommt die Milchpumpe ohne Kabel aus, ist geräuscharm und über eine kostenlose Smartphone-App steuerbar. Einerseits verkörpert das Produkt durch seine Intention eine zukunftsgerichtete Lebensweise und ist andererseits ästhetisch durch runde Formen und sanfte Pastelltöne an vertraute, gar technikferne, weiblich codierte Designelemente angelehnt.⁷

³ Bundesministerium für Familie, Senioren, Frauen und Jugend, Hrsg. 2018. Mutterschutzgesetz: Leitfaden zum Mutterschutz. Bundesministerium für Familie, Senioren, Frauen und Jugend.
⁴ Bösl, Elsbeth. 2017. Medizintechnik und Lifestyle-Produkt: Milchpumpen, Muttermilchdiskurs, Stilldiskurs und Konzepte von Mutterschaft. In Mutterschaften sichtbar machen: Sozial- und kulturwissenschaftliche Beiträge, hrsg. v. Eva Tolasch u. Rhea Seehaus, S. 43–47, hier S. 48.
⁵ OECD. 2014. OECD Family database OECD, Paris, vgl. http://www.oecd.org/social/soc/oecdfamilydatabase.htm CO1.5: Breastfeeding Rates, last updated, 01.10.2009.
⁶ Elvie. o.D., vgl. https://www.elvie.com/shop/elvie-pump, zul. abgerufen am 13.10.2019.
⁷ Bösl. 2017. Medizintechnik und Lifestyle-Produkt, S. 49.

Despite the facts of these findings, researchers and, these days, social media influencers are increasingly speaking up to expose the »breast is best« mantra as a myth, or at least make it less dogmatic – a balance between »breastfeeding friendly« and »compulsory breastfeeding«.⁴

According to the Organisation for Economic Co-operation and Development (OECD), breastfeeding rates in Norway and Denmark are close to 100 percent, whereas they are at their lowest in France, and well below average in Ireland.⁵ In the UK the number of mothers who breastfeed is also fairly low, as is the length of time they breastfeed for. Clearly, there is a connection between breastfeeding rates and the different laws, levels of maternity protection, and parental leave legislation that govern a country – and this also applies to the acceptance and use of breast pumps. British company Elvie is one of many up-and-coming ventures to emerge in the so-called femtech industry. Following the release of their pelvic floor trainer, in 2018 the company launched »the world's first silent wearable breast pump«.⁶ It is aimed at modern working mothers who want to be independent and mobile. The pump is wireless, quiet, and can be controlled via a free smartphone app. Functionally, it is a future-oriented lifestyle product, yet aesthetically, with its rounded shape and soft pastel colours, it is based on familiar, technologically-distant even, female-coded design elements.⁷

³ Bundesministerium für Familie, Senioren, Frauen und Jugend (ed.), Mutterschutzgesetz: Leitfaden zum Mutterschutz (14th edn., 2018).
⁴ Elsbeth Bösl, »Medizintechnik und Lifestyle-Produkt: Milchpumpen, Muttermilchdiskurs, Stilldiskurs und Konzepte von Mutterschaft,« in Mutterschaften sichtbar machen: Sozial- und kulturwissenschaftliche Beiträge, edited by Eva Tolasch and Rhea Seehaus (Berlin/Toronto: Barbara Budrich, 2017), 43–57, here 48.
⁵ OECD, OECD Family database OECD, Paris, 2014, http://www.oecd.org/social/soc/oecdfamilydatabase.htm CO1.5: Breastfeeding Rates.
⁶ Elvie, n.d., cf. https://www.elvie.com/shop/elvie-pump.
⁷ Bösl, »Medizintechnik und Lifestyle-Produkt,« 49.

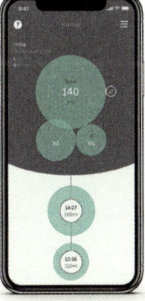

Elvie Pump / GB 2018 / Milchpumpe und App-Anwendung / *Breast Pump and App-Device* / Chiaro Technology und / *and* Elvie

Anti-Rauch-Kampagne auf HfG-isch Wenn es Dinge gab, die an der avantgardistischen Hochschule für Gestaltung mit Sitz auf dem Ulmer Kuhberg genauso salonfähig waren, wie in der Stadtgesellschaft selbst, dann gehörte das Rauchen sicherlich dazu. Während heute in Deutschland alle Tabakwaren mit einem Warnhinweis versehen sein müssen, waberte die Erkenntnis, dass der blaue Dunst gesundheitsschädlich ist, in den 1950er und 1960er Jahren langsam in die Gesellschaft. Das Magazin Der Spiegel veröffentlichte 1964 eine ganze Ausgabe unter der Frage: »Sind Zigaretten gefährlich?«. Darin breitete man die Geschichte der einstigen »Wunderdroge« aus und legte dar, wie die neuesten Forschungen in Amerika gar die Tabakaktien an der Wall Street zu Fall brachten und die Meinungen in zwei Lager gespalten waren, in sogenannte »Pro-« und »Antibacs« [Engl. Abkürzung für pro-tobacco, anti-tobacco].[8] Und an der HfG? Ganz seismografisch wurde im Studienjahr 1963/64 erstmals die Gestaltung einer Anti-Rauch-Kampagne zur Aufgabe im Fach Visuelle Kommunikation bei Dozent Adolf Zillmann. Bezüglich der Umsetzung ist die Wahl der Strategie, die das »Anti« in der Werbung stützen soll, höchst aufschlussreich. Generell ist die Narration anhand von erzeugten Bildern der Männlich- oder Weiblichkeit ein probates Marketinginstrument. Das Beispiel par excellence – um im Feld zu bleiben – ist in der Tabak-Werbung die Figur des »Marlboro-Mannes«. Ein weißer Mann, ein schlanker Cowboy, der die Freiheit und deshalb auch das Rauchen liebt. Anstatt wie heute mit den faktischen gesundheitlichen Folgen des Rauchens die Anti-Rauch-Kampagne zu einer aufklärerischen Kampagne zu machen, greifen die HfG Studierenden dasjenige Narrativ auf, das die Tabakindustrie seit jeher für sich nutzt: nämlich ein Gefühl zu verkaufen. Bloß drehen sie die Botschaft offensiv um. Ihre Werbefiguren gegen das Rauchen sind Mädchen und Jungen, die qualmen. Das, was die Jugend ursprünglich zum Rauchen verführte, das Erwachsen-Wirken, wird hier umgekehrt und so lauten die Botschaften, die an rauchende Jungen appellieren: »Nur Paffprotzen! Keine Männer!« und das paffende »Dämchen« ist »dämlich«. Ob Pro oder Anti: Werbung ist die offensichtlichste Veranschaulichung unserer menschlichen Empfänglichkeit für Vorbilder oder zumindest visuelle Prototypen, an denen wir unsere Identität abarbeiten – wozu auch Geschlecht gehört.

[8] Vgl. Hentschel, Manfred W. u. Petermann, Jürgen. »Wie gut«. In DER SPIEGEL, Nr. 4/1964, 22.01.1964, S. 60–68, https://www.spiegel.de/spiegel/print/d-46162828.html, zul. abgerufen am 11.10.2019.

Ulm School of Design (HfG Ulm) Anti-Smoking Campaign If there was anything that Ulm's avant-gardist design school and the city's residents both found socially acceptable, it was smoking. These days, all tobacco products in Germany must include warning labels by law, but in the 1950s and 1960s society was only slowly beginning to realise that cigarette smoke is harmful to health. In 1964, German magazine Der Spiegel dedicated a whole issue to the question: »Are cigarettes dangerous?« It told the story of a product once seen as a »miracle drug«, described how the latest research in America caused tobacco shares to tumble on Wall Street and explained how opinion was divided into pro- and anti-tobacco camps.[8] And at the HfG? In the 1963/64 academic year, plugged into the spirit of the times, lecturer Adolf Zillmann tasked his visual communication students to design their very first anti-smoking campaign. The strategy they chose to »sell« the anti-tobacco stance is very revealing. The use of narratives based on stereotyped images of masculinity and femininity is a tried and tested marketing tool. In tobacco advertising, the example par excellence is the figure of the »Marlboro Man«: a slim, white male cowboy who loves freedom – and therefore smoking, too. Rather than turning the anti-tobacco campaign into an educational one full of facts about the health effects of smoking, as is often done today, the HfG students deployed a narrative technique oft-used by the tobacco industry: the selling of a feeling. What they did was simply turn the message on its head. The characters that appear in their anti-smoking ads are young cigarette-puffing girls and boys. The very thing that seduced these youngsters into taking up smoking in the first place – the allure of adulthood – is reversed: The message to young boys who smoke is: »This won't make you a man!«, while cigarette-smoking young ladies are shown as »gormless girlies«. Whether pro or anti, advertising is the most vivid illustration of our susceptibility to role models, or visual prototypes at least, that we use to build our own identities – and that includes gender.

[8] Cf. Manfred W. Hentschel, Jürgen Petermann, »Wie gut,« DER SPIEGEL, No. 4/1964, Jan. 22, 1964, 60–68, https://www.spiegel.de/spiegel/print/d-46162828.html.

1

2

Nur Paffprotzen! Keine Männer!

3

Ist es nicht grotesk?
Sie versucht doppelt elegant zu wirken.
Es gilt nämlich als ladylike, eine Zigarette graziös
in einer Hand zu halten. Und das glaubt man heute.
Dabei ist es hochgradig unvernünftig
sich mit selbstmörderischen Attributen zu dekorieren.
Es gibt doch Möglichkeiten echter Eleganz!

Dämchen?

dämlich!

1–5 **Anti-Rauch-Kampagne** / *Anti-Smoking Campaign* / HfG Ulm / Studienjahr / *Semester* 1963 / 64 / Visuelle Kommunikation / *Visual Communication* / Dozent / *Lecturer:* Adolf Zillmann / Entwurf / *Design:* unbekannt / *unknown* / Sign. 2.0989, 2.0993, 2.0992, 2.0997, 2.1017 / HfG-Archiv / Museum Ulm

1

Gendermarketing: Nein, danke! Gendermedizin: Ja, bitte! »Ist Suzy zuhause?« Mit seinem Auftritt als »Mike« im Bayer-Werbespot (1963) für das Medikament »Children's Aspirin« wird der kleine Ted »Teddy« Quinn berühmt. Leider könne die kleine Suzy nicht zum Spielen zu ihm rauskommen, sie habe eine Erkältung und der Doktor sagt, sie müsse im Bett bleiben, erklärt ihm die Mutter an der Haustür. Schmerzen und Fieber habe sie aber nicht, weil sie ihrer Tochter Aspirin gegeben habe. Das erleichtert Mike offenbar, denn er sagt, das sei auch das, was er bei einer Erkältung von seiner Mutter bekäme. »Weil sie dich liebt! Und wenn du dich besser fühlst, fühlt auch sie sich besser«, sagt Suzys Mutter zu ihm herunterkniend und Mike antwortet freudestrahlend: »Mütter sind so, ja, so sind sie!«– Aus dem Off kommt eine männliche Stimme, die in dieser abschließenden Szene der Mutter am Bett der kleinen, kranken Suzy schließt: »Es gibt Ihnen so ein Selbstvertrauen zu wissen, dass Sie immer das Beste geben. Verlassen Sie sich stets auf Bayer Kinder-Aspirin mit Orangen-Geschmack. Sie und Ihr Kind werden sich beide schnell besser fühlen.«

Das Pharmazieunternehmen griff mit seiner Fernsehwerbung ein zeittypisches Frauenbild der 1960er Jahre auf und appellierte sogar über die Verpackung: »Mothers: Buy Flavored Bayer Children's Aspirin!« (Abb. 3). Auch für Print-Anzeigen wurde das Narrativ aufgegriffen: Für Kinder sei das Schmerzmittel »sanft wie der Kuss einer Mutter« (Abb. 2); eine im Haus arbeitende Frau verkündet, sie nehme Aspirin gegen Erschöpfung durch

Gender Marketing: No, thanks! Gender Medicine: Yes, please! »Is Suzy home?« Little Ted »Teddy« Quinn found fame after appearing as »Mike« and uttering these words in the 1963 TV commercial for Bayer Children's Aspirin.[11] Sadly, little Suzy can't come out to play: Answering the knock at her front door, Suzy's mother explains to Mike that her daughter has a cold and the doctor has told her to stay in bed. But Suzy has no pain or fever because mother has given her aspirin. Clearly reassured, Mike says his mother also gives him aspirin when he has a cold. »That's because she loves you!«, says Suzy's mother kneeling down to him, »And when you feel better, she feels better too«. Beaming with joy, Mike replies: »Mothers are like that, yeah, they are!« At the end of the closing scene, which sees mother at sick little Suzy's bedside, a male voiceover cuts in: »It gives you such confidence to know you're giving the best. Always rely on new orange-flavored Bayer aspirin for children. You and your child will both feel better, fast.«

The pharmaceutical company featured stereotypical images of the 1960s woman in their TV commercials and even on on their packaging: »Mothers: Buy Bayer Flavored Children's Aspirin!« (fig. 3). Such gendered depictions were also used in print ads: For children, the pain reliever is described as »gentle as a mother's kiss« (fig. 2); housewives take aspirin to relieve the fatigue of housework; while men working outdoors take the pills to ease cold-related muscle aches and fever (fig. 1). All this is typical of Western advertising created in the context of the time. What is less typical,

Hausarbeit; ein Mann bei der Arbeit im Freien erklärt, er nehme das Medikament gegen schmerzende Muskeln und Fieber bei einer Erkältung (Abb. 1). All das ist werbetechnisch typisch angesichts der westeuropäischen Kultur und vor dem zeitlichen Hintergrund. Weniger typisch ist es hingegen, dass Medikamente – über die Werbung hinaus – gestalterisch vermarktet werden, wie wir es z. B. aus der Kosmetikindustrie kennen. Nahezu jedes Produkt, Shampoo, Duschgel oder Rasierer scheint es da in einer Ausführung nach heteronormativer Geschlechterlogik, also »for men« und für Frauen, zu geben. Dabei ist es die Medizin betreffend keineswegs so, dass Unterschiede zwischen Geschlechtern keine Rolle spielen würden und der Mann weiter als Norm gelten könnte – zumindest lässt sich das nicht zuletzt mit der Begründung der sogenannten »Gendermedizin« feststellen, die seit 1997 auch von der Weltgesundheitsorganisation (WHO) unter dem Aspekt des »Gender-Mainstreaming« unterstützt wird.[9] Aus verschiedenen Gründen werden nach wie vor Frauen zu selten oder gar nicht für Medikamententests hinzugezogen, intergeschlechtliche Menschen kommen nicht vor. Dabei ist es mehr als offenbar, dass allein Hormonhaushalte, die eine Auswirkung auf die körperliche Verarbeitung von Medikamenten haben, je nach Geschlecht verschieden sind. In Bezug auf das Medikament Aspirin hatte beispielsweise eine groß angelegte Studie von 2005 zum Resultat, dass das Mittel bei vielen Frauen und damit nicht wie bei Männern eine signifikante Auswirkung auf ein Herzinfarktrisiko hat, dafür Acetylsalicylsäure (ASS) aber das Risiko für einen Schlaganfall bei Frauen senken kann.[10]

[9] Keiner, Dirk. 2015. »Der kleine Unterschied«. In Pharmazeutische Zeitung, Ausg. 41, 15.10.2015, https://www.pharmazeutische-zeitung.de/ausgabe-412015/der-kleine-unterschied/, zul. abgerufen am 13.10.2019.
[10] Levin, Richard I. 2005. The Puzzle of Aspirin and Sex. New England Journal of Medicine. 352: 1366–1368, DOI: 10.1056/NEJMe058051.

however, is that this creative marketing of medicines – aside from the advert itself – is very like cosmetics advertising: for example, almost every product, be it shampoo, shower gel, or razors, is available in a version based on a heteronormative gender logic, i.e. one version for men and another for women. And yet, it cannot be said that differences between the sexes play no role in medicine, nor that the male should still be considered the norm – thinking validated by the argument for so-called gender medicine, which has been supported by the World Health Organization (WHO) since 1997 through its work on »gender mainstreaming«.[9] For various reasons, women are still too rarely, if at all, involved in clinical trials, while intersex people are completely ignored. Yet there is no doubt that hormone levels alone – which affect the way the body processes medicines – differ depending on one's sex. With reference to aspirin, the results of a large-scale study in 2005 showed that the medicine does not have such a significant impact on the risk of a heart attack for women as it does for men, whereas acetylsalicylic acid (ASA) is more likely to lower women's risk of a stroke.[10]

[9] *Dirk Keiner, »Der kleine Unterschied,« Pharmazeutische Zeitung, No. 41, Oct. 15., 2015, https://www.pharmazeutische-zeitung.de/ausgabe-412015/der-kleine-unterschied/.*
[10] *Levin, Richard I. 2005. The Puzzle of Aspirin and Sex, New England Journal of Medicine 352 (2005): 1366–1368, DOI: 10.1056/NEJMe058051.*

1 **Bayer Aspirin** / US 1959 / Bayer Aspirin Werbeanzeige / *Ad* / Unternehmen: / *Company:* Bayer Corp. U.S.

2 **Gentle as a Mother's Kiss...** / US 1954 / Bayer Aspirin Werbeanzeige / *Ad* / Unternehmen: / *Company:* Bayer Corp. U.S. / Ladies' Home Journal / Ausg. / *Ed.* 07.1954

3 **Aspirin Pillendose** / *Drug packaging* / US ca. 1959 / Hersteller: / *Manufacturer:* Bayer Corp. U.S. / Sammlung / *Collection* Hans (Nick) Roericht / Sign. RS.007 / HfG-Archiv / Museum Ulm

2

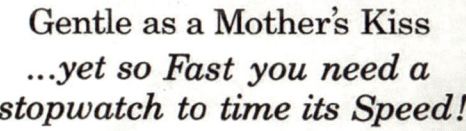

Gentle as a Mother's Kiss
...yet so *Fast* you need a stopwatch to time its Speed!

Only Bayer Aspirin Offers Both This *Proof* of Gentleness and *Proof* of Speed

WHEN YOU'RE IN PAIN, you *need* relief that's *gentle*. And the gentleness of Bayer Aspirin has been proved by its safe use by millions of people. The fact is that no other pain reliever can match its record of safety. Even for small children, doctors prescribe *gentle* Bayer Aspirin.

And when you're in pain, you *want* relief that's *fast*. Bayer Aspirin gives you amazingly fast relief. Here's one reason why: When you drop a Bayer Aspirin tablet into a glass of water, it starts to disintegrate almost instantly—so fast you need a stopwatch to time its speed. The same thing happens in your stomach. It's ready to go to work with amazing speed, to make you feel better—*fast*.

So whenever you suffer from an ordinary headache, take Bayer Aspirin for *gentle* relief and *fast* relief. And when you buy aspirin, don't look for a bargain. The *best* always costs more. So to be sure you are getting the *best*, buy *Bayer* Aspirin.

Get the best—get
BAYER ASPIRIN

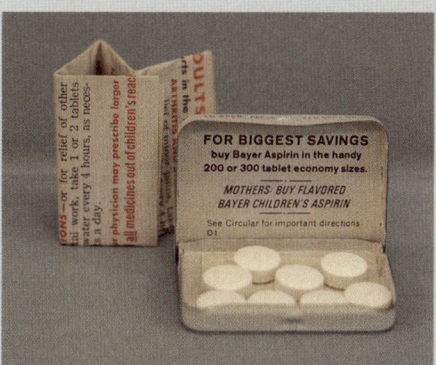

3

Haushalt und Wohnen /
Household and Living

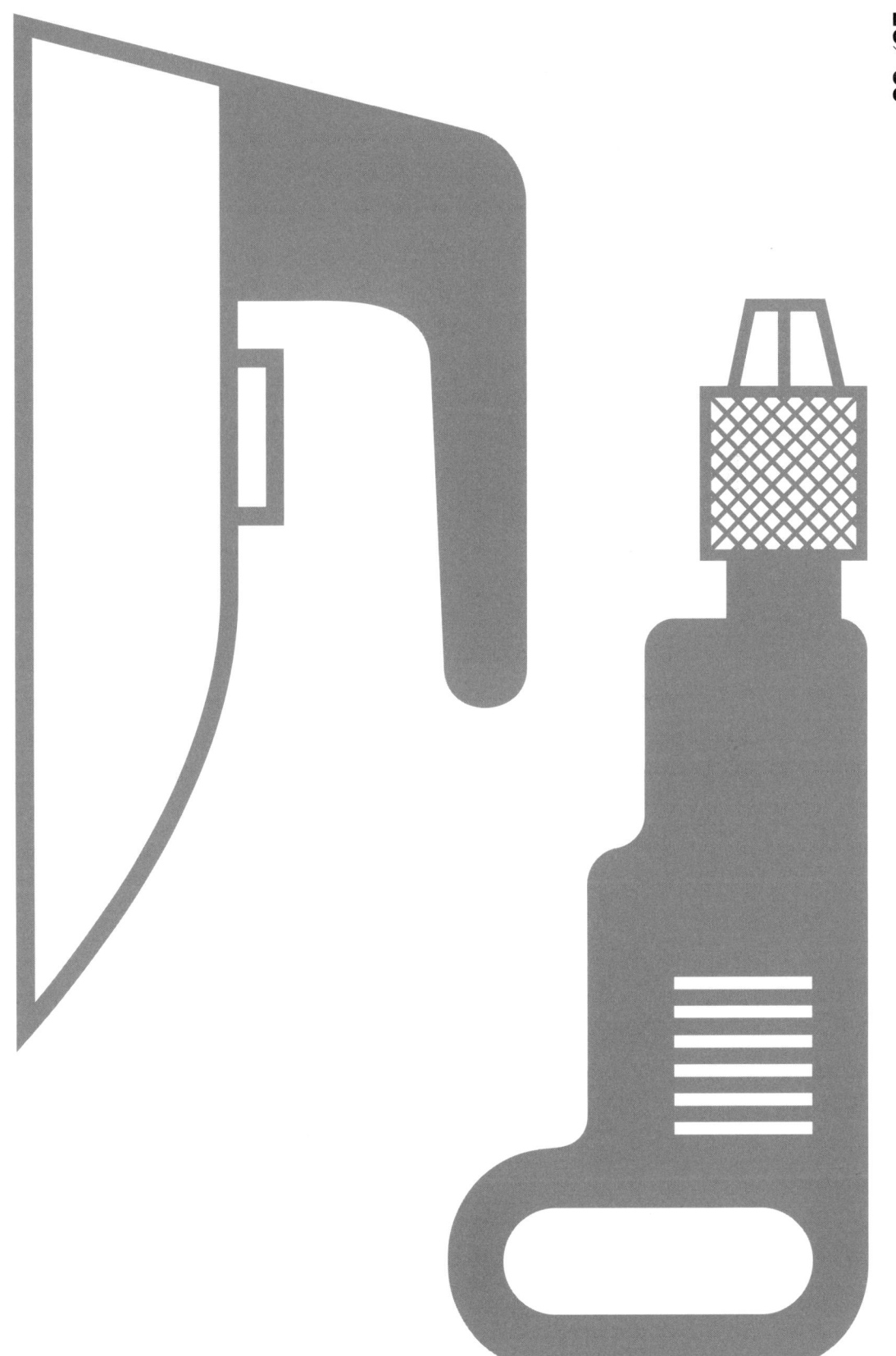

My Home is my Castle Im privaten Raum entscheiden wir. Das zumindest ist die Individualität, die wir hochhalten, wenn wir entscheiden, womit wir uns im eigenen Haushalt umgeben und wie wir unseren privaten Lebensraum gestalten. Er repräsentiert uns persönlich, im Gegensatz zum öffentlichen Raum. Dafür sind nicht bloß die Dinge, sondern auch soziale Rollen relevant.

Viel stärker als heute waren die familiären Rollen in der deutschen Nachkriegszeit aufgeteilt. Ein Bereich, der nach dichotomer Geschlechterlogik bis heute noch weitgehend weiblich assoziiert ist, ist die Hausarbeit. Beispielhaft dafür, dass mit der Entwicklung von Haushaltstechnologien auch Geschlechterrollen verknüpft wurden, zeigen das Aufkommen der vollautomatischen Waschmaschine und der Mikrowelle, wie Sandra Buchmüller in ihrer Dissertation »Geschlecht Macht Gestaltung – Gestaltung Macht Geschlecht« (2018) verdeutlicht. Das Hightech-Konzept, mit der sich Mikrowelle ursprünglich an »junge, dynamische, alleinstehende Männer« richtete, ging ebenso wenig auf, wie die Erwartung der 1950er Jahre, die Waschmaschine sei ein Beitrag zur Emanzipation der Hausfrau – deren Arbeitsbereich und Zeitaufwand verlagerte sich lediglich auf andere Tätigkeiten im gleichen Handlungsfeld.[1] Wiederum die Gestaltung einer Sanitäreinheit (1961/62) belegt, dass die Kategorie »Gender« auch in den funktionalistischen Entwürfen der ehemaligen HfG Ulm eine Rolle spielt. Eine Tabelle dient der systematischen Analyse und schlüsselt auf, wer in einer klassischen Familienkonstellation aus Mutter, Vater, Kind innerhalb eines Tages welche Tätigkeit im Badezimmer verrichtet. Während hier für das Rasieren nur der Mann auftaucht, ist die Frau für das Kinder baden und Wäsche waschen zuständig. Solche Trennungen zu hinterfragen, die sich eben mit an Dingen manifestieren, war das Anliegen zweier Aicher-Scholl-Kollegiatinnen aus dem Teilprojekt des Produktdesignkurses. Das Ergebnis: eine Installation unter dem Titel »Küche vs. Werkstatt«.

Unter dem Stichwort »Smart Home« werden heute digitale Systeme gehandelt, die das Zuhause sowie damit verbundene Tätigkeiten vernetzen und uns im Alltag intelligent assistieren sollen. Wie auch anderswo tritt genauso im Bereich der sogenannten Künstlichen Intelligenz (KI) zu Tage, dass diese Systeme dafür mit gewissen Normen gefüttert werden müssen, die wiederum auch Ergebnis und Spiegel soziokultureller Art sind – Menschen formen Dinge, Dinge formen Menschen. Sprach-Assistenzsysteme der großen Tech-Firmen Apple, Google, Microsoft und Amazon sind überwiegend weiblich stilisiert, KI-Systeme der Finanz-Branche männlich und werden deshalb anhaltend kontrovers diskutiert. »Q« (2019) ist das Ergebnis einer Herangehensweise, Stereotype und binäre Geschlechternormen nicht auf Technik zu reproduzieren, entstanden aus der Kollaboration zwischen der Organisation Copenhagen Pride und dem Tech-Unternehmen Virtue Nordics: »Q« als »erste genderlose Stimme« ist eine Verschmelzung

My Home is my Castle In the private sphere it's up to us. At least this is the individuality we uphold when it comes to our decisions about the things we choose to surround ourselves with in our own households and the design of our private habitat. It represents us personally, as opposed to the public space. Not just things, but also social roles are relevant here.

In post-war Germany the different family roles were divided far more strictly than today. In keeping with dichotomous gender logic, domestic work is a realm that has a primarily female connotation to this day. That the development of household technologies was also tied to gender roles is exemplified in the advent of the fully automatic washing machine and the microwave oven, as Sandra Buchmüller points out in her dissertation Geschlecht Macht Gestaltung – Gestaltung Macht Geschlecht (2018). The high-tech concept by which microwaves originally addressed »young, dynamic bachelors« proved to be as unsuccessful as the expectation in the 1950s that the washing machine would contribute to the emancipation of the housewife – ultimately, her work space and time expenditure merely shifted to other tasks in the same sphere.[1] In turn, the concept for a sanitary unit (1961/62) also reflects that gender played a role in the functionalist designs at the former Ulm School of Design. A chart for systematic analysis breaks down who, in a classic family constellation of mother, father, and child, performs which activity in the bathroom over the course of a day. While shaving is only attributed to the man, the woman is responsible for bathing the children and doing the laundry. To challenge such divisions and how they manifest in things was the concern of two Aicher-Scholl-Kolleg students from the product design course subproject. The result: an installation titled »Kitchen vs. Workshop«.

Today, the catchword »smart home« refers to digital systems that network the household and related activities and are supposed to intelligently assist in our daily lives. As elsewhere, it is evident in the realm of so-called artificial intelligence (AI) that the corresponding systems have to be fed with certain norms, which, in turn, are a result of and mirror a sociocultural reality – what we design, designs us back. Voice assistant systems by the big tech firms Apple, Google, Microsoft, and Amazon predominantly bear a female stylisation, whereas AI components of the financial sector are male and therefore continue to elicit controversial debates. »Q« (2019), a collaboration between the Copenhagen Pride organisation and the tech company Virtue Nordics, evolved from the intention to not reproduce stereotypes and binary gender norms in technology: »Q – The First Genderless Voice« merges non-binary voice patterns and is transmitted on the neutrally perceived frequency range between 145 to 175 Hertz.

In his project titled »In A Parallel Universe« (2018) Eli Rezkallah caused quite the stir in social networks with an artistic perspective that employs

nicht-binärer Stimmenmuster und deren Übertragung auf einem neutral geltenden Frequenzbereich von 145 bis 175 Hertz.

Mit einer künstlerischen Perspektive sorgte Eli Rezkallah unter dem Titel »In A Parallel Universe« (2018) unter Einsatz des »Gender-Swapping« für Aufsehen in den sozialen Netzwerken: Er vertauscht die dargestellten männlichen und weiblichen Rollen von Reklamen der 1940er und 1950er Jahre. Vor allem im Nebeneinander der historischen und künstlerischen Versionen offenbaren sich absurd wirkende Konstruktionen von sozialen Rollenbildern und deren zeitlicher Wandel. Übertragen auf vermeintlich neutrale Alltagswerkzeuge, eröffnet ein solcher Umkehreffekt erstaunliche Perspektiven auf unsere Seh- und Nutzungsgewohnheiten. Die Kombination oder Umkehrung zweier weiblich oder männlich kodierter Produkte findet sich als Mittel sowohl in der angewandten Designforschung (Karin Ehrnberger: Bohrer »Dolphin«, Stabmixer »Mega Hurricane«), wie auch in der Produktwelt von Werkzeughersteller Bosch (Akkuschrauber »IXO«) oder im durchgeführten Schulprojekt als »neutral« intendierter Entwurf (Akkuschrauber »Akita Multitask Future 2000«) wieder.

[1] Vgl. Buchmüller, Sandra. 2018. Geschlecht Macht Gestaltung – Gestaltung Macht Geschlecht, S. 96–97.

»gender swapping«: He swaps the male and female roles portrayed in adverts of the 1940s and 1950s. Above all, the juxtaposition of the historical and artistic versions reveals absurd constructions of social role models and their transformation over the course of time. Translated to allegedly neutral tools of the everyday, such a reversal reveals surprising perspectives on our viewing and usage habits. The combination or reversal of two female or male connoted products is also found in applied design research (Karin Ehrnberger's drill »Dolphin«, hand blender »Mega Hurricane«), in the product range of tool manufacturer Bosch (cordless screwdriver »IXO«), or in the school project as a »neutrally« intended design proposal (cordless screwdriver »Akita Multitask Future 2000«).

[1] *Sandra Buchmüller, Geschlecht Macht Gestaltung – Gestaltung Macht Geschlecht (Berlin, Logos, 2018), 96–97.*

System Design at the HfG Ulm: »The Adaptable Flat« (1964) and »Sanitary Units for the Living Area« (1961/62)

The application of design to systems was also a cornerstone of the interdisciplinary educational principles at the Ulm School of Design (HfG Ulm). In this context, functionalism assumed a guiding role. In order to come to a result, a design solution, a profound understanding and the analysis of given circumstances, processes, and conditions were imperative. Above all, with an objective to design for all – but does that also imply neutrality? In the 1950s and 1960s, when the HfG Ulm was still in operation, the realm of the household was characterised by gender roles even stronger than today. Hence, it is worth taking a look at the designs in this realm.

For their diploma thesis in product design at the beginning of the 1960s, the students Robert Gräff, Walter Kiehlneker, Dieter Reich, and Heinz Wäger joined forces. Under the supervision of Hans Gugelot, they conceived »The Adaptable Flat – A System of Industry Products«. On the basis of sociological, psychological, and physiological factors, they systematically developed a design strongly characterised by functional modularity and individualisation. At an earlier point, Walter Kiehlneker and Heinz Wäger already worked on the development of sanitary units in a course led by Walter Zeischegg, which returned in part in the diploma thesis, and thus can be seen as a preliminary draft. In both cases family usage habits were integrated into the analysis. For Wäger's design, which was purchased by the Bern-based company Troesch & Co.,[2] this meant: Which family member is potentially using which unit of the bathroom at what time and for which activity? What is interesting here are the parameters employed to underpin a visual analysis for answering this set of questions as well as the design of the sanitary unit (fig. 1): First, there is the assumption of a traditional family constellation of father, mother, and child. The chart indicates that the activity of shaving was only attributed to the man (presumably his morning shave). Makeup, on the other hand, is reserved for the woman, four times a day; »manicure« and »pedicure« are assigned to the man and the child, in the mornings and evenings. The woman, in turn, takes care of »doing the laundry« and »bathing the children«. Without doubt, this reflects conceptions typical for their time, which would probably look different today but are interesting for a number of reasons: On the one hand, it seems that the (male) assumptions are used to analyse the usage of a bathroom and, on the other, to introduce role models of the time in the design process. The outlined approach is oriented upon functional aspects and is gender-specific in certain regards, thus it is in no way neutral. This illustrates that not only things but also spaces and their usage are determined by notions of gender.

Many successful designs of the HfG Ulm and their appraisal as timeless design indicate that there

Zeitliche Verteilung wesentlicher Verrichtungen im Hygieneraum

	6 - 7	7 - 8	8 -11	11-14	14-17	17-19	19-20	20-24
Hände-waschen	ⓅⓂ.	ⓅⓂⓀ	Ⓟ.Ⓚ	ⓅⓂⓀ	Ⓟ.Ⓚ	Ⓕ.Ⓚ	ⓅⓂⓀ	ⓅⓂ.
Gesicht-waschen	ⓅⓂ.	ⓅⓂⓀ	...	ⓅⓂⓀ	......	......	ⓅⓂⓀ	ⓅⓂ.
Zähne-putzen	ⓅⓂ.	ⓅⓂⓀ	...	ⓅⓂⓀ			ⓅⓂⓀ	
Kämmen	ⓅⓂ.	ⓅⓂⓀ	...	ⓅⓂⓀ			ⓅⓂ.	...
Haare-waschen					Ⓟ..		Ⓚ .Ⓜ	
Rasieren	.Ⓜ.							
Make-up			.Ⓟ..		Ⓟ...		Ⓟ...	Ⓟ...
Manicure			.ⓂⓀ				.ⓂⓀ	
Kinder-baden			Ⓟ.Ⓚ		Ⓟ.Ⓚ			
Wäsche-waschen				Ⓟ..				
Unterkörper-waschen				Ⓟ..	Ⓟ..		ⓅⓂⓀ	
Körper-entleeren	ⓅⓂ.	ⓅⓂⓀ	Ⓟ..	ⓅⓂⓀ	Ⓟ..	Ⓟ.Ⓚ	ⓅⓂⓀ	ⓅⓂ.
Füsse-waschen				ⓅⓂ			ⓅⓂⓀ	
Pedicure			.ⓂⓀ				.ⓂⓀ	
Duschen	ⓅⓂ.	Ⓟ...	......	......	Ⓚ	ⓅⓂⓀ	...	ⓅⓂ.
Baden			Ⓟ.Ⓚ				.ⓂⓀ	

Ⓟ = Frau   Ⓜ = Mann   Ⓚ = Kind

1 Zeitliche Verteilung wesentlicher Verrichtungen im Hygieneraum / *Time distribution of the main activities in the hygiene room* / Studienjahr / *Semester* 1961/62 / HfG Ulm / Abt. Produktgestaltung / *Dept. Product Design* / Systematische Analyse für die Gestaltung einer Sanitäreinheit / *Systematic analysis for the design of a sanitary unit* / Dozent: / *Lecturer:* Walter Zeischegg / Student: Heinz Wäger / Sign. Ze.AZ. 236 / HfG-Archiv / Museum Ulm

2 Sanitäreinheit für den Wohnbereich / *Sanitary Unit for the Living Area* / Studienjahr / *Semester* 1961/62 / HfG Ulm / Abt. Produktgestaltung / *Dept. Product Design* / Modell / *Model* / Dozent: / *Lecturer:* Walter Zeischegg / Student: Walter Kiehlneker / Sign. M 142 / HfG-Archiv / Museum Ulm

sondern auch Räume und deren Nutzung sind unter diesem Blickwinkel von Geschlechtervorstellungen geprägt.

Viele erfolgreiche Entwürfe der HfG Ulm und das Preisen dieser als zeitlose Gestaltung sprechen dafür, dass es zumindest der Anspruch war, »für alle« zu entwerfen. Dennoch bleibt es – wie in vielen anderen Bereichen auch – schwierig, etwa von »neutraler Gestaltung« zu sprechen. Oder anders formuliert: Wie können Dinge, die von Menschen gestaltet werden, neutral sein, wenn diejenigen, die gestalten, es auch nicht sind, ja nicht sein können? Zumeist verschleiert der Anspruch »für alle« hinter einer vermeintlichen Neutralität, dass beispielsweise Geschlecht überhaupt eine Rolle spielt. Der Funktionalismus, der diesen Anspruch ausweist, läuft daher auch Gefahr, »genderblind« zu sein, respektive unhinterfragte Konzepte der Gestaltenden in die Gestaltung zu übertragen.[3] Dies zeigt sich weniger offenbar in den Ergebnissen als vielmehr anhand vorausgehender Entwurfsprozesse selbst.

[2] In einem »Ideenwettbewerb für einen Sanitär-Installationsblock« des 22. Juni 1962, den die Firma Troesch & Co. in Bern veranstaltete, gewann Gerhard Mayer den 3. Preis und der Entwurf von Heinz Wäger wurde angekauft (s. Hochschule für Gestaltung (Hg.): ulm 6, Zeitschrift der Hochschule für Gestaltung, Ausg. Oktober 1962, S. 35).

[3] Vgl. u. a. Becker, Katja u. Herling, Claudia. 2017. Der Einfluss von Gender im Entwicklungsprozess von digitalen Artefakten. In Gender und Design – zum vergeschlechtlichten Umgang mit dem gestalteten Alltag, hrsg. v. Uta Brandes u. Sigrid Metz-Göckel, Gender, Zeitschrift für Geschlecht, Kultur und Gesellschaft 3, vol. 9 (2017), 26–44; Van Oost, Ellen. 2003. Materialized Gender; Buchmüller, Susanne. 2018. Geschlecht Macht Gestaltung – Gestaltung Macht Geschlecht.

was at least an aspiration to design »for all«. However, it remains difficult – as in many other realms – to speak of »neutral design«. Or in other words: How can things that are designed by humans be neutral, when the ones who design are not, nor even can be? Often the claim »for all« tagged behind a presumed neutrality conceals, for example, that gender plays a role at all. A functionalism that builds upon this claim therefore runs the risk of being »gender blind«, including the transfer of unquestioned concepts of the designers into the design.[3] This is less obvious in the results but clearly readable in the preceding design processes.

[2] *In an »Idea Competition for a Sanitary Installation Block« of June 22, 1962, organised by the Bern-based company Troesch & Co., Gerhard Mayer won 3rd prize and the design by Heinz Wäger was purchased. See: Hochschule für Gestaltung (ed.), »ulm 6,« Journal of the Hochschule für Gestaltung (October 1962): 35.*

[3] *Cf., amongst others: Katja Becker and Claudia Herling, »Der Einfluss von Gender im Entwicklungsprozess von digitalen Artefakten,« in: Gender und Design – zum vergeschlechtlichten Umgang mit dem gestalteten Alltag, edited by Uta Brandes and Sigrid Metz-Göckel, Gender, Zeitschrift für Geschlecht, Kultur und Gesellschaft 3, vol. 9 (2017): 26–44; Ellen Van Oost, Materialized Gender (Cambridge, MA: MIT Press, 2003); Susanne Buchmüller, Geschlecht Macht Gestaltung – Gestaltung Macht Geschlecht (Berlin: Logos, 2018).*

3 **Die anpassbare Wohnung – Ein System von Industrieprodukten** / *The Adaptable Flat – A System of Industry Products* / DE 1964 / Diplomarbeit mit Modellen / *Diploma thesis with models* / HfG Ulm / Abt. Produktgestaltung / *Dept. Product Design* / Hauptreferent: / *Head lecturer:* Hans Gugelot / Studierende: / *Students:* Robert Graeff, Walter Kiehlneker, Dieter Reich, Heinz Waeger / Sign. 65.9 / HfG-Archiv / Museum Ulm

»Wie könnte Ihre Wohnung aussehen? Machen Sie sich an's Einrichten!« So lautete die Aufforderung an die Ausstellungsbesucher*innen von den zwei Aicher-Scholl-Kollegiatinnen Lena K. und Annika Ruß. Sie nahmen an dem Produktdesignkurs des Kollegs teil und haben nach einem Zusammenhang zwischen Vorlieben bei der Wohnungseinrichtung und Geschlecht gefragt. Dafür haben sie ein interaktives Einrichtungsspiel für die Ausstellung entworfen. Besucher*innen waren eingeladen, aus vorausgewählten Abbildungen von Zimmerpflanzen, Sitzmöbeln, Leuchten, Teppichen u. Ä. auf einer weißen Fläche ihre bevorzugte Wohnzimmereinrichtung zusammenzustellen. Dazu gehörte die Möglichkeit, dies fotografisch zu dokumentieren, und zwar zusammen mit einer auszufüllenden Karte in Bezug auf die Daten Geschlecht (m/w/d) und Alter (s. Abb. 1–3). Wenngleich das fotografische Material keine Schlüsse bezüglich Wohnungseinrichtung und Geschlecht bzw. Alter zulassen, konnte anhand der über 200 ausgefüllten Kärtchen eine Statistik hinsichtlich Alter und Geschlecht der Besucher*innen erstellt werden (s. Abb. 4–5).[4]

Die zweiteilige Auswertung zeigt, dass das Durchschnittsalter (gesamt) mit 35,4 Jahren überdurchschnittlich niedrig ist, wenn man davon ausgeht, dass als das typische Museumspublikum die Altersgruppe 60+ gilt. Dabei waren den Angaben zufolge von sehr jungen Besucher*innen bis in das Alter von 78 Jahren alle Altersgruppen vertreten. Überdurchschnittlich scheint mit 71 Prozent auch die Anzahl derjenigen, die sich als weiblich identifizieren (Durchschnittsalter 34 Jahre), gegenüber 21 Prozent, die die Option männlich (Durchschnittsalter 39,6 Jahre) und vier Prozent, die die Option divers (Durchschnittsalter 32,1 Jahre) wählten. Es zeigt sich anhand der Ergebnisse, dass sich entweder überdurchschnittlich viele Besucherinnen dem Einrichtungsspiel zuwandten und/oder, dass das Interesse am Ausstellungsthema besonders bei Frauen hoch war. Auch wenn oder gerade weil wir in einer Mehrheitsgesellschaft leben, werten wir als kulturelle Institution die Annahme der Option divers sowie Mehrfachnennungen (zusammen neun Prozent) als bestärkendes Zeichen dafür, denjenigen, die sich selbst weder als männlich noch als weiblich identifizieren, eine Stimme zu geben. Geschlecht ist ein wichtiger Teil der menschlichen Identität und auch oder erneut gerade wenn wir Kategorien zu unserer Selbstvergewisserung als wichtig erachten, dürfen diese nicht dazu führen, Personen die Teil der Gesellschaft sind, schlichtweg außen vor zu lassen.

[4] Bei über 2.000 erfassten Gesamtbesucher*innen beträgt die Auswertung von über 214 Karten immerhin zehn Prozent der Besucher*innen-Anteile.

1

2

3

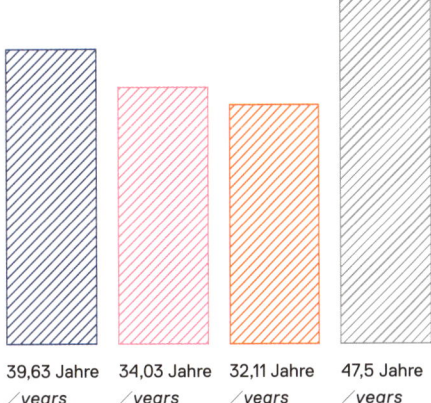

39,63 Jahre / years   34,03 Jahre / years   32,11 Jahre / years   47,5 Jahre / years

4 Auswertung nach Durchschnittsalter je Geschlecht männlich / weiblich / divers / andere (Mehrfachnennung) / *Evaluation by average age per gender male / female / diverse / other*

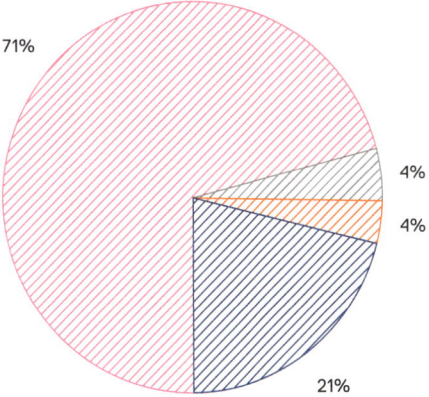

71%
4%
4%
21%

5 Auswertung nach Geschlecht männlich / weiblich / divers / andere (Mehrfachnennung) / *Evaluation by gender male / female / diverse / other*

Einrichtungsspiel / *Furnishing game* / DE 2019 / Aicher-Scholl-Kolleg / Produktdesignkurs / *Product design course* / Dozent: / *Lecturer:* Uli Häussler / Konzept und Umsetzung: / *Concept and realisation:* Lena K., Annika Ruß

Beispiele fotografisch dokumentierter Ergebnisse mit zugehörigen Angaben zu Alter und Geschlecht: / *Examples of photographically documented results with corresponding information on age and gender:*

1 männlich / *male* / 38 Jahre alt / *Years old*
2 weiblich / *female* / 4 Jahre alt / *Years old*
3 männlich / *male* / 50 Jahre alt / *Years old*

»**How could your apartment look like? Go ahead and furnish it!**« read the invitation by the two Aicher-Scholl-Kolleg students Annika and Lena, asking exhibition visitors to participate in the game. They had participated in the college's product design course and posed the question whether furnishing preferences and gender are connected. To this end, they developed an interactive furnishing game for the exhibition. On a white surface, visitors were asked to compose their preferred living room interiors from preselected images of room plants, seating furniture, lamps, carpets, and other items. There was also the opportunity to document it with a camera, along with a form with questions relating to sex (m/f/d) and age (fig. 1–3). Although the photographic material did not provide any conclusions in terms of the interiors and gender or age, the 200 completed forms facilitated statistics regarding the age and sex of the visitors (fig. 4–5).[4]

The two-part evaluation shows that the average age (in total) of 35.4 years was distinctly low, given that the reported age group of museum visitors is 60+. However, based on the provided data – from very young visitors up to the age of 78 – all age groups were represented. At 71 percent, the number of people who identify themselves as females (average age 34 years) seems above average, in comparison to the 21 percent who chose the male option (average age 39.6 years) and four percent, who checked »diverse« (average age 32.1 years). The results show that either an above-average number of female visitors played the furnishing game and/or that the exhibition topic was particularly popular amongst women. Even though, or precisely because we live in a majority society, we, as a cultural institution, regard the choice of the option »diverse« as well as multiple answers (nine percent in total) as an encouraging signal to give those people, who identify themselves neither as male nor as female, a voice. Gender is an important part of human identity; and even though, or again precisely when we deem categories important for our self-assurance, they should not lead to the simple exclusion of persons who are part of our society.

[4] Although there was a total of over 2.000 documented visitors, the evaluation of more than 200 cards still pertains to 10 percent of the visitors.

Butler und Dienstmädchen sind von gestern? Wenn es um Künstliche Intelligenz, kurz KI, und deren Einsatz für »smarte« Assistenzsysteme geht, könnte man den Eindruck gewinnen, diese veralteten Rollenbilder seien zurück; natürlich ins digitale Zeitalter übertragen, bezeichnet als »Intelligent Personal Assistants«. Sprachassistenzsysteme sind längst keine Zukunftsmusik mehr, sondern in der Software und den Geräten der jeweiligen großen Tech-Companies von Microsoft, Google, Amazon und Apple verbaut. Genannte Unternehmen haben ihre jeweiligen Systeme »Siri«, »Cortana« und »Alexa« getauft, ihnen eine Stimme gegeben, in der Regel eine weibliche, wie auch die Namen signalisieren. Dass all diese Konzepte für intelligente, zukunftsweisende Technologien so selbstverständlich dasselbe Muster der weiblichen, hilfsbereiten Dienstleistungskraft aufgreifen, ist ein Hauptkritikpunkt der entfachten Debatte. Tatsächlich wurden weitere Fragen aufgeworfen, die aufzeigen, dass wir vor einem größeren Diskurs und vielen offenen Fragen bezüglich »Embodiment of Design«[5] stehen: Braucht Künstliche Intelligenz ein Geschlecht? Wer bestimmt über Normen, mit denen die KI »gefüttert« wird? In welchem Verhältnis stehen wir als Mensch zur Technik und welchen Umgang möchten wir dazu pflegen? Während in Fachkreisen schon darüber diskutiert wurde, ob z. B. Roboter eine techniknahe physische Erscheinung zur Wahrung des Charakters erhalten sollten, ist es bei den Sprachassistenzen so, dass diese vielmehr nur Programme sind. Gleichzeitig sind sie uns aber über die Stimme – das einzige Wesen des Programms und zugleich Steuerungselement – viel näher. »Q – The First Genderless Voice« ist die Antwort einer Kollaboration u. a. des LGBTQ-Netzwerks Copenhagen Pride und Technikunternehmens Virtue Nordics, von Linguist*innen, IT-Spezialist*innen und Sounddesigner*innen. Sie haben fünf Stimmen von nicht-binären Personen aufgenommen, diese zu einer Stimme verarbeitet und anhand einer Befragung von über 4.600 Personen aus ganz Europa verfeinert. Der Frequenzbereich von »Q« liegt zwischen 145 und 175 Hertz, einem als neutral empfundenen Bereich zwischen männlicher und weiblicher Stimmfrequenz. Laut eigenen Angaben soll »Q« eine dritte Option sein, ähnlich wie das dritte Geschlecht »divers«. Ein damit verbundenes Anliegen: Statt das Zweigeschlechtersystem und damit verbundene Stereotype auf Technologien zu übertragen, wie es die meisten Unternehmen machen, sollte innovative Technologie den gesellschaftlichen Entwicklungsprozess begleiten.[6] Zusätzlich interessant an »Q« ist, dass es eine grafische Visualisierung für den Kurzclip und die Webseite gibt: eine organisch wirkende, pulsierende Membran, abstrakt-biologisch und fluid, ästhetisch angelehnt an die Vorstellung von Stimmbändern.

[5] Gemeint sind Strategien oder Mechanismen, die mit Ideen und Konzepten von Verkörperung im Feld von Gestaltung als Abstraktion einhergehen. Unter diesem Themenschwerpunkt erschien auch eine Ausgabe des form Design Magazines (Sep/Okt 2018, Nr. 279).
[6] Siehe Antwort auf die Frage »Why did we make Q?« auf https://genderlessvoice.com/about, zul. abgerufen am 23.11.2019.

Butler and maid are of yesteryear? When we speak about artificial intelligence (AI) and its application in »smart« assistant systems, one might get the impression that these outdated role models are back; of course, translated into the digital age as »intelligent personal assistants«. Voice assistant systems are no longer dreams of the future – they are being built in the software and devices of the big tech firms like Microsoft, Google, Amazon, and Apple. These companies have baptised their systems »Siri«, »Cortana«, and »Alexa«, and gave them a voice, usually a female one, as the names suggest. The fact that all of these concepts for intelligent, trendsetting technologies are adopting the same pattern of a helpful female servant so naturally is the main point of criticism in the heated debate. Indeed, other questions arose, which show that we are facing a much broader discourse and many open questions about the »embodiment of design«[5]: Does AI need a gender? Who decides on the norms which are fed into AI? How do humans relate to technology and what type of conduct do we want to have with it? While expert groups have already discussed whether robots, for example, should have a physical appearance that confirms the technological character, voice assistants are only programs. At the same time, however, with their voice – being the only true essence of the program as well as the control element – they are much closer to us. »Q – The First Genderless Voice« is the outcome of a collaboration between the LGBTQ network Copenhagen Pride and the technology company Virtue Nordics, between linguists, IT specialists, sound designers, and other parties. They recorded five voices of non-binary persons, combined them into one voice, and refined it based on a survey of more than 4600 people from all across Europe. The frequency range of Q lies between 145 and 175 Hertz, which is perceived as being neutral between male and female voice frequencies. Q should be a third option, similar to the third sex term »diverse«. Accordingly, the objective is to not translate the binary system and related stereotypes into technologies, as most companies do, but to accompany social development processes with innovative technology.[6] Another interesting aspect of Q is the graphic visualisation for a short video clip and the website: a seemingly organic, pulsating membrane, abstract-biological and fluid, aesthetically reminiscent of vocal cords.

[5] What is meant here are strategies or mechanisms that coincide with ideas and conceptions of embodiment in design as abstractions. An edition of the design magazine form (Sept./Oct. 2018, no. 279) was dedicated to this topic.
[6] See the answer to the question »Why did we make Q?« on https://genderlessvoice.com/about.

Move me

153Hz Perceived Neutral Frequency

Q – The First Genderless Voice / DK 2019
/ Frame KI-Stimme auf: / Frame AI-voice on: www.genderlessvoice.com / Idee und Umsetzung: / Idea and realisation: Copenhagen Pride, Virtue Nordic, Equal AI, Koalition Interactive, thirtysoundsgood

Haushalt und Wohnen / Household and Living

Küche vs. Werkstatt Nicht nur Dinge allein, sondern ganze Räume und die Summe der tätigkeitsspezifischen Geräte können Vorstellungen von Geschlecht unterworfen sein. Bekannteste, stereotype Beispiele dafür sind insbesondere die Küche als »das Reich der Frau« mit Topf, Suppenkelle und Lappen und die Einreihung dieser in die Pflichten der Hausfrau bis in die Mitte des vergangenen Jahrhunderts, Stichwort: Küche, Kirche, Kinder. Andererseits die Werkstatt als das »Refugium des Mannes«, die Enklave im Haushalt, das Reich von Hammer, Schrauben und Bohrer. Judith Hoerder und Jessy Tieu aus dem Produktdesignkurs im Aicher-Scholl-Kolleg haben sich gefragt was passiert, wenn man die Utensilien, die Werkzeuge der jeweiligen Räume, ihrer eigentlichen typischen Funktion beraubt und sie in den jeweils anderen Kontext überträgt? Die an die Ausstellungsfläche angrenzende Küche funktionierten die beiden für ihre Installation »Küche vs. Werkstatt« um: Der Kühlschrank bestückt mit Farbdosen, Arbeitshandschuhen, Säge und Schutzbrille landete auf der Küchenarbeitsplatte, gepudert mit Weizenmehlstaub. Auf gegenüberstehender Werkbank fanden sich Küchenwaage und Topfhandschuhe zwischen Sägespänen und ein Spanholzscheit auf dem Kuchenheber arrangiert. Wie eine Intervention fügte sich die Installation als eine Art begehbares Stillleben in die Ausstellung »Nicht mein Ding« und deren Bereich »Haushalt und Wohnen« ein. Das Moment der Irritation haben sich die beiden Kollegiatinnen dabei zu Nutze gemacht, um zugleich geschlechtsspezifische Konnotationen hinsichtlich von Dingen in Haushalt und Freizeit aufzuzeigen.

Kitchen vs. Workshop Not only things but complete spaces and the sum of the tools and appliances, which are specific to certain activities, can be subjected to notions of gender. One of the most familiar stereotypical examples is the kitchen, the »domain of the woman«, together with pot, ladle, and cleaning rag, and its integration in the duties of the housewife up to the middle of last century – keywords: kitchen, church, children. On the other hand, the workshop is the »refuge of the man«, an enclave within the household, the domain of hammer, screws, and drill. Judith Hoerder und Jessy Tieu from the Aicher-Scholl-Kolleg product design course pondered what would happen if one were to divest the utensils, the tools of each space, of their typical original functions and transfer them into the respective other context. The two participants adapted the kitchen adjacent to the exhibition space for their installation »Kitchen vs. Workshop«: The fridge was equipped with paint tins, work gloves, and saw, safety goggles landed on the kitchen counter, dusted over with wheat flour. On the workbench standing opposite one found a kitchen scale and oven gloves between sawdust and chipboard placed on a cake lifter. The installation integrated in the exhibition »Not My Thing« and the section »Household and Living« as a kind of walk-in still-life intervention. The two students used the moment of irritation as a strategy to point out gender-specific connotations of everyday things in the household and leisure time.

Küche vs. Werkstatt Kitchen vs. Workshop / DE 2018/19 / Installation / Aicher-Scholl-Kolleg / Produktdesignkurs *Product design course* / Dozent: *Lecturer:* Uli Häussler / Konzept und Umsetzung: *Concept and realisation:* Judith Hoerder, Jessy Tieu

Der »Akita Multitask Future 2000« ist das von Alicia gestaltete Ergebnis zur Aufgabenstellung der Schulprojektwoche, ein »neutrales« Produkt zu entwerfen. Ihre Umsetzung erweist sich als Beispiel einer rationalen Herangehensweise im Rahmen der binären Geschlechterlogik: Das entworfene Haushaltsgerät ist in erster Linie ein Akkuschrauber mit integriertem Radio und wird durch verschiedene Aufsätze wie zum Multifunktionsprodukt, das in der Küche und im Heimwerken einsetzbar ist. Dahinter steht die von außen nachvollziehbare Gleichung, etwas männlich und weiblich assoziiertes – wie hier: Akkuschrauber und Rührgerät – miteinander zu kombinieren, um so zu etwas »Neutralem« zu kommen. Diese Herangehensweise mag vermeintlich zu einfach wirken und doch ist es ideentechnisch dem Prinzip nahe, das Werkzeughersteller Bosch für sein Erfolgsprodukt »IXO« samt Aufsätzen anwendet (s. Bosch »IXO«, S. 100). Zudem ist erkennbar, wie sehr einerseits geschlechtsspezifische Zuschreibungen und andererseits die gleichzeitige Übertragung auf Dinge bereits in jungem Alter erkannt werden.

The »Akita Multitask Future 2000« Alicia presented the »Akita Multitask Future 2000« in response to the task to design a »neutral« product in the Project Week. Her idea is exemplary of a rational approach in the framework of binary gender logic: The household appliance design is a cordless screwdriver with an integrated radio, whose different heads make it a multifunctional product, which can be used in the kitchen and for home improvement. Behind the idea is the easily identifiable equation of combining two items with a male and female connotation – here, a cordless screwdriver and a mixer – to arrive at something »neutral«. This approach might seem all-too simple, yet at its essence it is close to the principle that tool manufacturer Bosch applies to its successful product line »IXO« with its attachment heads (see Bosch »IXO«, p. 100). Moreover, it is a clear example of how both gender-specific ascriptions and their simultaneous translation into things are already perceived at a young age.

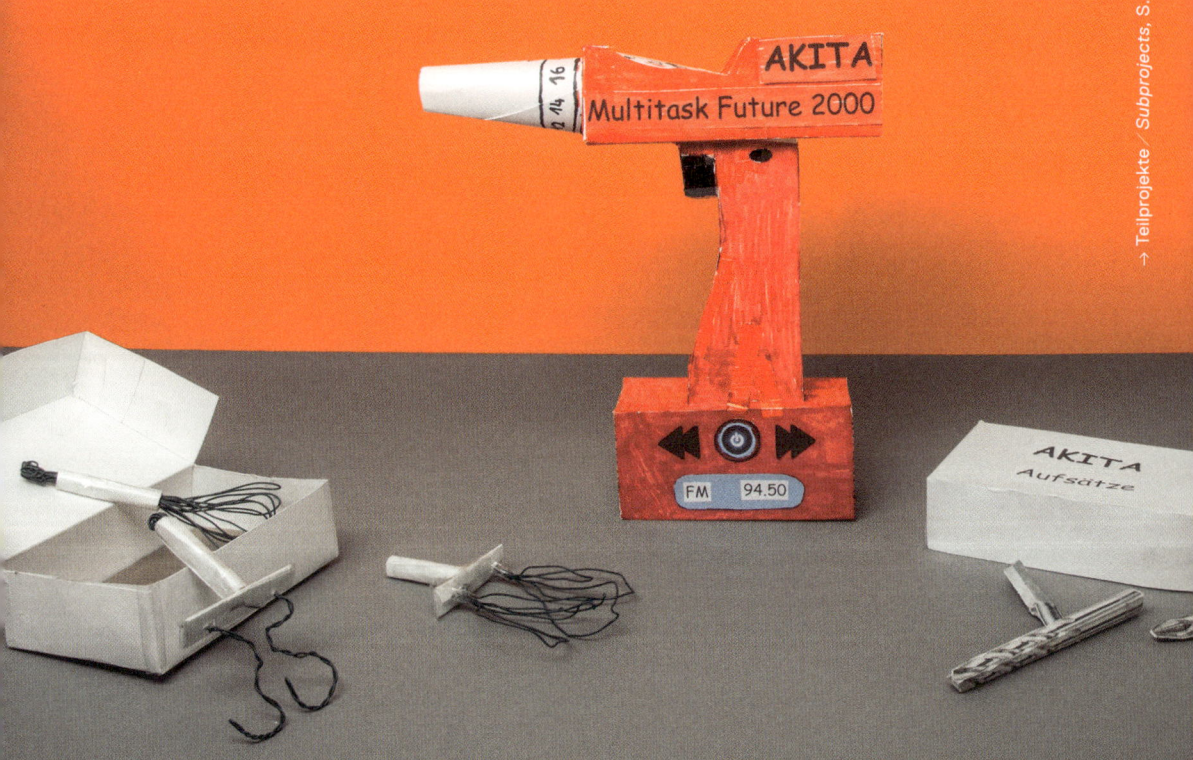

Akita Multitask Future 2000 ╱ DE 2018 ╱ Mock-up multifunktionaler Akkuschrauber ╱ *Multifunctional cordless drill* ╱ Schulprojekt mit einer 9. Klasse der Realschule Dornstadt ╱ *School project with 9th grade pupils from Realschule Dornstadt* ╱ Werbeslogan: Der Akkuschrauber für SIE und IHN! ╱ *Advertising slogan: The Cordless Drill for HER and HIM!* ╱ Entwurf: ╱ *Design:* Alicia

Visualisierung von Gendernormen im Design: Bohrer »Dolphia« und Stabmixer »Mega Hurricane« Wie sehen technische Gegenstände aus, die wir im Haushalt benutzen? Eigentlich sind uns die hierbei gängigen Gestaltungsparameter aus dem Alltag sehr vertraut – und doch wirken die Ergebnisse aus dem Forschungsprojekt »Visualisierung von Gendernormen im Design« (2006) etwa befremdlich und gleichzeitig Augen öffnend.[7] Ausgangspunkt dieser angewandten Designforschung von Karin Ehrnberger ist die Feststellung, dass Stereotype hinsichtlich des binären Geschlechtersystems (männlich, weiblich) auf Gestaltung übertragen wird, die so wiederum zum Fortbestehen dichotomer Normen beiträgt. Also geschlechtsspezifisches Design, ohne dass die Funktion der Dinge selbst einen klar erkennbaren Zusammenhang zu Geschlecht hätte (s. Abb. 2). Vielmehr sind diese Zusammenhänge meist tradierte Vorannahmen darüber, wer diese Produkte kauft oder verwendet. Im Sinne von Jacques Derridas philosophischem Begriff der »Dekonstruktion« und einem Verständnis von Design als kritische Praxis wird in dem Projekt per Analyse die Gestaltungssprache zweier typischer Haushaltsgeräte – Bohrer und Handmixer – zerlegt und

Visualising Gender Norms in Design: »Dolphia« Drill and »Mega Hurricane« Mixer How do the technical objects we use in our households look like? Generally speaking, we are quite familiar with common design parameters from everyday life – yet the results of the research project »Visualising Gender Norms in Design« (2006) seem somewhat peculiar and eye-opening at the same time.[7] The departure point for this applied design research by Karin Ehrnberger was the conclusion that stereotypes based on a binary gender system (male, female) are transferred to design, which in turn contributes to the persistence of gender-dichotomous norms – gender-specific design without the respective functions having any clear connection to gender (fig. 2). Instead, these connections are primarily owed to traditional assumptions about who is buying or using these products. Inspired by Jacques Derrida's philosophical term »deconstruction« and an understanding of design as a critical practice, the project analytically dissects the design language of two common household appliances – a drill and a hand blender – and transfers it to the respective other appliance (fig. 1). The result are two prototypes: the »Mega Hurricane« mixer with its precision and speed, and the »Dolphia« drill

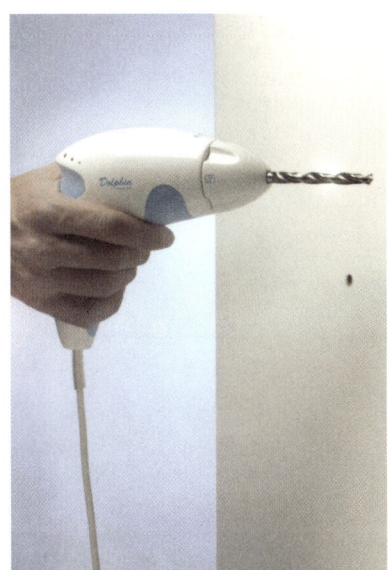

1

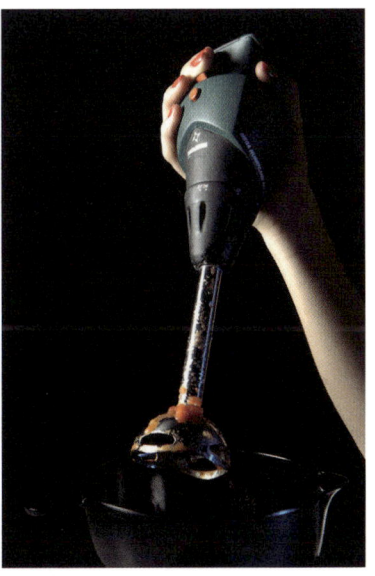

auf das jeweils andere Gerät übertragen (s. Abb. 1). Das Ergebnis sind zwei Prototypen: Zum einen der Präzision und Schnelligkeit vermittelnde Stabmixer »Mega Hurricane« und zum anderen der soft wirkende Bohrer »Dolphia« (s. Abb. 1). Zu dieser Strategie des Vertauschens der physischen Produktsprache gehört das passende »Wording«, die Benennung der Produkte und deren visuelle Inszenierung. Zu den Ergebnissen der Forschung zählt, dass sich mit dem Vertauschen auch das Verhalten zu und die Erwartungen an das Produkt ändern. Es zeige sich, so resümieren die Forscherinnen, dass Gendernormen mit Design zwar unweigerlich verknüpft seien, es aber gleichzeitig auch bedeute, dass beides je nach Zeit, Ort und Kontext wandelbar ist.[8]

[7] Ehrnberger, Karin; Räsänen, Mina u. Ilstedt, Sara. 2012. Visualising Gender Norms in Design: Meet the Mega Hurricane Mixer and the Drill Dolphia. International Journal of Design, 6 (3), 85–98.
[8] Vgl. ebd.

with its soft appearance (fig. 1). This strategy of switching the physical product language is paired with a corresponding wording of the products and their visual staging. It was also noted that along with this switching also the behaviour and the expectations towards the product change. What this demonstrates, as the researchers conclude, is how gender gender norms bear a connection with each design but that both can be renegotiated in time, place, and context.[8]

[7] *Karin Ehrnberger, Minna Räsänen, and Sara Ilstedt, »Visualising Gender Norms in Design: Meet the Mega Hurricane Mixer and the Drill Dolphia,« International Journal of Design 6, no. 3 (2012): 85–98.*
[8] *Ibid.*

1 **Bohrer »Dolphia« und Stabmixer »Mega Hurricane«** / *»Dolphia« drill and »Mega Hurricane« mixer* / SE 2006 / Angwandte Designforschung zur Visualisierung von Gendernormen im Design / *Applied design research on visualising gender norms in design* / Entwurf: / *Design:* Karin Ehrnberger

2 **Transformer-Figur und Bohrer** / *Transformer figure and drill* / Barbie-Puppe und Stabmixer / *Barbie doll and mixer* / SE 2006 / Forschungsarbeit: / *Design research:* Karin Ehrnberger

Haushalt und Wohnen / Household and Living

Bosch »IXO« Zu der eigenen Unternehmenskultur und -strategie des Technologie- und Dienstleistungsunternehmens Robert Bosch GmbH zählt nach eigenen Angaben das Diversity-Management.[9] Darunter fallen Aspekte wie z. B. Herkunft, Alter und sexuelle Orientierung sowie Gender. Deshalb engagiert sich das Unternehmen des Gründers Robert Bosch, der sich schon für kulturelle Vielfalt einsetzte, für Lohngleichheit, unterstützt Netzwerke wie »RBg« (Bosch LGBTI Netzwerk) oder »women@bosch« (gegründet 1995) sowie Trainings für vorurteilsfreie Personalentscheidungen bzw. gegen Unconscious Bias.[10] Dabei dient aktives Diversity-Management nicht nur der Mitarbeiter*innen-Kultur und dem Arbeitsklima. Das Unternehmen hat für sich erkannt, dass unterschiedliche Sichtweisen als Kreativitätsmotor für Impulse und neue Ideen fungieren können. Gemischte Teams würden außerdem »bessere Leistungen erbringen, häufiger Innovationen entwickeln, unterschiedliche Märkte besser verstehen und schneller auf Veränderungen reagieren können«.[11] Ein Resultat soll auch der Bosch »IXO« sein, der sich mit insgesamt über 18 Mio. umgesetzten Exemplaren zum weltweit meistverkauften Elektrowerkzeug gemausert hat. Der Produktname für den kompakten Akkuschrauber leitet sich von den drei Arten des Schraubenkopfes (Schlitz, Kreuz, Torx) ab. Zunächst war das Werkzeug 2003 eine Neuheit als das erste Elektrowerkzeug mit einem Lithium-Ionen-Akku. Dazu seitdem: kompakt und schnell zur Hand. Auch z. B. zur »Frauenhand«, die statistisch gesehen kleiner ist als die durchschnittliche Männerhand. Anstatt also das vielfach auftauchende Prinzip des »Pink it and shrink it« anzuwenden und einen solchen Akkuschrauber mit dem »Frauenlabel« zu versehen, hat Bosch das eigene Corporate Design beibehalten und das Produkt unter funktionalen Aspekten entwickelt. Die Palette derjenigen Produkte, die als Aufsätze für den »IXO« dienen, wurde seither stetig erweitert: vom Schrauben, Bohren, Zerschneiden, über Weinöffnen, Pfeffern, Salzen bis zum Anfeuern und Grasschneiden scheint alles möglich. Damit wurde der Akkuschrauber zu einem Multifunktionsgerät, einsetzbar in verschiedenen Bereichen, drinnen wie draußen. Auf eine Formel verkürzt: Ein Schrauber für alle und für alles. Diese Formel hat Bosch in eine visuelle Sprache für das Marketing übersetzt, das wiederum neben der Funktionalität und Qualität sicherlich ein weiterer Grund dafür ist, warum Bosch als Zielgruppe des »IXOs« zu gleichen Teilen Frauen und Männer ansprechen konnte (Abb. 1). Das gilt allerdings nicht nur für das IXO-Produkt, sondern z. B. für die Vermarktung der »YOUseries«. Abgesehen davon gibt es immer wieder Sondereditionen des »IXOs« inklusive zugehöriger Kampagnen. Diese fallen durch ihre Verschiedenartigkeit auf: Während die Edition aus einer Kooperation mit dem Edelstein- und Schmuckhersteller Swarovski sich offenbar an Frauen richtete (Abb. 5), zeigte sich der »IXO Gold&Black« (2018) zum 15-jährigen Jubiläum zwar in farblich anderem Kleid, jedoch sehr nah an der allgemeinen Intention, Männer und Frauen gleichermaßen anzusprechen (Abb. 2–3). Ganz im

Bosch »IXO« The technology company and service provider Robert Bosch GmbH states that diversity management is an integral part of its corporate culture and strategy.[9] This includes aspects such as cultural background, age, and sexual orientation as well as gender issues. For this reason, the company founded by Robert Bosch, who already advocated cultural diversity early on, supports equal pay, networks like »RBg« (Bosch LGBTI network), or »women@bosch« (established in 1995) as well as trainings for impartial human resource decisions and against unconscious bias.[10] Not only the employee culture and working atmosphere benefit from the active diversity management; the company realised that different perspectives can also give rise to creative impulses and fresh ideas. Furthermore, »mixed teams perform better, develop more innovations, have a better understanding of different markets, and are quicker to respond to change«.[11] One result of this approach is said to be Bosch's »IXO«, which turned out to be the best-selling electric tool worldwide with more than a total of 18 million items sold. The product name for the compact cordless screwdriver is derived from the three types of screw heads (slotted, cross-head, torx). The tool was initially a novelty in 2003 as the first electric tool with a lithium ion accumulator. And since then: compact and ready at hand. And a »woman's hand«, too, which statistically speaking is smaller than the average male hand. So instead of applying the widespread principle »pink it and shrink it« and tagging such a cordless screwdriver with a »woman's label«, Bosch maintained its own corporate design and developed the product according to functional aspects. The product range with heads for »IXO« has been continuously expanding: from screwing, drilling, and cutting to wine bottle opening, peppering, salting, and even setting fire and grass mowing – the possibilities are endless. In this way, the cordless screwdriver became a multifunctional tool that can be used in different areas, inside and outdoors. In short: a screwdriver for everybody and everything. Bosch translated this formula into a visual marketing language, which is certainly another reason, next to functionality and quality, why Bosch was able to appeal to women and men in equal measure as target groups (fig. 1). This not only applies to the »IXO« product line but also the marketing of the »YOUseries«, for example. Furthermore, there are always new »IXO« special editions being launched, together with corresponding campaigns. And they are remarkably diverse: While the edition from a cooperation between the crystals and jewellery manufacturer Swarovski was obviously directed at women (fig. 5), the »IXO Gold&Black« (2018) on the occasion of the products' 15th anniversary exhibited an unusual colour range, yet was very close to the general intention to appeal to men and women in equal measure (fig. 2–3). In the spirit of the individualisation trend, Bosch used the »IXO 6 Colour Edition« to launch a style contest as online marketing strategy. The colour of the winning design: raspberry red (2019) (fig. 6).

1

2

3

Zeitgeist eines Individualisierungstrends machte Bosch 2019 den »IXO 6 Colour Edition« zum Ausgangspunkt eines Style Contests als Online-Marketing – Farbe des Siegerdesigns: Himbeerrot (2019) (Abb. 6).

[9] Robert Bosch GmbH (29.05.2017): Interview: Diversity-Management bei Bosch. Fünf Fragen an Heidi Stock, Leiterin Talent Management und Diversity, Robert Bosch GmbH. https://www.bosch-presse.de/pressportal/de/de/interview-diversity-management-bei-bosch-106696.html, zul. abgerufen am: 14.10.2019.

[10] Robert Bosch GmbH: Vielfalt ist unser Vorteil. Diversity-Webseite weltweit, https://www.bosch.com/de/karriere/vielfalt/, zul. abgerufen am 14.10.2019.

[11] Robert Bosch GmbH (Mai 2017): Aktives Diversity-Management bei Bosch. In: Presse-Information: Bosch kompakt, 2018, 13 S., Mappe 106624, Download 05.12.2018, via https://www.bosch-presse.de/pressportal/de/de/diversity-management-bei-bosch-106624.html

[9] Robert Bosch GmbH, »Interview: Diversity-Management bei Bosch. Fünf Fragen an Heidi Stock, Leiterin Talent Management und Diversity, Robert Bosch GmbH,« 29.05.2017, https://www.bosch-presse.de/pressportal/de/de/interview-diversity-management-bei-bosch-106696.html.

[10] Robert Bosch GmbH, »Vielfalt ist unser Vorteil. Diversity-Webseite weltweit,« https://www.bosch.com/de/karriere/vielfalt.

[11] Robert Bosch GmbH, »Aktives Diversity-Management bei Bosch,« in Presse-Information: Bosch kompakt, (2018), 13, Mappe 106624, https://www.bosch-presse.de/pressportal/de/ de/diversity-management-bei-bosch-106624.html; and in English: Robert Bosch GmbH, »Diversity Management at Bosch,« 19.11.2019, https://www.bosch-presse.de/pressportal/de/en/ proactive-diversity-management-at-bosch-106701.html.

4

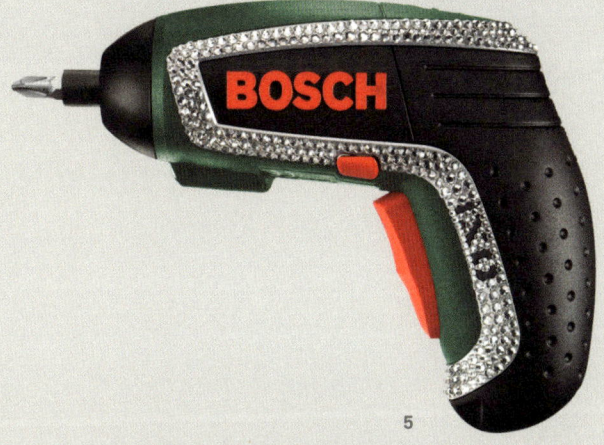

5

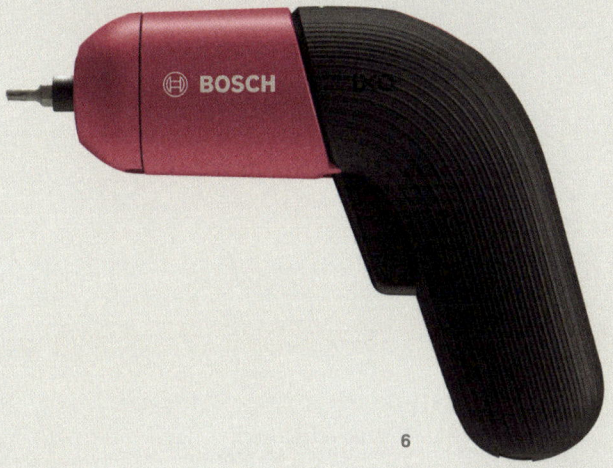

6

1 **Bosch IXO Classic Edition und Zubehör** / *and Attachments* / DE 2019 / IXO Collection Aufsätze: / *Adapters:* Home, DIY & Handicraft / Robert Bosch Power Tools GmbH

2–3 **Bosch IXO Gold&Black** / DE 2018 / Limitierte Sonderedition zum 15-jährigen Jubiläum / *Limited 15th anniversary edition* / Robert Bosch Power Tools GmbH

4 **Bosch IXO Classic Edition** / DE 2019 / Werbefotografie / *Advertising photography* / Robert Bosch Power Tools GmbH

5 **Bosch IXO Swarovski** / DE 2010 / Limitierte Sonderedition, Kooperation mit Swarovski / *Limited special edition, collaboration with Swarovski* / Robert Bosch Power Tools GmbH

6 **Bosch IXO Colour Edition** / DE 2019 / Siegerdesign des IXO Style Contests / *IXO Style Contest's winning design* / Robert Bosch Power Tools GmbH

Schulprojekt: Gestaltung eines »genderneutralen« Produktes Rollschuhe, die über eine App gesteuert werden, eine Tasse, die bei Zeitnot und Vergesslichkeit »mitdenkt« und eine Tasse, die durch eine integrierte Heizspirale das Getränk warmhält – das sind Entwürfe der Schüler*innen als Antwort auf die Frage danach, wie Dinge aussehen könnten, die »für alle« gestaltet sind. Bei der Ideenfindung und Umsetzung standen neben Funktionalität und Innovation auch Gestaltungsparameter wie Form, Farbe und Typographie im Vordergrund. Die Süßigkeiten-Box »Bon Bohnen« wurde deshalb sehr bunt gestaltet. Bei der »Mitdenk-Tasse« kann sogar aus einer Farbskala ausgewählt und die Form des Henkels individuell bzw. unter ergonomischen Gesichtspunkten angepasst werden. Die Hintergrundfarbe der Rollschuh-App kann über die angezeigten Mars- und Venussymbole gesteuert werden.

School project: Design of a Gender-Neutral Product Roller skates controlled by an app, a cup that »thinks« about time pressure and forgetfulness, and a cup that keeps the beverage warm with an integrated heating coil: These were the students' designs in response to the question how things designed »for all« could look like. In the idea development and realisation process, design parameters such as form, colour, and typography played an important role, next to functionality and innovation. The candy box »Bon Bohnen«, for example, received a very colourful appearance. The »thinking« cup also comes in a range of colours to choose from and the form of the handle is individually adaptable according to ergonomic needs. The background colour of the roller skates app can be adjusted via the displayed Mars and Venus symbols.

Gestaltung eines »genderneutralen« Produktes / *Design of a »Gender-Neutral« Product* / DE 2018 / Schulprojekt mit einer 9. Klasse der Realschule Dornstadt / *School project with 9th grade pupils from Realschule Dornstadt* / Konzeption und Durchführung: / *Concept and realisation:* / Susanne Umscheid (Produktdesignerin / *product designer*) / Fabian Karrer (Grafikdesigner / *graphic designer*)

1 Bon Bohnen / DE 2018 / Entwurf: / *Design:* Robin

2 X-Pro 3D Print Smartphone Cover / DE 2018 / Entwurf: / *Design:* Felix

3 Scary Bee Parfüm / *Perfume* / DE 2018 / Entwurf: / *Design:* Michi

4 Black & White Smartphone Cover / DE 2018 / Entwurf: / *Design:* Vanessa

5 **Potty** / DE 2018 / Entwurf: / Design:
Laura, Lauri

6 **Mitdenk-Tasse** / *The Thinking Cup* /
DE 2018 / Entwurf: / *Design:* Damian

7 **MG Armbanduhr** / *Wrist watch* /
DE 2018 / Entwurf: / *Design:* Mirko

8 **H&D Rollschuh-Sneaker steuerbar via Smartphone-App** / *Sneaker with wheels controlled via smartphone app* / DE 2018 / Entwurf: / *Design:* Hanna, Deniz

Kosmetik und Gender-Marketing / *Cosmetics and Gender Marketing*

Pink stinks? Körperpflege und -modifikation betreiben wir alltäglich: Wir verändern unsere äußerliche Erscheinung nicht nur durch Kleidung, sondern bearbeiten unseren Körper regelrecht durch eine Vielzahl von Produkten und Dingen. Während die Welt des Schminkens als kosmetische Maßnahme bis heute vorwiegend weiblich assoziiert ist, gilt geschlechtsspezifisch die Bartrasur oder -pflege als männliches »Territorium«. Die Rasur an sich ist dabei alles andere als eine geschlechtsspezifische Tätigkeit. Körperbehaarung und deren Nicht-/Entfernung ist dem kulturellen und zeitlichen Wandel unterworfen: Während in den 1950er und 1960er Jahren die Glattrasur als modisch galt und dem Braun »sixtant« zu Ruhm verhalf, sind Bartpflegetools und -mittel heute mehr denn je gefragt und sogenannte »Barber Shops« stehen hoch im Kurs.

Verpackung und Formgebung zeitgenössischer Kosmetik- und Hygieneprodukte sowie deren Vermarktung sind, ähnlich wie beim Spielzeug, hochgradig und binär gegendert bzw. nach männlich und weiblich getrennt. In den Drogerien stehen wenige, teilweise schwarze Regale bereit, um die hochleistungsfähig anmutenden Rasierer »Mach3Turbo« sowie Duschgel in benzinkanisterartigem Verpackungsdesign an den Mann zu bringen. Den elegant geschwungenen »Venus«-Rasierer in einer weißen und pastellfarbenen Umgebung findet man neben einem Überangebot an weiteren Produkten für Frauen. Welchen Einfluss das Marketing großer Konzerne auch auf gesellschaftliche Debatten wie beispielsweise toxische Maskulinität haben kann, zeigt die Kampagne der Rasierer-Marke »Gillette« für eine »neue Männlichkeit«, die im Januar 2019 viel Aufsehen erregte. Die Reaktionen, die bis zum Boykott-Aufruf reichten, bewiesen symptomatisch, was Liz Plank zum Ausgangspunkt ihrer Publikation von »For The Love of Men« (2019) macht: »Während bei der Infragestellung der Geschlechterstereotypen und -erwartungen an Frauen große Fortschritte erzielt wurden, sind selbige Fortschritte für Männer nicht zu verzeichnen.«[1]

Dass wiederum für die Vermarktung auch eine systematische Preisdifferenzierung angewandt wird, bezeichnet als »Gender Pricing«, belegt eine Studie der Antidiskriminierungsstelle des Bundes (2017).[2] Vor allem bei Dienstleistungen wie z. B. einem Frisierangebot, besteht ein hohes Preisungleichgewicht: Der Preisunterschied beträgt 59 Prozent bei 381 gleichartigen Dienstleistungsvarianten, je nachdem ob ein Mann oder eine Frau die Leistung in Anspruch nimmt. Als »Pink Tax« wird eine Preisunterscheidung bezeichnet, die auf die Annahme zurückgeht, Frauen seien bereit, mehr Geld für Körperpflege auszugeben. Auf Gender-Marketing aufmerksam zu machen und gegen diskriminierende Werbung vorzugehen, ist ein Ziel der gemeinnützigen Protest- und Bildungsorganisation Pinkstinks. Dazu unterhält sie u. a. Initiativen wie den Positivpreis für gendersensible Werbung »Pinker Pudel« und das Online-Tool »Werbemelder*in« (Abb. 1–2).

Pink stinks? We groom and modify our bodies on a daily basis: Not only do we change our appearance with clothes, we also downright work over our bodies with a plethora of products and things. While the world of makeup as a cosmetic treatment is widely associated with women to this day, shaving or grooming the beard is seen as a male »territory«. On the other hand, shaving per se is everything but a gender-specific act. Body hair and its (non-)removal is subject to change in culture and over time: For example, clean shaving was in fashion in the 1950s and 1960s, helping Braun's »sixtant« rise to fame, whereas today beard grooming tools and products are in high demand along with so-called barber shops popping up everywhere.

Similar to toys, the packaging and design of contemporary cosmetic and hygiene products as well as their marketing are rigorously gendered on a binary basis or divided into the categories male/female. Drug stores allocate a few, often black shelves to appeal to men, filled with the apparently high-performance »Mach3Turbo« razors or shower gels in petrol canister styled packaging design. The elegantly curved »Venus« razors can be found in a white and pastel coloured display next to an abundance of other products targeted at women. That the marketing of major corporations can also fuel debates in society such as toxic masculinity is illustrated in the campaign for the razor brand »Gillette« promoting a »new masculinity«, which garnered great attention in January 2019. The reactions, including calls for boycott, exemplified what Liz Plank stated in the introduction to her publication For The Love of Men (2019): »While great strides have been made in challenging the gender stereotypes and expectations for women, the same progress has not happened for men.«[1]

A survey of the Federal Anti-Discrimination Agency (2017) substantiated that marketing, on the other hand, also involves a systematic price difference, known as »gender pricing«.[2] Especially with services like those of hairdressers, there is a high imbalance in the costs: The difference amounts up to 59 percent for 381 similar service variants, depending on whether a man or a woman makes use of them. The term »pink tax« points to another differentiation in pricing, which builds upon the assumption that women are willing to spend more money on body care. Raising awareness for gender marketing and opposing discriminating advertising are the objectives of the nonprofit protest and education platform Pinkstinks. Its initiatives include the positive award for gender-sensitive advertising »Pinker Pudel« [Pink Poodle] and the online tool »Werbemelder*in« [Ad Alert] (fig. 1–2).

[1] Liz Plank, For The Love of Men. A New Vision for Mindful Masculinity (New York: St. Martin's Press, 2019), n.p.
[2] Antidiskriminierungsstelle des Bundes, Hrsg., Iris an der Heiden und Prof. Dr. Maria Wersig. Preisdifferenzierung nach Geschlecht in Deutschland: Forschungsbericht. (Baden-Baden: Nomos, 2017).

[1] Originalzitat: »While great strides have been made in challenging the gender stereotypes and expectations for women, the same progress has not happened for men.« Plank, Liz. 2019. For the Love of Men. A New Vision for Mindful Masculinity, o.S.
[2] Antidiskriminierungsstelle des Bundes, Hrsg., Iris an der Heiden und Prof. Dr. Maria Wersig. 2017. Preisdifferenzierung nach Geschlecht in Deutschland: Forschungsbericht. Baden-Baden: Nomos.

1

1 **www.werbemelder.in** ⁄ Werbemelder*in ist ein vom BMFSFJ (Bundesministerium für Familie, Senioren, Frauen und Jugend) beauftragtes und von Pinkstinks Germany ausgeführtes Monitoring-Projekt, um Sexismus in der Werbung sichtbar zu machen. Über Webseite oder App kann abfotografierte Werbung eingesendet werden, die auf einer interaktiven Karte sichtbar gemacht und eingeordnet wird. ⁄ *Werbemelder*in [Ad Alert] is a monitoring project commissioned by the German BMFSFJ (Federal Ministry for Family Affairs, Senior Citizens, Women and Youth) and carried out by Pinkstinks Germany to make sexism in advertising visible. Photographed advertisements can be sent in via website or app, which will then be visualized and classified on an interactive map.*

Pinkstinks Germany e.V. ist eine gemeinnützige Protest- und Bildungsorganisation, die sich u. a. mit Workshops für Kinder und Jugendliche, Online-Kampagnen sowie Beratung und Bildungsmaterialien gegen jede Form von Diskriminierung stellt und sich für Geschlechtersensibilität und Persönlichkeitsentfaltung einsetzt. Seit 2018 vergibt sie gemeinsam mit dem Gesamtverband Kommunikationsagenturen (GWA e.V.) zudem jährlich den Award »Pinker Pudel« (Abb. 2). Dabei handelt es sich um einen Positivpreis für geschlechtergerechte Werbung, also Kampagnen, die mit Geschlechterrollenstereotypen brechen. So auch schon der Titel der Auszeichnung selbst; er bezieht sich auf die abfällige Bezeichnung »Lila Pudel« für emanzipierte Männer. Die Jury zeichnete etwa 2018 u. a. das Baumarktunternehmen Hornbach AG mit der Kampagne »Wir haben nie gesagt, dass es einfach wird« der Werbeagentur Heimat aus, 2019 gewann die Agentur VICE Media mit »Standard Evolved« für den Automobilhersteller Opel AG den Publikumspreis. Darüber hinaus betreibt Pinkstinks Germany e.V. das Online-Tool »Werbemelder*in« (Abb. 1), das mit Bundesmitteln gefördert wird: Der Verein informiert und prüft digital eingereichte Kampagnen hinsichtlich sexistischer Diskriminierung, eingestuft nach den Kategorien »nicht sexistisch, sexistisch, stereotyp« und »Grauzone«.

*Pinkstinks Germany e.V. is a nonprofit protest and education platform, which fights against all forms of discrimination and for gender sensitivity and personal development by organising workshops for children and youth and online campaigns or providing counselling and educational materials. Since 2018, together with the Gesamtverband Kommunikationsagenturen (GWA e.V.) [General Association of Communication Agencies] it has awarded the annual »Pinker Pudel« (fig. 2), a positive prize for gender-neutral advertising campaigns that break with stereotypical gender roles. The title of the award speaks for itself – it references the derogatory German term »Lila Pudel« [purple poodle] for emancipated men. For example, in 2018 the jury honoured the Hornbach AG building supplies company campaign »Wir haben nie gesagt, dass es einfach wird« [We've never said it's gonna be easy] by the ad agency Heimat; the 2019 winner of the audience award was the agency VICE Media with »Standard Evolved« for car manufacturer Opel AG. In addition, Pinkstinks Germany e.V. runs the online tool »Werbemelder*in« (fig. 1), with the support of federal funding: The association informs about and checks digitally submitted campaigns for sexist discrimination according to the categories »not sexist, sexist, stereotypical«, and »grey zone«.*

2 **www.pinker-pudel.de** ∕ Der »Pinke Pudel« ist Deutschlands erster Positivpreis für geschlechtergerechte Werbung. Pinkstinks Germany e.V. zeichnet jährlich Kreative aus, die in Werbekampagnen mit Geschlechtsrollenstereotypen brechen und gesellschaftliche Vielfalt feiern. ∕ *The »Pink Poodle« is Germany's first positive award for gender-sensitive advertising. Annually, Pinkstinks Germany e.V. honors creative people who successfully break with gender role stereotypes in advertising campaigns and celebrate social diversity.*

1

Rasieren: Braun und Gillette Zum heutigen amerikanischen Mutterkonzern Procter & Gamble gehören auch die Unternehmen Braun und Gillette. Der erste seriengefertigte Trockenrasierer von Max Braun war das Modell »S 50« (1950), dessen patentiertes Scherfoliensystem eine absolute technische Neuheit war. Durch die Zusammenarbeit mit der Hochschule für Gestaltung Ulm kam 1962 ein weiteres neuartiges Modell auf den Markt, das mit über acht Millionen Exemplaren zum waschechten Verkaufsschlager avancierte: der Braun »sixtant« (s. Abb. 1). Entworfen haben ihn Gerd A. Müller und der Ulmer Dozent Hans Gugelot als eine Weiterentwicklung der vorangegangenen »SM«-Modelle. Neben technischen Neuerungen war eine gestalterische Entscheidung so revolutionär wie die Plexiglashaube des »Schneewittchensargs«, dem »SK4« von Braun, an dem Gugelot ebenfalls beteiligt war: Die Verschalung des »sixtant« war entgegen aller gängigen Badutensilien und -geräte der Zeit nicht weiß oder elfenbeinfarben, sondern schwarz. Etwas, was unter den Rasierern für Männer bis heute nicht wegzudenken ist und sie markant von Damenrasierern unterscheidet. Lediglich 1971 will es der Zeitgeist, dass sowohl der »sixtant« für Männer wie auch der Braun »Lady-Shaver« in poppigem, damals angesagtem Orange daherkommen (s. Abb. 3), die Mehrzahl der Nachfolgemodelle ist als Herrenrasierer schwarz bzw. als Frauenrasierer weiß.

Shaving: Braun and Gillette Today Braun and Gillette are subsidiaries of the US American parent company Procter & Gamble. The first serially produced dry shaver by Max Braun was the model »S 50« (1950), whose patented shaving foil system represented an absolute technical breakthrough. In 1962 a cooperation with the Ulm School of Design resulted in another novelty on the market, which turned out to be a true bestseller with eight million pieces sold: Braun's »sixtant« (fig. 1). Gerd A. Müller and the Ulm teacher Hans Gugelot designed it as a follow-up product of the previous »SM« models. Beside technical improvements, one design decision was as revolutionary as the »Snow White's coffin« Plexiglas case of Braun's »Phonosuper SK 4«, likewise developed with Gugelot's participation: Contrary to all commonplace bathroom utensils and appliances of the time, the »sixtant« case was not white or ivory coloured but black. A feature which next to no razor for men can be imagined without hitherto, and distinctively marks the difference to razors for women. Only in 1971, owed to the zeitgeist, did both the »sixtant« for men and Braun's »Lady Shaver« come in a pop orange, the colour trend of the era (fig. 3), whereas the majority of the successor models were once again black for men and white for women.

The »Venus« and »Mach3« razors by manufacturer Gillette are time and again used as examples for strongly binary, gender-coded products. In the beginning of 2019, a short film by the company

Als Beispiele für stark binär bzw. zweigeschlechtlich codierte Produkte werden immer wieder die Rasierer »Venus« und »Mach3« des Herstellers Gillette herangezogen. Mit einem Kurzfilm sorgte das Unternehmen Anfang 2019 für eine Kontroverse und Überraschung – positiver wie negativer Art. Unter dem Titel »We Believe: The Best Man Can Be« wurde ein filmischer Clip gelauncht, mit dem das Unternehmen laut eigenen Angaben auch die Bedeutung des 1989 eingeführten Slogans »The Best a Man Can Get« hinterfragt (s. Abb. 2). Dieses eigene Hinterfragen erfolgt einleitend mittels Bildern vor dem Hintergrund zeitgenössischer Debatten um Sexismus, die #MeToo-Bewegung oder toxische Männlichkeit. Im weiteren Verlauf entwickelt sich die Narration zu einer Aufforderung an Männer, u. a. übergriffiges oder Frauen bevormundendes Benehmen sowie ein Ermutigen zu gewalttätigem und konkurrierendem Verhalten nicht durch Platitüden wie »Boys will be boys«, also zu Deutsch etwa: Männer sind halt so, zu entschuldigen. Stattdessen sei es an der Zeit, so lässt sich zusammenfassen, Rollenklischees und toxische Männlichkeit, die vor allem auch für das Selbst schädlich sind, abzulegen. Organisationen, die mit ihrer Arbeit dieses Ziel fördern, so kündigte Gillette in gleichem Zuge an, werde das Unternehmen in den kommenden drei Jahren jeweils durch eine Million Dollar unterstützen. Gillette erhielt einerseits viel Lob dafür, den eigenen enormen Einfluss und Beitrag zum Aufrechterhalten oder -brechen binärer Genderstereotype zu erkennen. Andererseits erntete das Unternehmen massive Kritik u. a. verbrämt als misandrische, linkspolitische Propaganda gefolgt von Umsatzeinbußen. Die Reaktionen darauf sind ein Gradmesser dafür, wie sehr das Thema Geschlecht als Teil unserer Identität emotional beladen ist und polarisiert und wie wenig das stereotype Männlichkeitsbild – das auch Gillette bislang wiederholte – überhaupt Risse erfahren hat.

elicited controversy and surprise – both positive and negative in nature. Under the title »We Believe: The Best Man Can Be«, the firm released a film clip that claims to question the message of their slogan »The Best a Man Can Get«, introduced in 1989 (fig. 2). This self-reflection initially unfolds through imagery taken from present-day debates on sexism, the #MeToo movement, or toxic masculinity. The narrative develops into an appeal to men not to excuse, for example, abusive or patronising conduct towards women or encourage violent and competitive behaviour with shibboleths like »boys will be boys«. Instead, to sum up the clip, it's time to overcome role clichés and toxic masculinity, which in the end only do damage to oneself. In the same breath, Gillette announced that it would support organisations that pursue this goal in their work, each with one million dollars in the coming three years. Gillette was widely praised for recognising its own enormous influence and contribution in perpetuating or breaking binary gender stereotypes. At the same time, the company drew massive criticism that it was spreading misandric, left-wing propaganda, which was followed by a decline in sales. These reactions illustrate the emotional and polarising charge of the gender issue as part of our identity and how little the stereotypical image of manhood – that Gillette also reiterated before – has been marred.

3

1 **Braun sixtant SM 31** ⁄ Elektrorasierer ⁄ *Electric shaver* ⁄ DE 1962 ⁄ Produktfotografie ⁄ *Product photography* ⁄ Hersteller: ⁄ *Manufacturer:* Braun AG ⁄ Entwurf: ⁄ *Design:* Gerd Alfred Müller und ⁄ *and* Hans Gugelot ⁄ Privatarchiv ⁄ *Private archive* G. Gugelot

2 **»We Believe: The Best Man Can Be«** ⁄ US 2019 ⁄ Videostills Gillette Kurzfilm-Kampagne ⁄ *Video stills Gillette short film campaign* ⁄ Unternehmen: ⁄ *Company:* Procter & Gamble ⁄ Produktion: ⁄ *Production:* Kim Gehrig ⁄ 1:46 Min.

3 **Lady-Shaver** ⁄ DE 1971 ⁄ Damen Elektrorasierer ⁄ *Ladies electric shaver* ⁄ Hersteller: ⁄ *Manufacturer:* Braun AG ⁄ Entwurf: ⁄ *Design:* Florian Seiffert ⁄ Sammlung Compensis ⁄ *Compensis collection* ⁄ HfG-Archiv ⁄ Museum Ulm

Unisex or what? Gender-neutral packaging design? How might it look like – and anyway, does something like neutral design even exist? One cosmetic product, whose packaging has changed little since the 1920s and is conceived as unisex, is »Nivea« (fig. 4). Starting with the unmistakable metal can of the design classic in a blue-and-white colour scheme, the cream is world-renowned and popular as a product for everyone and everything when it comes to body care. A television spot from 1954 features women, men, and children, from home and abroad, advertising as faces for the cream.[3] The principle of a gender-specific expansion of the product line is present here, too: As is the case with other articles and applications in the cosmetics sector, but notably often in the other direction, it is now men who are explicitly targeted. The tag »for men« is an effective method to highlight this, which not only appears in »Nivea's« product range. The shaving soap of 1924 was the first specific cosmetic for men. The latest trick: the musk-scented cream in a common »Nivea« can with a dark-blue metallic look and the tried-and-tested »MEN« branding (fig. 3).

Lesser known as such but a classic amongst unisex products is the over 200-year-old toilet water »4711 Echt Kölnisch Wasser«. The original »Eau de Cologne« carried the first coloured perfume label, and its design – like the formula and the »Molanus bottle« introduced in 1820 – has virtually gone unchanged to this day. The eponymous so-called conscription number of the house 4711 dates back to the time of the French occupation in the early nineteenth century, which was also responsible for the fact that the former medicinal tincture for oral intake became a fragrance for external application in order to avoid having to disclose the formula. Already in the 1920s »4711« was promoted as a scent for women as well. »Always spring-fresh!« was the slogan in the 1930s, and in the 1950s the typical enamel labels should appeal to a female clientele (fig. 2). As a unisex product that radiated youth, »4711« was also presented as a massage, travel, and refreshing tincture to dab onto the skin, an »invigorating freshness« that is »always with you« and a »mindful hospitality« at the house party that's »always at hand« for all (fig. 1).[4] To this day, the »party package« with ten miniature bottles belongs to its assortment.

»Creating a Society Open to Diversity through Gender Neutral Packaging Design« is the title of the twice honoured master thesis by Saana Hellsten, now a design entrepreneur, for Pratt School of Art and Design, New York. Her initial motivation was to identify and criticise the participation of packaging design in the iteration of gender stereotypes. To this end, she investigated common practices in the field of household product design and analysed, in particular, the visual language of cosmetic and hygiene products. Although razors, for example, come in different shapes, Hellsten explains, this is owed, however, to functional parameters related to shaving various parts of the body and thus not

1 »Party« / DE 1959 / Werbefilm 4711 Echt Kölnisch Wasser / *Promotional film 4711 Original Eau de Cologne* / Produktion: / *Production:* Muelhens GmbH & Co. KG / 1:03 Min.

2 »mit 4711 immer frühlingsfrisch« / *»with 4711 always spring-fresh«* / DE 1956 / Reklameschild 4711 Echt Kölnisch Wasser / *Advertising sign 4711 Original Eau de Cologne* / Unternehmen: / *Company:* Muelhens GmbH & Co. KG / Wirtschaftswundermuseum

Bereich der Gestaltung von Haushaltsprodukten und analysierte insbesondere die visuelle Sprache von Kosmetik- und Hygieneprodukten. Obschon es z. B. bei Rasierern physische Unterschiede gibt, so Hellsten, seien diese aber funktionaler Natur in Bezug auf das Rasieren verschiedener Körperpartien und damit nicht notwendigerweise an ein Geschlecht gebunden. Ergebnis und zugleich Ziel ihrer Arbeit war eine Gestaltung, die weitaus mehr neutral bzw. »basic« ist: So entstand das Produkt- und Verpackungsdesign »BASIK«. Es zeichnet sich durch seine minimalistische (visuelle) Sprache – einer Kombination aus nötigsten Informationen und Piktogrammen, stapelbaren Verpackungen und Individualisierungsmöglichkeiten aus (s. Abb. 5). Das Design ist zugleich Resultat einer eigens konzipierten Umfrage mit über 400 Teilnehmer*innen.

[3] »Wo man sich pflegt« (1954). Eingebettet auf der Unternehmens-Webseite zur eigenen Markenhistorie, Upload via YouTube: https://youtu.be/OJLQWbz5qqI, zul. abgerufen am: 21.11.2019.
[4] »Party« (1959). Eingebettet auf der Unternehmens-Webseite zur eigenen Historie, Upload via YouTube: https://www.youtube.com/watch?v=wiBi1B8JGHA, zul. abgerufen am: 21.11.2019.

necessarily bound to a specific gender. The objective of her work resulted in a far more neutral or »basic« design – the product and packaging design »BASIK«. It is characterised by its minimalist visual language (a combination of just the most necessary information and pictograms), its stackable packaging, and options for individualisation (fig. 5). The design also integrates the results of a specially developed survey with more than 400 participants.

[3] *»Wo man sich pflegt« (1954). Embedded in the company's website in its brand history section, YouTube upload: https://youtu.be/OJLQWbz5qqI.*
[4] *»Party« (1959). Embedded in the company's website in its history section, YouTube upload: https://www.youtube.com/watch?v=wiBi1B8JGHA.*

3

4

5

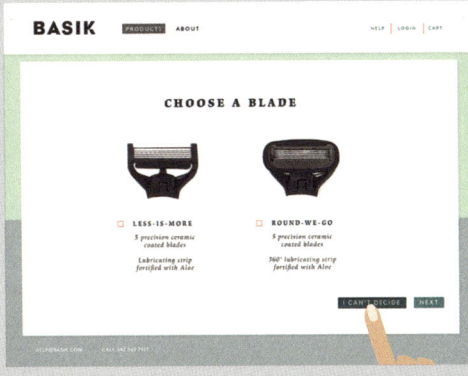

5

3 NIVEA MEN CREME ⁄ DE 2020 ⁄ Dosenverpackung ⁄ *Can packaging* ⁄ »Der Mann unter den Cremes« ⁄ *»The man among lotions«* ⁄ Hersteller: ⁄ *Manufacturer:* Beiersdorf AG

4 NIVEA TIN EVOLUTION ⁄ DE 2019 ⁄ Chronologie der Nivea Creme-Dosen ⁄ *Chronology of the Nivea Cream Cans* ⁄ Beiersdorf AG

5 BASIK ⁄ US 2014 ⁄ Masterarbeit: Verpackungsdesign als Gestaltungsmittel einer diversitäts-zugewandten Gesellschaft ⁄ *Master thesis: Creating A Society Open To Diversity Through Gender Neutral Packaging Design* ⁄ Stapelbare Kosmetik-Verpackungen und individualisierbare Rasierer ⁄ *Customizable razors and partially stackable cosmetic packaging* ⁄ Betreut von: ⁄ *Supervised by:* Warren Bernard, Santiago Piedrafita ⁄ *Pratt School of Art and Design* ⁄ Entwurf: ⁄ *Design:* Saana Hellsten

Gestaltung von »genderneutralen« Kosmetikverpackungen / Design of »Gender-Neutral« Cosmetic Packagings / DE 2018 / Schulprojekt mit einer 9. Klasse der Realschule Dornstadt / School project with 9th grade pupils from Realschule Dornstadt / Konzeption und Durch-führung: / Concept and realisation: Susanne Umscheid (Produktdesignerin / product designer) Fabian Karrer (Grafikdesigner / graphic designer)

1 **Tigeres Shampoo** / DE 2018 / Kosmetikverpackung / Cosmetic packaging / Entwurf: / Design: Meike S., Moritz / Werbeslogan: / Advertising slogan: Tigeres bändigt nicht nur deine Haare, sondern auch die Tigerin in dir! / Tigeres not only tames your hair but also your inner tigress!

2 **Kokos-Zitronen-Shampoo** / Coconut-Lemon Shampoo / DE 2018 / Kosmetikverpackung / Cosmetic packaging / Entwurf: / Design: Benjamin / Werbeslogan: / Advertising slogan: Jetzt neu! / Now new!

3 **Sommer & Winter Parfüm** / Summer & Winter Perfume / DE 2018 / Parfümverpackung / Perfume packaging / Entwurf: / Design: Ella / Werbeslogan: Für Sommer und Winter! / Advertising slogan: For summer and winter!

4 **Orange & Lemon** / DE 2018 / Kosmetikverpackung / Cosmetic packaging / Entwurf: / Design: Samuel / Werbeslogan: Jetzt mit den Düften Orange und Zitrone – das Duschgel für Frauen! / Advertising slogan: Comes now with orange or lemon scent – the shower gel for women!

Schulprojekt: Gestaltung eines »genderneutralen« Produktes Was könnten Unisex-Pflegeprodukte sein? Wie sollen sie verpackt sein? Wo hört Design auf und wo fängt Marketing an? Ausgehend von diesen Fragestellungen entwickelten die Schüler*innen einzeln oder im gemischten Duo eigene Produkte, die möglichst alle Geschlechter ansprechen sollen – eine Herausforderung. Die Bandbreite der gegenderten Pflegeprodukte in Drogeriemärkten regte eine große Anzahl von Schüler*innen zu einer Auseinandersetzung mit Kosmetikverpackungen an. Das Duschgel »Waldfrische« ist ein Ergebnis dieser Auseinandersetzung. Das Argument: Wald und Bäume sowie deren Duft sind zweifellos keinem Geschlecht zuzuordnen.

Nach dem Versuch, ein neutrales Produkt zu gestalten, war die anknüpfende Aufgabenstellung, genderspezifische Werbeanzeigen dafür zu entwerfen – so sollten Faktoren und Wechselwirkungen von Design und Marketingstrategien sichtbar werden. Die Verwirrung war zunächst groß: »Das macht doch gar keinen Sinn, ein neutrales Produkt zu gestalten, und dann Werbung nur für Männer oder Frauen zu machen!«. Das »Ginger Deo« wiederum wirbt mit seinem Versprechen »48 h epic win« nicht nur mit langanhaltendem Schutz, sondern auch Stärke und Sieg – für beide Geschlechter.

School project: Design of a Gender-Neutral Product What could unisex care products be? How should they be packed? Where does design end and where does marketing begin? Based on these questions, the students developed their own products, individually or in a mixed duo, which should appeal to all genders if possible – a challenge. The range of the changed care products in drugstores prompted a large number of school-children to deal with cosmetic packaging. The »Waldfrische« shower gel is a result of this discussion. The argument: forest and trees and their scent are undoubtedly not gender.

After trying to design a neutral product, the subsequent task was to design gender-specific advertisements for it – this should make the factors and interactions of design and marketing strategies visible. The confusion was great at first: »It makes no sense to design a neutral product and then only advertise for men or women!« The »Ginger Deodorant« in turn promotes with its promise »48 h epic win« not only with long-lasting protection, but also strength and victory – for both genders.

5 Wash-Up-Duschgel Zitrone ⁄ *Shower Gel Lemon* ⁄ DE 2018 ⁄ Kosmetikverpackung ⁄ *Cosmetic packaging* ⁄ Entwurf: ⁄ *Design:* Lea ⁄ Werbeslogan: Werd' nicht sauer, wenn die Frau mal wieder nervt, geh' duschen mit Wash-Up Zitrone! ⁄ *Advertising slogan: Don't get sour with your nagging wife, go have a shower with Wash-Up Lemon!*

6 Ingwer-Deo ⁄ *Ginger Deo* ⁄ DE 2018 ⁄ Kosmetikverpackung ⁄ *Cosmetic packaging* ⁄ Entwurf: ⁄ *Design:* Meike Z., Yannik ⁄ Werbeslogan: Mit Ingwer-Deo kannst auch du scharf sein! ⁄ *Advertising slogan: Get hot with the Ginger deo!*

7 Duschgel Waldfrische ⁄ *Shower Gel Forest Fresh* ⁄ DE 2018 ⁄ Kosmetikverpackungen ⁄ *Cosmetic packagings* ⁄ Entwurf: ⁄ *Design:* Lukas, Sina ⁄ Werbeslogans: Hol' dir die Frische des Waldes in die Stadt! ⁄ Dich verfolgt deine Männlichkeit bis unter die Dusche! ⁄ *Advertising slogans: Bring forest freshness to your city! ⁄ Your manhood hunts you down even under the shower!*

Design: Ausbildung und Beruf / Design: Education and Profession

Gender in Design Functionality, durability, and sustainability: These are just a few of the attributes that factor in to making »good« design. Indeed, the »Ten Principles of Good Design« developed by Dieter Rams in the 1970s are still often quoted mantra-like to this day. But even then, he realised that just as technology and culture constantly evolve, good design also evolves – and this should apply to design education, too. However, »gender« still seems to be something of a blind spot in both design – unless it's about its marketing – and design education. And this, despite the fact that designers always work for others, be it for a specific target group or with the aim of designing products for all.

The fact that no designer is or ever can be »neutral« clearly means there can be no such thing as neutral design. One could say that designers are faced with a kind of determinism.[1] Like product users and consumers, we are all saddled with culturally transmitted concepts of gender that serve to orient us in the world. But that, in and of itself, only becomes problematic when these gendered concepts are obsessively communicated in stereotypical ways and are allowed to become mechanisms of inclusion and exclusion. Gender in design – in a positive sense – does not mean to be incapable of action; rather it means acknowledging one's own and other more generally accepted notions, questioning and, if necessary, revising them. This could also mean incorporating gender into design, for example, where it may not previously have played a role, or only by way of unreflective assumptions, without any comparisons to reality. Because – and this is also clear – sociocultural concepts can shift.

Gender-sensitive design is one of the key approaches that can help make design more problem or solution oriented but also more innovative, too. In a positive perspective, adopting gender-sensitive or gender-specific strategies involves, above all, not replicating stereotypes that are at odds with the diverse societies we live in, and thus not contributing to their reinforcement. While it is not possible to measure gender in the same »objective« way one might measure the environmental friendliness of a product, we cannot allow sociocultural identities to be treated as biological and »natural«, nor can they be blanked out in a »gender blind« way. This applies to the identities of both designers themselves and product users. Initiatives such as Jaqueline Diedam's »Design for ...« board game (2016) and the »Gender Equity Toolkit«, developed in partnership with the AIGA design association, enable these issues to be approached in playful and reflective ways.

And what about the design profession? As in other occupational fields, the role of women is being increasingly debated – indeed, these discussions have already come quite a long way in many Western countries. In Germany, there has been an upturn in historical reappraisals of women's roles at the Bauhaus and the Deutsche

Und wie steht es um die Designberufe? Wie in anderen Berufsfeldern ist es die Rolle der Frauen, die hierbei zunehmend diskutiert wird – im westlichen Ausland bereits fortgeschritten. In Deutschland setzte zuletzt vermehrt die historische Aufarbeitung von Frauenrollen am Bauhaus oder den Deutschen Werkstätten Hellerau ein.[2] Allerdings scheint diese Reflexion nicht weit über den Zweiten Weltkrieg hinauszugehen. Ausnahmeprojekte sind dahingehend die zwei Bände »Frauen im Design: Berufsbilder und Lebenswege seit 1900« (1989) von Angela Oedekoven-Gerischer sowie das von ehemaligen HfG-lerinnen Gerda Müller-Krauspe, Ursula Wenzel sowie Petra Kellner initiierte Webseiten- und Buchprojekt »Frauen an der hfg ulm« (2003 / 2007). Gewissermaßen in der Zukunft liegt zum Zeitpunkt des vorliegenden Katalogs auch die Forschung »Der neue Mann und das Bauhaus. Männlichkeitskonzepte in der klassischen Moderne« (Mai 2020) von Anja Baumhoff, die damit die Perspektiven um Geschlechterrollen in der Designgeschichte und, so ist zu erwarten, die Gegenwart bereichert. Im Rahmen der Ausstellung und Publikation »Nicht mein Ding« ist es zusammen mit Christiane Wachsmann das Anliegen, ausgewählte Lebensläufe als Ausgangspunkt und Beleg für verschiedenartige Werdegänge von Männern und Frauen zusammenzustellen, die an der HfG Ulm studierten (S. 125–129). Sie zeugen einerseits von einer Avantgarde inmitten der 1950er und 1960er Jahre in Deutschland sowie deren private und berufliche Wege im Anschluss an diese Zeit.

Dass wiederum das Gestern und Heute eng miteinander verbunden sind, wird nicht zuletzt an zweierlei Fakten ersichtlich: Zum einen sind Narrationen über Designgeschichte weiterhin sehr männlich dominiert, woran auch Museen ihren Anteil haben. Die explizite Aufarbeitung einer Geschichte von Frauen im Design ist richtig und anhaltend wichtig, erhellt aber auch, dass dafür immer eben jene separaten Erzählstränge eröffnet werden, als ginge es um Parallelwelten. Aus beispielsweise museumswissenschaftlicher Sicht wäre es wünschenswert, diese Erzählungen nicht nur via Sonderausstellung zu einem Sonder-, respektive einem »Frauenthema« zu machen, sondern die Erkenntnisse in die Dauerausstellungen und damit in die Geschichtsschreibung zu integrieren. Dazu gehört auch die Frage, wenn Frauen (scheinbar) nicht vorkommen: Warum ist das so? Was wiederum zum zweiten Fakt führt: Die Zahl weiblicher Studierender und Absolventinnen von Design-Disziplinen liegt nicht selten über der der männlichen, jedoch tauchen sie in den Berufen dann nicht auf. Zwar steht eine adäquate Beantwortung nach dem Warum aus, es dürfte aber auch klar sein, dass es an Rollenvorbildern fehlt – historisch, in der Designausbildung und den Berufsfeldern. Letzteres führte die drei Absolventinnen

Werkstätten Hellerau in recent years.[2] Nonetheless, besides two exceptional projects – Frauen im Design: Berufsbilder und Lebenswege seit 1900 [Women in Design: Employment Histories and Life Paths since 1900] (1989) by Angela Oedekoven-Gerischer, and the website and book project »Frauen an der hfg ulm« [Women at the hfg ulm] (2003 / 2007) by Gerda Müller-Krauspe, Ursula Wenzel, and Petra Kellner from the former Ulm School of Design – such reexaminations do not seem to extend far beyond the Second World War. Although, at the time of writing this catalogue, Anja Baumhoff's book Der neue Mann und das Bauhaus. Männlichkeitskonzepte in der klassischen Moderne [The New Man and the Bauhaus. Concepts of Masculinity in Classical Modernity] is yet to be published (May 2020), her work is expected to enrich our perspectives on gender roles in the history of design and to the present day. And one of the aims of the »Not My Thing« exhibition is, with Christiane Wachsmann's contribution, to gather a selection of biographies that evidence and showcase the various career paths followed by those men and women who studied at Ulm School of Design (pp. 125–129). Biographies that bear witness to an avant-garde in Germany during the 1950s and 1960s as well as to the personal and professional life paths taken in later years.

And last but not least, two facts show how closely the past and present are linked: Firstly, design history narratives continue to be very male dominated, and museums also play their part in this. The explicit reappraisal of the history of women in design is necessary and of lasting importance, but such reappraisals also highlight how these stories are always told as separate narratives, as if they were parallel universes. From the scholarly museum perspective, it would be preferable, for example, not to turn women's stories into »special exhibitions«, but to integrate the findings into permanent exhibitions and therewith the general historiography. The (apparent) invisibility of women also begs the question: Why is this so? Which leads to the second consideration: The fact that the number of females studying and graduating from design disciplines is often higher than males, yet far fewer women are actually being employed in this field. Although the exact reasons for this remains unclear, one thing is certain: Historically, there has been a real lack of female role models in design education and in the professional field. This lack of women in graphic design was the motivation behind Silva Baum, Claudia Scheer, and Lea Sievertsen's »iphiGenia« award-winning diploma project »notamuse« (2018). Another initiative to come out of the international design community, which makes use of today's networked digital age, is the »Women Who Design« (2019) project: A Twitter directory that increases women's visibility and the diversity of the design industry.

Silva Baum, Claudia Scheer und Lea Sievertsen zu ihrem »iphiGenia«-prämierten Diplomprojekt »notamuse« (2018), welches das Fehlen weiblicher Vorbilder im Grafikdesign zum Ausgangspunkt hatte. Eine Initiative, die sich die Vernetzung unserer digitalen Welt zunutze macht und aus der internationalen Design-Community kommt, ist das Projekt »Women Who Design« (2019): Ein Twitter-Verzeichnis, um Frauen mehr Sichtbarkeit zu verschaffen und die Diversität der Branche zu erhöhen.

[1] Gemeint ist hier wie bereits im Vorwort eine gefühlte Ohnmacht, auf bestimmte Zusammenhänge aufgrund ihrer Vorbestimmtheit keinen Einfluss zu haben. Analog zum Designberuf ist es die Ohnmacht vor dem Hintergrund immer auch kulturelle Praktiken mitzugestalten, respektive nicht Nicht-Gestalten zu können, ähnlich wie es Daniel M. Feige beschreibt (s. Einführung, Katharina Kurz, S. 9).
[2] Siehe u. a.: Müller, Ulrike. 2019 [2009]. Bauhaus-Frauen. Meisterinnen in Kunst, Handwerk und Design; Staatl. Kunstsammlungen Dresden, Beyerle, Tulga u. Nemeckova, Klara. 2018. Gegen die Unsichtbarkeit. Designerinnen der Deutschen Werkstätten Hellerau, 1898 bis 1938; Otto, Elisabeth u. Rössler, Patrick. 2019. Bauhaus Women: A Global Perspective; Berg. Universität Wuppertal, Breuer, Gerda u. Meer, Julia. 2012. Women in Graphic Design 1890–2012.

[1] As mentioned in the introduction, what is meant here is a sense of powerlessness of having no influence certain contexts because of their predetermined nature – along the same lines in the design profession, there is a powerlessness rooted in the inescapability of shaping as well as not being able to shape cultural practices, as Daniel Martin Feige similarly describes (s. Introduction, Katharina Kurz, p. 9).
[2] See, for example: Ulrike Müller, »Bauhaus-Frauen. Meisterinnen in Kunst, Handwerk und Design,« 2009/2019; Staatl. Kunstsammlungen Dresden, Tulga Beyerle and Klara Nemeckova, »Gegen die Unsichtbarkeit. Designer innen der Deutschen Werkstätten Hellerau, 1898 bis 1938,« 2018; Elisabeth Otto and Patrick Rössler, »Bauhaus Women: A Global Perspective,« Berg. Universität Wuppertal, 2019; Gerda Breuer and Julia Meer, »Women in Graphic Design 1890–2012,« 2012.

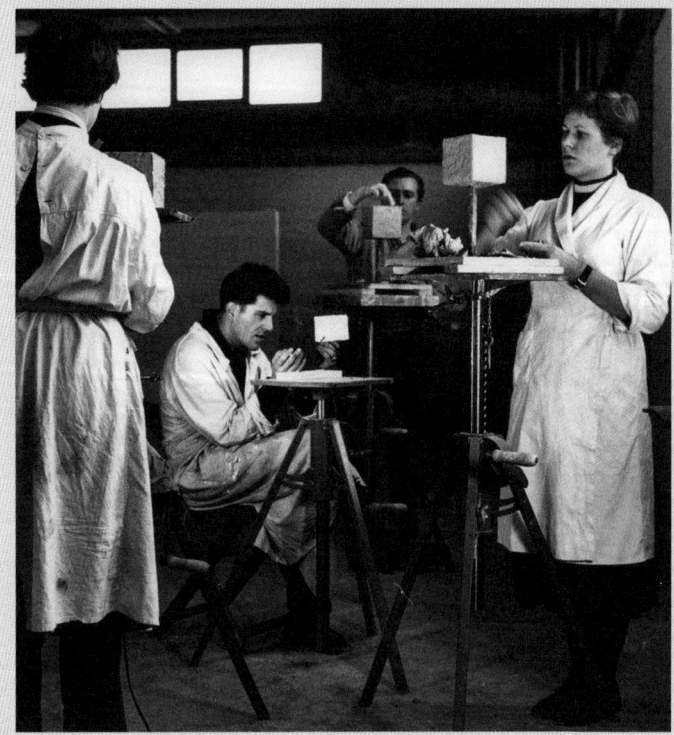

Studierende in der Gipswerkstatt / *Students working in the plaster workshop* / DE ca. 1955 / Margit Staber, Olivio Ferrari, Alexandre Wollner und Irmgard Philippi jeweils bei der Arbeit an einem Gipswürfel / *Each working on a plaster cube* / Sign. Dp. 90.9 / HfG-Archiv / Museum Ulm

Christiane Wachsmann **Frauen und Männer an der HfG – Lebensentwürfe der 1950er und 1960er Jahre** An der HfG trafen sich viele besondere, idealistisch gesonnene Menschen, die alle von der Vorstellung erfüllt waren, in dieser Zeit nach dem Faschismus eine neue Welt gestalten und aufzubauen zu wollen.

In Bezug auf die Geschlechterrollen waren es dabei vor allem die Frauen, die nach neuen Wegen suchten und Altes in Frage stellten. Das taten sie schon allein dadurch, dass sie sich um ein Studium an einer Hochschule bewarben: Ihr Bereich war dem allgemeinen gesellschaftlichen Verständnis der 1950er und 1960er Jahre nach der Haushalt und die Kindererziehung. So fand die höhere Ausbildung für Frauen dieser Zeit oft an Frauenfachschulen statt, wo sie mit den entsprechenden Kenntnissen für den vorgesehenen Berufsweg ausgestattet wurden. Wollten Frauen etwa nach einem geisteswissenschaftlichen Studium in einem ihrem Abschluss entsprechenden Beruf arbeiten, blieb ihnen oft nur die Wahl: Entweder verzichteten sie auf Kinder oder auf die Karriere.

Rechtlich waren Frauen in der Bundesrepublik bis 1972 ihren Ehemännern unterstellt, ohne deren Erlaubnis konnten sie keiner Berufsarbeit nachgehen. Dafür waren diese Ehemänner für die materielle Versorgung der gesamten Familie verantwortlich. Sie waren in der Berufswahl meist freier als die Studentinnen, es wurde aber auch von ihnen erwartet, dass sie im Berufsleben erfolgreich waren und Karriere machten.

Während die Studenten – weniger die Studentinnen – der 1950er Jahre noch von den eher konservativen Vorstellungen dieser Zeit über die Ehe geprägt waren, begann sich in den 1960er Jahren bereits ein anderer, freierer Lebensstil zu entwickeln.

Lebensentwürfe der 1950er Jahre Die jungen Leute, die in dieser Zeit zu studieren begannen, waren in ihrer Kindheit von den Idealen des Nationalsozialismus geprägt worden. Mann und Frau waren dort eindeutige Geschlechterrollen zugewiesen: Während die Frau als Mutter und Hausfrau für das Familienheim zuständig war, ging der Mann hinaus in die Berufswelt oder zog in den Krieg.

Wenn eine Frau heiratete, sah sie sich danach oft mit dem Anspruch konfrontiert, von nun an jeden beruflichen Ehrgeiz aufgeben und nur noch für Mann und Kind da sein zu dürfen – und oft genug blieb ihnen nichts übrig, als sich zu fügen. So erging es auch einer Reihe von HfG-Studentinnen, unter ihnen Irmgard Zeischegg: »die arbeiten von irmgard zeischegg zeichneten sich durch ein hohes ästhetisches niveau und diszipliniertes und methodisches vorgehen auf der grundlage einer sehr vorteilhaften analytischen begabung aus ... nach ihrer

Women and Men at the Ulm School of Design (HfG Ulm) – Life Planning in the 1950s and 1960s The HfG Ulm was a meeting point for many special, idealistic people, who were driven by the vision and will to shape a new world in this time after fascism. Regarding gender roles, it was women, above all, who searched for new paths and questioned the past. And they did so already by the mere fact that they applied to study at an academy: According to the prevailing social conceptions of the 1950s and 1960s, their domain was the household and parenting. Higher education for women primarily took place at women's technical colleges, where they could acquire the appropriate knowledge for their envisaged professional careers. If women, who completed studies in humanities, for example, wished to work in a profession related to their degrees, they often only had but two options: to refrain from having children or relinquish the career.

In the German Federal Republic, women were legally subordinated to their husbands – until 1972 they could not pursue professional work without their permission. In turn, these husbands were responsible for the material provision of the entire family. Although the majority of male students was more free in their choice of occupation than their female counterparts, they were expected to be successful in their work life and to climb up the career ladder. While male students of the 1950s – and less so the females – were still influenced by rather conservative notions of marriage, a new, more liberated lifestyle dawned in the 1960s.

Life Planning in the 1950s The childhoods of the young people who began studies in this time had been informed by the ideals of National Socialism. Man and woman were assigned distinct gender roles: The woman as mother and housewife was responsible for the family home; the man went out into the professional world or to war.

Once a woman got married, she was often confronted with the expectation to give up any professional ambitions and to care for the husband and children – and often enough they had no choice but to accept this fate. This was also the case for a number of female HfG students, such as Irmgard Zeischegg: »The works by Irmgard Zeischegg were distinguished by their high aesthetic level and a disciplined and methodical approach, based on a very expedient analytical talent [...] After her marriage Ms. Zeischegg left the School of Design upon her own request.« Otl Aicher, certificate for Irmgard Zeischegg, May 4, 1963

However, this also created opportunities for women, depending on their personality and interests, to develop their talents within the framework of the conventional role distribution and make contributions in their own right: »My marriage with Hermann Delugan brought me to South Tyrol, Italy. Main further activities:

verheiratung verließ frau zeischegg die hochschule für gestaltung auf eigenen wunsch.« Otl Aicher, Zeugnis für Irmgard Zeischegg, 4. Mai 1963

Je nach Persönlichkeit und Interessen bot das für die Frauen aber auch Chancen, sich im Rahmen der konventionellen Rollenverteilung zu entfalten und ihren eigenen Beitrag zu leisten: »Die Heirat mit Hermann Delugan brachte mich in der Folge nach Südtirol/Italien. Schwerpunkte der weiteren Tätigkeit: Mehrjähriges kunstpädagogisches Arbeiten mit 6–10-Jährigen; die Erziehung der eigenen drei Kinder und Mitdenken im Büro meines Mannes.« Ellinor Hirschfeld-Delugan (1989)[3]

Die Männer hatten in dieser Zeit weder den Anspruch noch den Zwang, sich gesellschaftlich neue Rollen zu erschließen. Ihr Betätigungsfeld war und blieb die bezahlte Berufsarbeit. Pioniere waren sie dennoch – und bekamen das unter Umständen auch zu spüren, vor allem, wenn sie selbständig arbeiten wollten. »in der ersten zeit galt es, kunden zu finden und ihnen klar zu machen, was wir sind, was wir können und welche vorteile sich aus einer zusammenarbeit mit uns ergeben könnte.« Karl-Heinz Bergmiller (2008)[4]

Lebensentwürfe der 1960er Jahre Mitte der 1960er Jahre kamen immer mehr Studierende nach Ulm, die kurz vor Kriegsende oder danach geboren waren. Sie gehörten einer neuen Generation an, die den Faschismus nur noch vom Hörensagen kannte und weniger von ihm geprägt war. Als »1968er« setzte sich eine Reihe von ihnen für einen neuerlichen Wandel der Gesellschaft ein, hin zu mehr Freiheit und Demokratie.

Frauen, die an der HfG studierten, mussten sich noch immer ihren Platz erkämpfen: Ihre Emanzipation, die mühsame Suche nach einer neuen Rolle, erfolgte auch in dieser Zeit oft gegen den Widerstand ihrer Partner. Mitunter gab es aber auch ein wirkliches Interesse von beiden Seiten an einem beruflichen wie familiären Miteinander, wie etwa bei Kinga und Andras Dózsa-Farkas, die 1970 in München gemeinsam ein Designbüro gründeten und gleichberechtigt betrieben. »Erfolge: zwei Kinder und viele Produkte auf dem Markt.« Kinga Dózsa-Farkas (1989)[5]

Das war in dieser Zeit allerdings ein eher ungewöhnliches Modell. Fast klassisch dagegen ist die Suche nach einem neuen Berufsfeld nach der Familienphase – oder der Trennung vom Lebenspartner, die in dieser Zeit zunehmend zur Option wurde. Während im studierten Beruf die Erfahrung fehlte und die Männer die entscheidenden Positionen bereits besetzt hielten, begannen etwa Frauke Decurtins, Marlies Poss oder Ursula Wenzel ein weiteres Studium und wurden in ihren neuen Berufen erfolgreich.

So hatten die Frauen – diejenigen der Vorkriegs- wie der Nachkriegsgeneration – in gewisser Hinsicht auch große Freiheiten; meist allerdings erst, nachdem die Familienphase vorbei war. Manche von ihnen konnten sich innerhalb der Partnerschaft entfalten, andere sahen sich in dieser neuen Lebensphase auf sich selbst gestellt.

several years of work in art education with 6 to 10-year-olds; raising my own three children, and sharing my ideas in the office of my husband.«
Ellinor Hirschfeld-Delugan (1989)[3]

In this time men had neither the ambition nor the pressure to pursue new social roles for themselves. Their field of occupation was and remained paid professional work. Nevertheless, they were pioneers – and occasionally came to experience the effects, above all, when they wanted to work independently. »In the beginning it was about finding clients and making it clear to them what we are, what we can do, and which advantages there are in cooperating with us.«
Karl-Heinz Bergmiller (2008)[4]

Life Planning in the 1960s By the mid-1960s the number of HfG Ulm students who were born shortly before the end of the war or thereafter had increased. They belonged to a new generation who only knew of fascism from hearsay and were less influenced by it. As a part of the '68 movement, a number of them strove for change in society and more freedom and democracy.

Women who studied at the HfG Ulm still had to fight for their place: Their emancipation, the tiresome search for a new role, was often faced by resistance from their partners in this time as well. Sometimes, however, there was a genuine interest on both sides in an equal coexistence in both professional and family life – as was the case with Kinga and Andras Dózsa-Farkas, who co-founded a design office in Munich in 1970 and ran it as equal partners. »Achievements: two children and many products on the market.«
Kinga Dózsa-Farkas (1989)[5]

Albeit, this was a rather uncommon model in this time. The almost classic scenario for women, on the other hand, was the search for a new occupation after the family upbringing phase – or separation from the life partner, which increasingly became an alternative in the 1960s. Whereas experience was lacking in the studied profession and the key positions were already occupied by men, women like Frauke Decurtins, Marlies Poss, or Ursula Wenzel began new studies and became successful in their professions.

In this light, women – those of the pre-war and post-war generation alike – also had a great deal of freedom in a certain sense; usually, however, only once the family phase was over. Some of them could blossom within their partnerships, while others would pursue this new life phase on their own.

Not all men were satisfied with the expectations that accompanied their prescribed roles either. For Helmut Müller-Kühn or Klaus Hofmann, for example, it was even more difficult to revoke these ideals than it was for women. By rejecting the pursuit of a career and performing a typical masculine role, they broke taboos and were sometimes confronted with deeply ingrained

Studierende in der Metallwerkstatt / *Students working in the metal workshop* / DE 1958 / Sign. D. 5.0039 / HfG-Archiv / Museum Ulm

Auch nicht alle Männer dieser Zeit waren mit den Erwartungen, die die vorgegebenen Rollen an sie stellten, glücklich. Für Helmut Müller-Kühn oder Klaus Hofmann etwa war es schwerer als für die Frauen, sich diesen Idealen zu entziehen. Indem sie sich dem Karrierestreben verweigerten, brachen sie Tabus und mussten sich mitunter mit tiefsitzenden Vorurteilen auseinandersetzen, die mit der Weigerung, eine typisch männliche Rolle einzunehmen, zugleich ihre männliche Identität in Frage stellten.

Bewerbungs- und Studienstatistik Zwischen 1952 und 1968 bewarben sich insgesamt 1.040 Studienwillige an der HfG. Davon traten 648 ihr Studium auch wirklich an. Sowohl bei denjenigen, die sich um ein Studium bewarben, als auch bei denjenigen, die letztlich an der HfG studierten, betrug der Frauenanteil jeweils 15 Prozent. Das war für diese Zeit ein ausgesprochen hoher Prozentsatz.

Abschluss des Studiums Von den insgesamt 236 diplomierten HfG-Studierenden waren 90 Prozent Männer, 10 Prozent Frauen. Gegenüber dem Frauenanteil bei Eintritt in die Hochschule war der Anteil derjenigen, die ihr Studium auch tatsächlich beendeten, also um ein Drittel gesunken.

[3] Landesgewerbeamt Baden-Württemberg / Design Center Stuttgart, Oedekoven-Gerischer, Angela (Hg.). 1989. Frauen im Design: Berufsbilder und Lebenswege seit 1900. / Women in Design: Careers and Life Histories since 1900, S. 278.
[4] Bergmiller, Karl-Heinz. 2008. »rückblick – von rio de janeiro,« In hfg ulm: Die Abteilung Produktgestaltung – 39 Rückblicke, hrsg. von Karl-Achim Czemper, S. 24.
[5] Landesgewerbeamt Baden-Württemberg, Frauen im Design, S. 322.

prejudices, which also called their male identity into question.

Applicants and Students Statistics *Between 1952 and 1968 there was a total of 1040 applicants for studies at the HfG Ulm. 648 of them actually commenced studies. In both the category of applicants and those who actually studied at the HfG Ulm, the ratio of women amounted to 15 percent. It was an exceptionally high percentage for this time.*

Graduation *Of the total of 236 HfG Ulm graduates, 90 percent were men and 10 percent women. Hence, in comparison to the ratio of women admitted for studies at the HfG Ulm, the percentage of actual graduates had sunk by a third.*

[3] *Landesgewerbeamt Baden-Württemberg / Design Center Stuttgart, Angela Oedekoven-Gerischer (eds.), Frauen im Design: Berufsbilder und Lebenswege seit 1900. / Women in Design: Careers and Life Histories since 1900 (Stuttgart: Design Center Stuttgart, Haus der Wirtschaft, 1989), 278.*
[4] *Karl-Heinz Bergmiller. »rückblick – von rio de janeiro,« in hfg ulm: Die Abteilung Produktgestaltung – 39 Rückblicke, edited by Karl-Achim Czemper (Dortmund: Verlag Dorothea Rohn, 2008), 24.*
[5] *Landesgewerbeamt Baden-Württemberg, Frauen im Design, 322.*

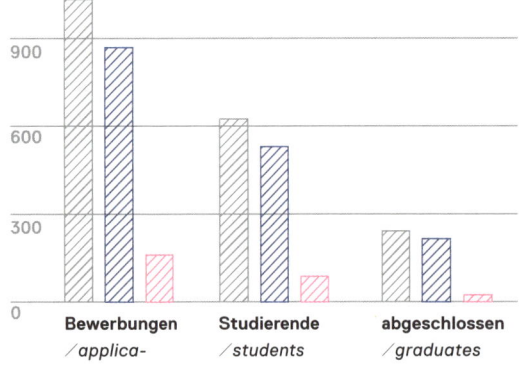

Auswertung der Bewerbungen, Studierenden und Absolvent*innen an der HfG Ulm nach Geschlecht
gesamt / männlich / weiblich / *Evaluation of applications, students and graduates at the HfG Ulm by gender* total / male / female

Grundlehre im großen Hörsaal /
Foundation course in the large auditorium /
DE ca. 1955 / Foto: / *Photography:*
Eva Koch-Hörmann / Sign. Dp. 117.022. /
HfG-Archiv / Museum Ulm

Karl-Heinz Bergmiller (geb. 1928). Studium der Produktgestaltung an der HfG Ulm. Arbeit als selbstständiger Designer in Brasilien, Gründung der Escola Superior de Desenho Industrial (ESDI) in Rio de Janeiro gemeinsam mit seinem HfG-Kommilitonen Alexandre Wollner. *Karl-Heinz Bergmiller, born 1928, studied product design at the HfG Ulm. Work as self-employed designer in Brazil, founder of the Escola Superior de Desenho Industrial (ESDI) in Rio de Janeiro together with his fellow HfG student Alexandre Wollner.*

Helmut Müller-Kühn (1929–2017) Studium der Produktgestaltung an der HfG Ulm. Arbeit als Assistent von Hans Gugelot, danach Aufbau und Leitung der Abteilung Produktgestaltung der Firma Krupp. Ab 1981 freier Künstler im Emsland. *Helmut Müller-Kühn, born (1929–2017), studied product design at the HfG Ulm. Work as assistant of Hans Gugelot, then establishment and head of the product design department of the company Krupp. From 1981 independent artist in the Emsland region of Lower Saxony.*

Frauke Koch-Weser verh. Decurtins (1934–2014). Studium der Produktgestaltung an der HfG Ulm. Nach der Kinderphase Ausbildung und Arbeit als Erwachsenenbildnerin. *Frauke Koch-Weser, md. Decurtins (1934–2014) studied product design at the HfG Ulm. After raising her children, studies and work in adult education.*

Marlies Matthies verh. Poss (geb. 1944). Studium der Produktgestaltung an der HfG Ulm. Arbeit als Designerin bis zur Geburt des ersten Kindes. Später Studium Kunsterziehung, Arbeit als Lehrerin, Dozentin und Bildhauerin. *Marlies Matthies, md. Poss, born 1944, studied product design at the HfG Ulm. Work as designer up to the birth of her first child. Thereafter studies in art education, work as a teacher, lecturer, and sculptor.*

Kinga Gebefügi verh. Dózsa-Farkas (geb. 1943). Studium der Produktgestaltung an der HfG Ulm. Gemeinsames Büro mit ihrem Mann András Dózsa-Farkas. *Kinga Gebefügi, md. Dózsa-Farkas, born 1943, studied product design at the HfG Ulm. Runs an office together with her husband András Dózsa-Farkas.*

Ursula Wenzel (geb. 1943). Studium der Visuellen Kommunikation an der HfG Ulm. Arbeit als Fotojournalistin, später Studium Kunstwissenschaften, freie Arbeit als Journalistin und Webdesignerin. *Ursula Wenzel, born 1943, studied visual communication at the HfG Ulm. Work as photo journalist, thereafter studies in art history, independent work as journalist and web designer.*

Ellinor Hirschfeld verh. Hirschfeld-Delugan (geb. 1928). Studium der Produktgestaltung an der HfG Ulm. Danach Familienphase und Mitarbeit im Büro ihres Mannes. *Ellinor Hirschfeld, md. Hirschfeld-Delugan, born 1928, studied product design at the HfG Ulm. Thereafter family phase and cooperation in her husband's office.*

Irmgard Philippi verh. Zeischegg (1921–1993). Studium der Visuellen Kommunikation an der HfG Ulm. Nach der Trennung von ihrem Mann Weiterbildung und Arbeit als Werk- und Zeichenlehrerin, später als Projektleiterin beim Deutschen Paritätischen Wohlfahrtsverband. *Irmgard Philippi, md. Zeischegg (1921–1993) studied visual communication at the HfG Ulm. After separating from her husband, further education and work as craft and drawing teacher, thereafter as project manager at the Deutsche Paritätischer Wohlfahrtsverband [German Parity Welfare Association].*

Klaus Hofmann (1941–2004). Studium der Visuellen Kommunikation an der HfG Ulm. Arbeit als angestellter und selbstständiger Grafiker, seit 1992 Landwirt und Künstler in Portugal. *Klaus Hofmann (1941–2004) studied product design at the HfG Ulm. Work as employed and independent graphic designer, since 1992 farmer and artist in Portugal.*

Selbstbehauptungen – Frauen an der HfG ulm (2007) An der ehemaligen Hochschule für Gestaltung Ulm studierten seinerzeit 98 Frauen, aus 19 Ländern, von insgesamt 642 Studierenden. Während, wie mittlerweile bekannt ist, die Frauen am Bauhaus in das Kunsthandwerk bzw. vor allem in die Textilabteilung geschoben wurden, gab es solche Beschränkungen an der HfG Ulm offenbar nicht. Verglichen mit dem Frauenanteil unter den Mitarbeiter*innen (50 Prozent) war ihr Anteil unter dem Lehrkörper (2 Prozent) und den Studierenden (15 Prozent) allerdings eher gering. Obwohl mit der Begründung des HfG-Archivs eine wissenschaftliche Auseinandersetzung mit der Schule und ihrer Bedeutung eingesetzt hat, ist im Vergleich dazu die Rolle der Frauen kaum erforscht. Dieser Umstand war zugleich Anlass für die ehemaligen Studentinnen Gerda Müller-Krauspe und Ursula Wenzel sowie Petra Kellner, ein Online-Archiv, ergänzt um eine Printpublikation zu »Frauen an der HfG ulm« zu initiieren. Das Projekt ist als »Spurensuche und Spurensicherung aller Frauen, die an der HfG ulm studierten, lehrten oder als Mitarbeiterinnen tätig waren«[6] zu verstehen. Das Projekt stellt mit Lebensläufen, Werdegängen und Interviews einen wichtigen Fundus und eine außerordentliche Grundlage aus erster Hand für noch ausstehende Fragen bzw. deren Beantwortung dar.[7]

[6] Zitiert nach https://frauen-HfG-ulm.de, zul. abgerufen am 18.11.2019.
[7] Nach neuesten Recherchen und der Öffnung des privaten Gugelot Familienarchivs konnte eine weitere Frau, nämlich Marie-Hélène »Malke« Gugelot, als bisher unbekannte, kurzzeitige Mitarbeiterin eruiert werden – der Beitrag »Seitwärts der Avantgarde: Malke Gugelot und die Ehefrauen im Kuhberg-Kosmos« (2020) ist zumindest ein weiterer Beitrag dazu, den Rollen anhand der starken Verquickung von Privatem und Beruflichem rund um das moderne Hochschulprojekt näher zu kommen, Kurz, Katharina u. Wachsmann, Christiane. 2020. Seitwärts der Avantgarde: Malke Gugelot und die Ehefrauen im Kuhberg-Kosmos. In Hans Gugelot – Die Architektur des Design, hrsg. v. HfG-Archiv / Museum Ulm u. Christiane Wachsmann.

Assertiveness – Women at the HfG Ulm (2007)
Out of a total of 642 students, 98 women from 19 different countries studied at the former Ulm School of Design (HfG). While, as we now know, women at the Bauhaus were pushed into doing handicrafts, and textiles in particular, it seems there were no such restrictions at the HfG. However, compared to the ratio of women employed by the school (50 percent), their numbers among the teaching staff (2 percent) and students (15 percent) were rather low. Although the establishment of the HfG-Archiv has enabled scholars to examine the school and its importance, the role of women there has hardly been researched at all. This omission led Gerda Müller-Krauspe, Ursula Wenzel, and Petra Kellner to create an online archive and accompanying print publication entitled Women at the HfG Ulm. Their project aims to secure »traces of all the women who studied, lectured, or were members of the staff at the HfG Ulm«.[6] With its biographies, career histories, and interviews, it represents a remarkable pool of first-hand sources that will help shed light on some unanswered questions.[7]

[6] *Quoted from http://frauen-hfg-ulm.de.*
[7] *New research and the opening of the Gugelot family's private archive have revealed the existence of a previously unknown female temporary employee named Marie-Hélène »Malke« Gugelot – the text »Seitwärts der Avantgarde: Malke Gugelot und die Ehefrauen im Kuhberg-Kosmos« [On the Sidelines of the Avant-Garde: Malke Gugelot and Wives in the Kuhberg Cosmos] (2020) represents another contribution to our understanding of the private and professional roles these women held within this modern university. Cf. Katharina Kurz and Christiane Wachsmann, »Seitwärts der Avantgarde: Malke Gugelot und die Ehefrauen im Kuhberg-Kosmos,« in Hans Gugelot – Die Architektur des Design, edited by HfG-Archiv / Museum Ulm / Christiane Wachsmann (Stuttgart: avedition, 2020).*

Frauen an der hfg ulm – Lebensläufe und Werdegänge / *Women at the HfG Ulm – Curricula and personal histories* / DE 2003 / Frame www.frauen-hfg-ulm.de / Projektgruppe: / *Project group:* Petra Keller, Gerda Müller-Krauspe, Ursula Wenzel

»notamuse – A New Perspective on Woman Graphic Designers in Europe«

»notamuse« (dt. »keine Muse«) ist eine Initiative von Silva Baum, Claudia Scheer und Lea Sievertsen, die auf eine Masterarbeit an der HAW Hamburg zurückgeht. Der Titel ist zugleich Anlass und Ziel des Projekts: Ausgehend von der Feststellung, dass sowohl während der Ausbildung wie auch auf Konferenzen die immer gleiche, einseitige Narration wiederholt und männliche »Designgrößen« gepriesen werden, entschieden die Drei, diese Perspektive aufzubrechen. Was ist mit weiblichen Vorbildern? Wie steht es um die Frauen, die in dieser Branche tätig sind? Sie führten dazu 22 Interviews mit Designerinnen, Soziologinnen, Gender-Forscherinnen sowie Netzwerk-Gründerinnen. Das Ergebnis veröffentlichten sie zunächst in Form einer Webseite und schickten 2018 die Crowdfunding-Kampagne zur Realisierung als Buchprojekt hinterher – erfolgreich, sodass die großformatige Publikation (2019) mit über 400 Seiten nicht nur inhaltlich ein Gegengewicht zu den bisherigen Erzählungen darstellt. Der Intention, den Blick für mehr Diversität im Grafikdesign zu öffnen und Frauen, die eben »keine Musen« sind, sondern Sichtbarkeit verdienen, kommen sie mit der Präsentation und Dokumentation von über 60 europäischen Designerinnen sowie deren Arbeiten nach. Das International Gender Design Network (iGDN) zeichnete das Projekt 2018 mit dem »iphiGenia Gender Design Award« aus.

»notamuse – A New Perspective on Women Graphic Designers in Europe« Silva Baum, Claudia Scheer, and Lea Sievertsen's »notamuse« project came out of their master's thesis undertaken at Hamburg University of Applied Sciences (HAW Hamburg). The title itself offers a clue as to what prompted the project and its ultimate aim: fed up with hearing – both throughout their education and at almost every conference – the same one-sided narrative endlessly repeated and exclusively male designers being hailed as »design stars«, the three women decided to challenge this perspective by asking: What about female role models? What about the women who work in this industry? They conducted interviews with 22 female designers, sociologists, gender researchers, and network founders, first publishing the results in the form of a website. In 2018, they launched a successful crowdfunding campaign to develop the project as a book, which came out as a large-format, 400-page publication in 2019. The project not only represents a counterbalance to earlier narratives, in terms of content – by presenting and documenting over 60 European female designers and their work, it also succeeds in spotlighting the diversity that exists in graphic design and women who are »notamuse« but deserve more visibility. The International Gender Design Network (iGDN) awarded the project the iphiGenia Gender Design Award in 2018.

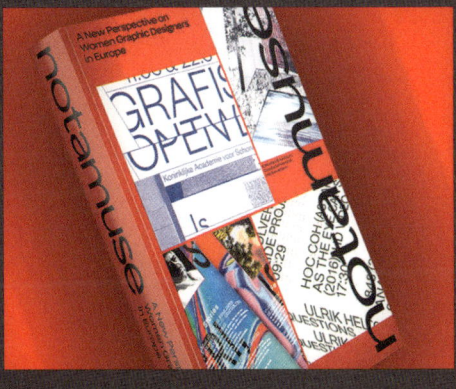

notamuse – A New Perspective on Woman Graphic Designers in Europe / DE 2018 / 19 / Webseite und Buch / Website and book / Masterarbeit im Bereich Kommunikationsdesign, Editorial Design an der / Master thesis in communication design, editorial design at the HAW Hamburg / Betreut von: / Supervised by: Prof. Dr. Anke Haarmann, Prof. Heike Grebin / Verlag: / Publisher: niggli / Konzept und Gestaltung: / Concept and Design: Silvia Baum, Claudia Scheer, Lea Sievertsen

»Design for …« ist ein Simulations-Brettspiel, das Spielende in die Rolle als Designer*innen versetzt. Entworfen hat es Illustratorin Jaqueline Diedam während ihres Studiums an der Köln International School of Design (KISD). Das Spiel ist als Werkzeug für Theorie und Praxis des Designs zu verstehen, das einen spielerischen Zugang zu den Themen Gender und Design bietet, ohne diesbezügliches Vorwissen vorauszusetzen. Das Konzept folgt einer partizipativen Spielidee nach Eva Brandt, bei der es nicht um klassisch-kompetitive Gewinnsituationen, sondern um das Initiieren von Prozessen geht, die eine Diskussion und Erkenntnis befördern. Während die Spieler*innen in Teams an ihren Design-Konzepten des »was« und »für wen« feilen, müssen sie durch das Passieren von Spielfeldern häufig umdenken, ihre Entwürfe konkretisieren und verändern; von der Make-Up-Verpackung für Senior*innen bis zur Bier-Werbekampagne für Jurist*innen ist alles denkbar. Eine weitere Person begleitet als Moderation den Ablauf und insbesondere den Spielausgang sowie damit die Ergebnisse und Erfahrungen. Letztlich geht es nicht um eine Handreichung für »gutes Design«, sondern darum, die Relation zwischen Gender und Design sicht- bzw. erfahrbar sowie Designer*innen auch auf ihre soziale Verantwortung aufmerksam zu machen, die sie mit der Gestaltung von Dingen und Konzepten haben. Der Austausch über das Anstoßen von Denkprozessen ist das höchste Gut dieses Spiels, den es auf eine unterhaltsame, interaktive und offene Art und Weise in Gang zu bringen sucht.

»Design for …« is a board game that has players take on the role of designers. It was designed by illustrator Jaqueline Diedam while studying at the Köln International School of Design (KISD). The game is a tool for the theory and practice of design that offers a playful way to approach topics such as »gender and design« without presuming any prior knowledge. It is based on a participatory game concept devised by Eva Brandt, which avoids the classic win-lose competition of most board games; instead, it is about initiating situations that encourage discussion and knowledge acquisition. Players work in teams on their design concepts, prompted by »what« and »for whom« briefing cards (from cosmetics packaging for older people to beer advertising campaigns aimed at lawyers, anything is possible), and they often have to rethink, concretise, or change their designs as they pass through the playing fields. One player, nominated as moderator, oversees the action, experience, and outcome of the game. Ultimately, it is not about creating »good design« as such, but about making the relationship between gender and design tangible and visible, as well as making designers aware of the social responsibility they have when designing objects and developing concepts. The game's greatest asset is the exchange of ideas and thought processes that it hopes to instigate in an entertaining, interactive, and open manner.

Design for… / DE 2016 / Brettspiel / Board game / Sprache: Englisch / *Language: English* / Basierend auf qualitativen Interviews im Rahmen der Abschlussarbeit im Fachbereich Integrated Design / *Based on qualitative interviews in context of the Bachelor's thesis in Integrated Design* / Köln International School of Design (KISD), TH Köln / Entwurf: / *Design:* Jaqueline Diedam

Gender Equity Toolkit Mit der Intention, Genderstereotype zu durchbrechen, erarbeitete die Soziologin und Designerin Leyla Acaroglu für die Initiative »Women Lead« des internationalen Designverbunds AIGA das »Gender Equity Toolkit«. Anfänglich war die Frage, was die Umstände dafür sind, die Frauen offenbar zurückhalten, Ausgangspunkt für Einzelinterviews im Jahr 2015. Es zeigte sich, dass sowohl Männer als auch Frauen sich im Arbeitsumfeld unter Druck fühlten, Rollenbildern zu entsprechen. Diese Erkenntnis führte dazu, dass Acaroglu Workshops initiierte, um das Toolkit zu erarbeiten. An Diskussionen über Gender und Führungsrollen nahmen über 80 Personen teil und wiederum weitere 70, die die entwickelten Übungen testeten. Auch außerhalb der Design-Community leitete die Designerin Workshops dazu bei den United Nations (UN) und Google, London. Das Toolkit soll mit seinen Übungen Quelle und Unterstützung für die Arbeit professioneller Designer*innen sein und ein Hilfsmittel, mit Empathie gegen Gender-Bias einzutreten. Es ist für Mitglieder des Netzwerks sowie online erhältlich und als DIY-Version per Download zugänglich.

Gender Equity Toolkit With the aim of breaking gender stereotypes, sociologist and designer Leyla Acaroglu developed the »Gender Equity Toolkit« for the professional design association AIGA's Women Lead Initiative. Initially, a series of one-to-one interviews was conducted in 2015 in to investigate the circumstances that prevent women from progressing to positions of leadership. It soon became apparent that both men and women feel pressured to conform to certain roles and expectations in the workplace. This insight led Acaroglu to organise a round of workshops to develop the toolkit. More than 80 people took part in discussions about gender and leadership roles, and another 70 took part in testing the resources that were subsequently developed. Workshops were organised outside of the design community, too: at the United Nations (UN) and Google's London offices, for example. The toolkit and its activities are intended to be used a resource to support the work of professional designers and help fight gender bias through empathy. It is available for members of the AIGA network and online as a downloadable DIY version.

Gender Equity Toolkit ∕ US 2016 ∕ Sprache: Englisch ∕ *Language: English* ∕ Herausgeber: ∕ *Publisher:* AIGA Women Lead Initiative ∕ Toolkit-Design: Leyla Acaroglu, Disrupt Design ∕ Visual Design: Adler Design

Gestaltungsfaktoren Drei maßgebliche Faktoren, die die grundsätzliche Gestaltung und dessen Ergebnis prägen, sind Form, Farbe und Material. Obwohl sie im wahrsten Sinne des Wortes nur an der Oberfläche dessen kratzen, was Design bedeutet, sind das auch die Parameter, die uns als denjenigen, die nicht am Prozess beteiligt sind, maßgeblich visuell oder haptisch reizen. In Zusammenhang damit sind es nicht unbedingt die Reize selbst, sondern auch die Vorstellungen, die mit der Nutzung verbunden sind. Visuelle Reize werden von Personen, die sehen können, ganz unmittelbar verarbeitet. Bezüglich des Zusammenspiels dieser Komponenten ist es vor allen Dingen so, dass sie uns in Sekundenschnelle Vorstellungen vermitteln, die auf unser Erfahrungswissen referieren: Ist ein Werkzeug handlich? Ist ein Stuhl bequem? Ist ein Automobil sportlich oder stadttauglich? Ist etwas »nicht mein Ding«? Diese Reaktion ist ein ganz unmittelbarer Ausweis dessen, dass wir die Dinge nicht nur anhand von Funktionalität bewerten, sondern auch mit unserer Identität abgleichen – deren Anteil auch Geschlecht ist. Beispiele zeigen, dass kulturelle Konzepte nicht nur von Nutzer*innen, sondern auch von denen, die gestalten, in die Dingwelt übertragen werden. Damit das funktioniert, müssen wir Teil eines kulturellen Kreises sein, der diese Zeichen lesen kann. Sie sind mitnichten universell, sondern zeitlichem und kulturellem Wandel unterlegen. Dieses Thema erschöpfend zu behandeln ist hier nicht möglich, jedoch mögen nachfolgend einzelne Objekte aus der Sammlung des HfG-Archivs exemplarische Fäden sein, die schier unendlich verfolgt werden könnten.

Ein gängiges Prinzip ist beispielsweise, Salz und Pfeffer sowie zugehörige Streuer oder -mühlen als untrennbares Paar der »Lebenswürze« miteinander zu assoziieren. In der Welt der Gestaltung wird dies nicht selten als Schwarz-und-Weiß-Kombination, sondern auch als heterosexuelles Paar, sprich Mann und Frau übersetzt. Wie im Fall von »Mr. und Mrs. Prickly« (1997) drückt sich das nicht zwangsläufig als menschenähnliche Form, sondern als Konzept aus (s. Abb. 1). Ein weiteres Beispiel ist der Flaschenöffner »party boy« (1979), entworfen von ehemaligem HfG-Student und Designer Horst Diener (s. Abb. 2). Das sprichwörtliche »Stehaufmännchen« wird zum Konzept, das die Idee hinter dem Öffner übersetzt: Durch die patentierte Konstruktionsweise kann er nie liegen, sondern richtet sich immerzu wieder auf. Ein witziges Detail, das den »party boy« zu einem beliebten Werbegeschenk machte. Eine ganze Reihe von »Boys«, namentlich u. a. »Transistor, Mini, Micro, Fernseh, Solo, Ocean, Elite, Tele und Phono Boy«, brachte das Unternehmen Grundig auf den Markt. Dabei handelt es sich um Fernseh- und Tongeräte, die in irgendeiner Weise tragbar oder mobil sind. Das erste Modell war der »Grundig Boy«, eines der ersten

Design Factors Shape, colour, and material are important factors that influence the overall design. Although they only scratch the surface of what design means, these are the parameters, visually and haptically, that most instantaneously appeal to us, as those not involved in the design process. That appeal is not just transmitted by these parameters, in and of themselves, but in the ideas associated with their use. For sighted people, this interplay of factors instantly transmits ideas visually, which relate to our empirical knowledge: Is this tool easy to handle? Is this chair comfortable? Is this a sports car or a city car? Is this »my thing« or »not my thing«? Such reactions prove we not only evaluate objects based on their functionality but also in relation to our own identities – and that includes gender. Several of the following examples illustrate that cultural concepts are transferred into the world of objects both by those who use them and those who design them. For this to work, it is necessary to be part of a cultural community that can read these shared signs – signs that are not universal, but can change over time and between cultures. It is beyond the scope of this catalogue to delve into this subject more deeply, however, each of the HfG-Archiv objects presented below could be used as a springboard to explore these ideas further.

Taking salt and pepper as one example, these two condiments and their shakers and grinders are often seen as inseparable or as some kind of »natural« pair. In the world of design, this pairing is often translated into a black-and-white colour combination or as a heterosexual couple (a man and a woman) – although the Mr. and Mrs. Prickly dip-moulded salt and pepper pots (1997) show that this coupling is not always expressed in human form but as a concept (fig. 1). The party boy (1979) bottle opener, designed by former HfG student and designer Horst Diener (fig. 2), offers another example. The »roly-poly man« becomes a concept that translates the idea behind the bottle opener: Thanks to its special patented form, it always rights itself no matter how many times it gets knocked over – an amusing detail that made the party boy a popular giveaway. Years earlier, the Grundig company had adopted the word »Boy« for a whole series of portable television and radio devices that they released onto the market: Transistor Boy, Mini Boy, Micro Boy, Fernseh Boy, Solo Boy, Ocean Boy, Elite Boy, Tele Boy, and Phono Boy, to name but a few. The first in this series – one of the earliest portable radios – was called the Grundig Boy. Founded in the 1940s, the then German company was based in territory occupied by the Americans and the name »Boy« was no doubt used to suggest youthfulness, coolness, and mobility, as well as to lend the products an international air. Mario and Dario Bellini were commissioned to design the Phono Boy (1968), a portable record player, under the original name GA 45 Pop – its round, functional design and loud and trendy colours were very much in tune with the spirit of the 1968

1

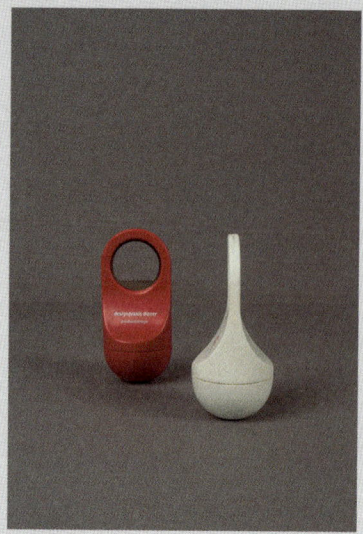

2

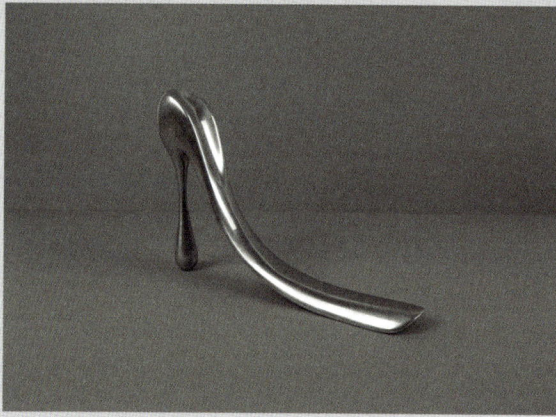

3

1 Mr. and Mrs. Prickly ⁄ GB 1997 ⁄ Salz- und Pfefferstreuer ⁄ *Salt and pepper shakers* ⁄ Hersteller: ⁄ *Manufacturer:* Inflate ⁄ Entwurf: ⁄ *Design:* Nick Crosbie ⁄ Sammlung Compensis ⁄ *Compensis Collection* ⁄ HfG-Archiv ⁄ Museum Ulm

2 party boy ⁄ DE 1979 ⁄ Flaschenöffner ⁄ *Bottle opener* ⁄ Hersteller: ⁄ *Manufacturer:* Berendson AG ⁄ Entwurf: ⁄ *Design:* design praxis diener, Horst Diener ⁄ HfG-Archiv ⁄ Museum Ulm

3 Shoehorn ⁄ GB 2004 ⁄ Schuhanzieher ⁄ Hersteller: ⁄ *Manufacturer:* habitat ⁄ Entwurf: ⁄ *Design:* Manolo Blahnik ⁄ Sammlung Compensis ⁄ *Compensis Collection* ⁄ HfG-Archiv ⁄ Museum Ulm

4 Cuddly Book »Siberian Ocean Blue« ⁄ FR 2018 ⁄ Artist's Book ⁄ Three Star Books ⁄ Künstlerin: ⁄ *Artist:* Sylvie Fleury ⁄ Museum Ulm

Kofferradios. Daneben, dass das damals deutsche Unternehmen seinen Sitz in den 1940er Jahren in besetztem amerikanischen Gebiet hatte, lässt die »Boy«-Reihe auf Assoziationen mit Jugendlichkeit, Coolness und Mobilität schließen, sowie die Intention erkennen, Internationalität auszustrahlen. Den »Phono Boy« (1968), einen transportablen Schallplattenspieler, gestalteten Mario und Dario Bellini als Auftrag und unter dem ursprünglichen Namen »GA 45 Pop« – sehr im Zeitgeist der Umbrüche der 1968er Generation in rundem, funktionalen Design und in poppigen Farbausführungen (s. Abb. 6). Genauso Pop-Art-inspiriert, jedoch weniger sachlich-funktional kommt 1969 das »Toot-A-Loop« Armreif-Radio des japanischen Herstellers Matshushita daher (s. Abb. 5). Dabei war es aber keineswegs so, dass sich dieses, an Schmuck erinnerndes Tool nur an Mädchen oder junge Frauen richtete, sondern generationen- und geschlechterübergreifend beworben wurde.

Ein weiteres Beispiel zeigt, dass Kooperationen im Design durch die Populärkultur zustande kommen und Profit versprechen: Die amerikanische Serie »Sex and the City« sorgte dafür, dass Schuhmoden-Designer Manolo Blahnik eine große Popularität in den 2000er Jahren erlangte. Das Unternehmen habitat tat sich mit ihm zusammen und vertrieb den von ihm gestalteten Schuhanzieher »Shoehorn« (2004) in Form eines Highheels (s. Abb. 3).

Dass die kommerzielle Industrie eine bestimmte, materialisierte Sprache anwendet, mit der sie einen »weiblichen Markt« forciert, thematisiert Künstlerin Sylvie Fleury mit ihrem »Cuddly Book« (2018) (s. Abb. 4). Eigentlich sind es Bücher: in mehreren Ausführungen hat sie die »Seiten« dieser monumentalen Objekte mit stark gefärbtem Kunstpelz überzogen und knüpft damit an eigene Arbeiten aus den 1990er Jahren zu Gender und Ambivalenz an. Nicht nur die Bücher selbst wirken dadurch so übertrieben wie gleichzeitig provokativ – mit »Cherry«, »Barbie Pink Frost« oder »Siberian Ocean Blue« ruft Fleury dasselbe Schema für die objektgebenden Farbnamen auf.

generation and the social upheavals of the era (fig. 6). Though a little less functional, the Toot-A-Loop bangle radio by Japanese manufacturer Matshushita that came out in 1969 was just as pop-inspired (fig. 5). Still, this gadget, which resembles a piece of jewellery, was never only aimed at girls or young women, but was advertised to all ages and genders.

A further example demonstrates how popular culture can lead to lucrative design collaborations: Shoe designer Manolo Blahnik became hugely popular in the 2000s thanks to the American TV series Sex and the City. The Habitat furniture company teamed up with Blahnik to launch the Shoehorn (2004), an accessory designed to resemble a high-heeled shoe (fig. 3).

Artist Sylvie Fleury's Cuddly Book (2018) addresses the fact that commercial industries use specific materialised language in order to manufacture »female markets« (fig. 4). The book is available in several versions: These huge objects are covered with brightly coloured fake fur that come in different shades – a reference to her own work from the 1990s on gender and ambivalence. Not only do the books themselves appear as exaggerated as they are provocative – with »Cherry«, »Barbie Pink Frost«, or »Siberian Ocean Blue« Fleury conjures up the same scheme for the object-giving color names.

4

5

5 Toot-A-Loop-Radio ⁄ JP 1969 ⁄ Armreifradio ⁄ *Bangle radio* ⁄ Hersteller: ⁄ *Manufacturer:* Panasonic, Matshushita ⁄ Entwurf: ⁄ *Design:* anonym ⁄ Sammlung Compensis ⁄ *Compensis Collection* ⁄ HfG-Archiv ⁄ Museum Ulm

6 Phonoboy ⁄ DE 1968 ⁄ Transportabler Plattenspieler ⁄ *Portable record player* ⁄ Hersteller: ⁄ *Manufacturer:* Grundig-Werke GmbH ⁄ Entwurf: ⁄ *Design:* Mario und *and* Dario Bellini ⁄ Sammlung Compensis ⁄ *Compensis Collection* ⁄ HfG-Archiv ⁄ Museum Ulm

6

Zig Zag, Tulip & Co. – Stuhldesign-Klassiker, mal anders befragt Das Wissen um die zuvor beschriebenen Fähigkeiten und Verhaltensweisen sowie darum, dass gestalterische Komponenten und deren Zusammenspiel gewisse Assoziationen wecken, haben wir für die Ausstellung »Nicht mein Ding – Gender im Design« aufgegriffen und eine interaktive Station entwickelt. Dass es vor allen Dingen Stühle sind, die dazu herangezogen werden, Design und Designgeschichte zu erhellen, wird nicht zuletzt daran deutlich, dass es überhaupt so etwas wie Miniaturen von Modellen gibt, die als Klassiker gelten. Aus der Miniatur-Reihe des Möbelherstellers Vitra haben wir acht Modelle ohne Armlehne und verschiedenster Form, Farbe und Materialität ausgewählt. Bis auf zwei der acht Entwürfe, der Zusammenarbeit von Ehepaar Charles und Ray Eames, sind alle »Design-Ikonen« Entwürfe von Gestaltern, entworfen zwischen 1926 und 2008 im westeuropäischen Raum. Dann haben wir Besucher*innen der Ausstellung gefragt: Welcher Stuhl wirkt auf Sie besonders feminin, maskulin oder neutral (s. Abb. 2)? Antworten konnten sie mittels farbigen Kunststoffbällen (klassisch codiert mit rosa, blau und orange), die sie durch eine Öffnung unterhalb der jeweiligen Miniaturen werfen. Diese konnten nebeneinander, integriert in einer Stellwand betrachtet werden. Umschritt man die Wand, war sowohl mehr über die Stühle (Entwurf, Modellbezeichnung, Jahr) zu erfahren, wie auch das bisherige Abstimmverhalten durch die Anhäufung der unterschiedlich farbigen Kunststoffbälle in Plexiglasröhren unmittelbar ablesbar. Über die Dauer der Ausstellung in Ulm hinweg haben wir das Abstimmverhalten dokumentiert und anschließend ausgewertet (s. Abb. 1; 3).

Vorweg: Auch wenn es sich nicht um einen abgesteckten Versuchsrahmen handelt, resultiert Dank der regen Beteiligung ein aussagekräftiges Bild aus den über 3.500 abgegebenen Gesamtstimmen, die per Ball abgegeben wurden. Dieses Bild ist nahezu deckungsgleich mit den Ergebnissen, die beispielsweise der Studie »Über die unbewusste und bewusste Vergeschlechtlichung von Produkten« (Brandes / Buchmüller / Stich 2001/2003) hervorgegangen sind und die wir für einen Abgleich mit unseren Ergebnissen hinzugezogen haben.[8] Dies gilt jedenfalls für Merkmale, die in der Studie als »männlich« und »weiblich« erfasst wurden, während neutral oder divers assoziierte Konnotationen nicht parallel aufgeführt vorkommen.

Die beiden Modelle, die als am wenigsten maskulin und zugleich am meisten weiblich wahrgenommen wurden, sind das Modell »Vegetal« sowie noch stärker der »Tulip Chair«. Dieser weist mit über 400 auch die meisten Gesamtstimmen vor und ist zugleich dasjenige Modell, welches offenbar am wenigsten als neutral gesehen wird. Beide Stühle haben rote Farbelemente, die offenbar in der Kombination mit runden, organischen

1

Zig Zag, Tulip & Co. – A Different Take on Classic Chair Designs The knowledge about the previously described capacities and behaviours, and about how design components and their interplay elicit certain associations was used to develop an interactive station for the »Not My Thing – Gender in Design« exhibition. That chairs, above all, are used to shed light on design and the history of design is not least owed to the fact that there is such a thing as a collection of miniature replicas of classic chair designs. We selected eight designs from this miniatures series of iconic chairs by the furniture manufacturer Vitra: all without armrests and made in a wide variety of shapes, colours, and materials. Every one but two of the eight »design icons« – which were designed by the couple Charles and Ray Eames – were made by male designers in Western Europe between 1926 and 2008. The miniature chairs were displayed side-by-side in transparent boxes embedded into a partition wall. Visitors were asked to select the chair they thought looked particularly feminine, masculine, or neutral (fig. 2) by placing plastic balls – colour-coded pink, blue, or orange respectively – into an opening below the respective replica chair. Visitors could then walk to the other side of the wall to read information about the chairs (design, model name, year) and find out how other people had voted by seeing how many balls of each colour the chairs had collected. Over the duration of the exhibition, a record of visitors' voting behaviour was documented and ater evaluated (fig. 1; 3).

Even though the experiment and expected results were not clearly defined from the outset, given that so many visitors took part, it was possible to attain an informative picture from the more than 3500 total votes cast per ball. This picture aligns very closely with the results from, for example, the study »Über die unbewusste und bewusste Vergeschlechtlichung von Produkten« [On the Unconscious

Sie haben die Wahl! / Welcher der Stühle wirkt auf Sie besonders *feminin*, *maskulin* und *neutral*? Werfen Sie je eine Kugel der entsprechenden Farbe durch die Öffnung und schauen Sie anschließend hinter die Wand. Wie haben die anderen Besucher*innen die Designikonen eingeordnet?

1–2 **Abstimmstation Stuhlminiaturen**
Voting unit chair miniatures / DE 2019
/ Leihgaben: / *Loans:* Vitra Design Museum

Formen sowie Kunststoff mit Weiblichkeit assoziiert werden. Das gilt insbesondere für das weiche, abnehmbare Kissen des »Tulip Chair«. Ohne dass die Namen der Modelle von vorn einsehbar gewesen sind, ist es bemerkenswert, dass diese beiden Stühle mit den organisch-floral-klingenden Namen, die ja auch das Design selbst unterstreichen, für feminin befunden wurden. Weniger eindeutig, aber dennoch prägnant als maskulin bewertete Modelle sind der »Zig Zag Stoel« und der noch davor liegende »LCM«. Obwohl die beiden sich auf den ersten Blick sehr unterscheiden, sind sie die einzigen beiden der insgesamt acht Modelle, deren Hauptmaterial Holz ist. Zudem ist vor allem der »Zig Zag Stoel« kantig, während der »LCM« mit seiner schwarzen, breiten Sitzfläche und Rückenlehne einigermaßen schwer wirkt, sich offen gebärdet und durch Metallstangen alle Elemente stabil miteinander verbindet. Im Vergleich zu den beiden Stühlen, die als besonders feminin gewertet wurden, ist bei diesen beiden besonders maskulin gewerteten Stühlen die Zahl der daneben abgegebenen Stimmen für neutral bemerkenswert hoch. Jedoch als besonders neutral gelten der Abstimmung zufolge der »DKR Wire Chair« und ganz vorn der »W1«, der älteste unter den acht Entwürfen (1926). Auch hierbei ist es in beiden Fällen und auch für das Modell »Selene« so, dass die anderen abgegebenen Stimmen für maskulin höher sind, als für feminin. Nahezu ausgewogen ist das Stimmverhältnis für neutral, feminin und (am niedrigsten) maskulin nur bei einem Modell: dem »Panton Chair«, der ausschließlich in der Farbe Blau präsentiert wurde. Die Vermutung liegt nahe, dass hier die Kombination von einzelnen, starken Parametern wie Kunststoff, glänzender Oberfläche, geschwungen, funktional (im Sinne von stapelbar), Blau, widersprüchliche oder jedenfalls eindeutige Reize geben, deren Gewichtung sich in der Kombination wiederum subjektiv auswirkt. Es bleibt offen, inwiefern die Wahrnehmung sich ändert, wenn der »Panton Chair« in einer der anderen Farben neben den anderen sieben Modellen zu sehen gewesen wäre. Auch wenn dieses Stuhl-Modell nicht als neutralstes gewertet wurde, bleibt eine weiterführende Frage offen: Wovon zeugt es noch, wenn es dasjenige Modell ist, dessen Wertung einerseits die diffuse und gleichzeitig die homogene, sprich ausgewogene Uneinigkeit ist? Klar ablesbar anhand aller Modelle ist die Tatsache, dass wenn eine weibliche Konnotation am stärksten ist, ist sie zeitgleich kaum neutral und absolut nicht maskulin. Andersherum ist es so, dass bei einer starken maskulinen oder neutralen Assoziation die jeweils andere immer nahe liegt, keines Falls aber die weibliche Konnotation. Es zeigt sich also im Kleinen einmal mehr, was wir eigentlich bereits sehr gut wissen: Männlichkeit hat sich als Norm etabliert, die häufig mit Neutralität gleichgesetzt wird.

and Conscious Gendering of Products], which we used as a comparison.[8] This applies at least to those characteristics recorded in the study as being considered particularly male or female, whereas the neutral or diverse connotations elicited in people were not specified parallel.

The two models that were perceived as being both the least masculine and the most feminine were the Vegetal Chair and, to an even greater extent, the Tulip Chair. With over 400 votes – the most votes received by any of the chairs – the Tulip Chair was also considered to be the least neutral. Both chairs have red-coloured elements, which, in combination with their rounded, organic shapes and the plastic they are made of, seem to be associated with femininity. And this is particularly true of the Tulip Chair's soft removable cushion. Despite the fact that the two chairs' organic floral-sounding names – attributes that also underlie the designs themselves – were not visible from the front, it is striking that they were still perceived to be feminine. The Zig Zag Chair and, even more so, the LCM Chair were both judged as being more masculine, albeit by a slightly lower margin than the »feminine« chairs. Although, at first glance, they look very different from each other, of the eight models they are the only two that are mainly made of wood. What's more, the Zig Zag Chair is particularly angular, while the LCM, with its wide black-coloured seat and backrest, looks heavy, open, and solidly connected together by a metal rod base. The number of neutral votes received by these two »masculine« chairs was remarkably high compared to those received by the two chairs that were rated particularly feminine. Overall, however, it was the DKR Wire Chair and the W1 Chair, the oldest of the eight designs (1926), that were considered the most neutral. Again, like the Zig Zag and LCM models, both these chairs (and the Selene design, too) received a higher number of masculine votes than feminine ones. Only the blue-coloured Panton Chair received a roughly equal number of neutral, feminine, and masculine votes (though the masculine vote was the smallest of the three). It is reasonable to assume, therefore, that the Panton Chair's very different but strongly evocative characteristics – the fact that it is made of plastic, has glossy surfaces, its curved shape, stackable functionality, and blue colour – give off clear, if contradictory, connotations that lead to very subjective choices. It's impossible to say whether the results would have been any different had the Panton Chair been displayed alongside the other models in a different colour. Even though this chair design was not rated the most neutral, another question arises: What does it mean if the votes the Panton Chair received were relatively evenly split – or inconclusive – in other words: that there was a kind of balanced disagreement? Looking at the results for all the chair designs, it is clear that when a chair is considered more female, it is very rarely seen as

[8] Siehe dafür vor allem die Kategorie »Sitzgelegenheiten (Sessel, Lounge Chairs, Stühle)«, nach: Brandes, Uta, Buchmüller, Sandra, Stich, Sonja. 2001/2003. Über die unbewusste und bewusste Vergeschlechtlichung von Produkten. Eine (meta)morphologische Studie in zwei Teilen (unveröff.), Auszüge in: Zentrum Frau in Beruf und Technik, ZfBT (Hg.). 2006. Gender & Design. Leitfragen. online veröffentl. unter: http://www.zfbt.de/veroeffentlichungen/dokumente/gender_design_2.81%20Leitfragen%20final.pdf, zul. abgerufen am: 12.10.2017.

neutral, and never as masculine. On the other hand, those designs that are considered more male are often also considered neutral, and vice versa, but were never seen as female. So, on a small scale, it once again confirms what we already knew: masculinity has become established as the norm, and is often equated with neutrality.

[8] See, in particular, the section »Sitzgelegenheiten: Sessel, Lounge Chairs, Stühle« [Seating: armchairs, lounge chairs, stools] on page 23 in: Uta Brandes, Sandra Buchmüller, and Sonja Stich (eds.), Über die unbewusste und bewusste Vergeschlechtlichung von Produkten. Eine (meta)morphologische Studie in zwei Teilen (Cologne: unpublished, 2001/2003); Excerpt from: Zentrum Frau in Beruf und Technik, ZfBT (ed.), Gender & Design. Leitfragen (2006), http://www.zfbt.de/veroeffentlichungen/dokumente/gender_design_2.81%20Leitfragen%20final.pdf.

3 **Auswertung der Abstimmstation je Stuhlminiatur nach** maskulin / feminin / neutral / *Evaluation of the voting unit per chair miniature by* masculine / feminine / neutral

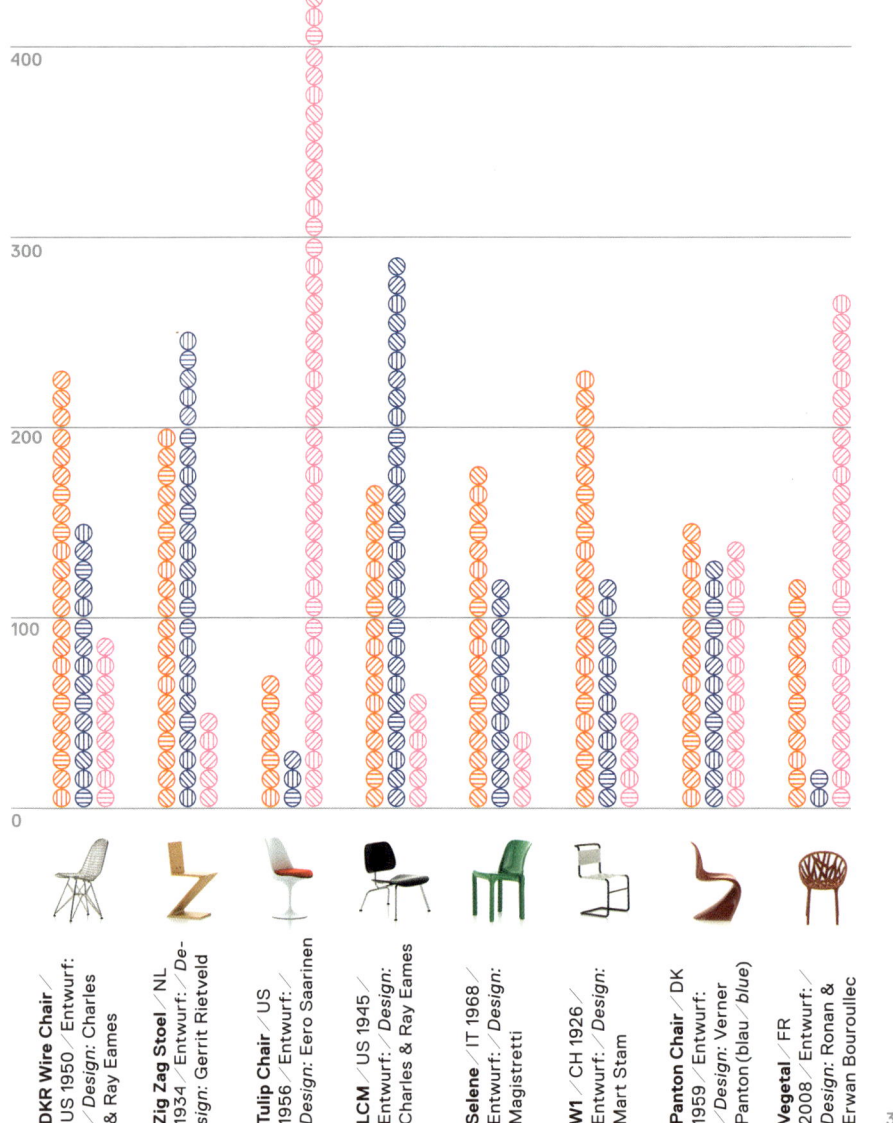

DKR Wire Chair / US 1950 / Entwurf: / *Design:* Charles & Ray Eames

Zig Zag Stoel / NL 1934 / Entwurf: / *Design:* Gerrit Rietveld

Tulip Chair / US 1956 / Entwurf: / *Design:* Eero Saarinen

LCM / US 1945 / Entwurf: / *Design:* Charles & Ray Eames

Selene / IT 1968 / Entwurf: / *Design:* Magistretti

W1 / CH 1926 / Entwurf: / *Design:* Mart Stam

Panton Chair / DK 1959 / Entwurf: / *Design:* Verner Panton (blau / *blue*)

Vegetal / FR 2008 / Entwurf: / *Design:* Ronan & Erwan Bouroullec

Confused, Ir/regular and In/correct – De-gendering Everyday Life **Drei Experimente einer angewandten Designforschung über das Thema Macht in Beziehung zu den Feldern Lesen/Schreiben.**

#1 Die Buchstaben der Typographie »Confused.tff« sind nicht in der Lage, sich zu entscheiden, welcher Buchstabe sie sind, da sie alle ihren jeweiligen Stamm mit einem anderen Buchstaben teilen. Daraus resultiert eine Vielzahl an unintentionalem Inhalt.

#2 Das Hinzufügen der Option »Irregular« (dt. ungeregelt) zu gängigen Typographien und den gewöhnlichen Optionen wie z.B. »Regular« oder »Bold«, erzeugt irritierende Effekte: Schriften, die ansonsten so stringent erscheinen, wirken in ihrer neuen Verschiedenartigkeit leicht unbehaglich und damit auch der Inhalt, den sie transportieren.

#3 Das Installieren der Datei »In/correct.plist« in den Favoriteneinstellungen eines Computers autokorrigiert eine ganze Wörtersammlung in jedem Programm. Von Word bis zu den E-Mails: Während des Eintippens werden die gegenderten Bedeutungen im Prozess ihres Entstehens regelrecht verdreht.

Confused, Ir/regular and In/correct – De-gendering Everyday Life Three experiments in applied design research that explore power in relation to reading/writing.

#1 The letters in the font »Confused.ttf« cannot decide what letter to be as they each share their body with a fellow letter establishing unintentional multiplicity in content.

#2 Adding the option of »Irregular« to the traditional options of »Regular«, »Bold« etc. in a number of the most used fonts enables a slightly uncomfortable diversity in what are usually very secure typographies, and hence, the content that they hold.

#3 And installing the »In/correct« file on one's computer autocorrects – in all programs from Word to emails – a library of words whilst typing distorting gendered-meaning in the process of its construction.

Confused, Ir/regular and In/correct – De-gendering Everyday Life / DE 2014 / Drei Videoarbeiten / *Three video pieces* / Entwicklung im Kontext des: / *Development in context of the:* International Gender Design Network (iGDN) / Forschung und Design: / *Research and design:* Michelle Christensen, Florian Conradi / 3:54 Min.

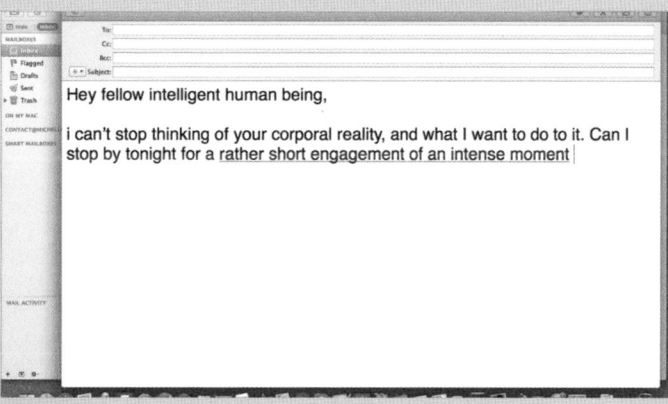

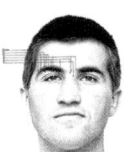

1–2 Tafeln: Entwicklung einer standardisierten Brillenfassung / *Panels: Development of a Standardised Eyeglass Frame* / DE 1958 / Ausstellungstafeln der »Mensa-Ausstellung« in der HfG Ulm / *Exhibition panels for the »Mensa Exhibition« at HfG Ulm* / Gestaltung: / *Design:* Otl Aicher / (1) Foto der Tafel 116: / *Photograph on panel 116:* Hermann Roth, Peter Seitz, Gui Bonsiepe, Herbert Lindinger, sowie (2) Tafel 118: / *and panel 118:* Hans G. Conrad, Deborah Sussman / Sign. T. 116–118 / HfG-Archiv / Museum Ulm

3 Entwicklung einer standardisierten Brillenfassung / *Development of a Standardised Eyeglass Frame* / Studienjahr / *Semester* 1956/57 / Modell einer Brillenfassung / *Eyeglass frame prototype* / Abt. Produktgestaltung / *Dept. Product Design* / Auftraggeber: / *Commissioned by:* Angerer, Linz / Dozent: / *Lecturer:* Hans Gugelot / Design: Herbert Lindinger / Sign. 58.0004 / HfG-Archiv / Museum Ulm

Durch die HfG-Brille An der ehemaligen HfG Ulm entwarf Student Herbert Lindinger im Studienjahr 1956/57 als Abteilungsarbeit der Produktgestaltung eine »Standardisierte Brillenfassung« (s. Abb. 3), die nach physiologischen Aspekten geformt und als »Unisex«-Modell präsentiert wurde. Dabei handelte es sich um eine Auftragsarbeit für die Firma Angerer, Linz, betreut von Dozent Hans Gugelot. Dieser wies Lindinger zu einer entsprechend systematischen Herangehensweise an. Dazu gehörten Sehfelduntersuchungen und die Vermaßung von Gesichtern, um ein Verhältnis bezüglich Form des Gesichts sowie der Augen und -brauen und deren Abstände zu bestimmen. »Noch heute existiert von diesen Studien eine Art fotografischer »Verbrecherkartei« aller damaligen Hochschulangehörigen, einschließlich Gugelots, fein säuberlich nach Augenbrauentypen sortiert« (Lindinger 1987, S. 47).[9] Die Tafeln, die anlässlich der hausinternen »Mensa-Ausstellung« (1958) erstellt wurden, zeugen von dieser und anderen Arbeiten, die die HfG als Aushängeschild ihrer Ausbildung und Designauffassung präsentierte (s. Abb. 1–2). Während standardisierte Brillenfassungen und -gläser heute zahlreich sind, ist hierbei ebenso zu bedenken, dass auch Brillengestelle modischen Trends unterworfen sind. Mit neuen technischen Möglichkeiten wie dem 3D-Druck ergeben sich zudem neue Entwicklungen: von der Standardisierung zur Individualisierung.

[9] Eine solche vollständige Akte ist im Bestand des HfG-Archivs leider nicht erhalten, sondern einige wenige Aufnahmen, die diese Vorgehensweise belegen, siehe Unterrichtsdatenbank HfG-Archiv: »Abteilungsarbeiten Produktform«, 1956–58, sowie »Untersuchungen für den Brillenrand (Augenbrauen), Sign. Dp. 043.019. Vgl. zu den zitierten Angaben: Lindinger, Herbert. 1987. Was hat Gugelot bewegt? In System-Design Bahnbrecher: Hans Gugelot 1920–65, Bd. 3, Industrial Design – Graphic Design, hrsg. v. Hans Wichmann, S. 38–49.

The Development of a Standardised Eyeglass Frame In the academic year 1956/57, HfG Ulm product design student Herbert Lindinger developed a »standardized eyeglass frame« (fig. 3), which incorporated physiological aspects and was presented as a »unisex« design Commissioned by Linz-based company Angerer, the project was supervised by lecturer Hans Gugelot, who advised Lindinger to adopt a systematic approach. This included visual field examinations and making facial measurements to determine the relationship between the form of a person's face, eyes, and eyebrows as well as correlated spacing between. »There still exists a collection of criminal-style 'mugshots' made of all the members of the school as part of the research for this project, including one of Gugelot, which were all neatly categorised according to different eyebrow types« (Lindinger 1987, p. 47).[9] The panels created for the school's in-house »Mensa Exhibition« (1958) feature this project and other work that the Ulm School of Design wished to spotlight as representative of their approach to and the teaching of design (fig. 1–2). Standardized eyeglasses and spectacle frames are commonplace today, but it should be borne in mind that they are subject to fashion trends. New technological advancements, such as 3D printing, for example, can also lead to new developments, including the shift from standardisation to individualisation.

[9] Unfortunately, no such records exist in the HfG-Archiv, all that remains are a few documents that list or mention the content of this research. See the HfG-Archiv teaching database: »Abteilungsarbeiten Produktform«, 1956–58, and »Untersuchungen für den Brillenrand (Augenbrauen)«, Sign. Dp. 043.019. Cf. Quoted from: Herbert Lindinger, »Was hat Gugelot bewegt?« in System-Design Bahnbrecher: Hans Gugelot 1920–65, edited by Hans Wichmann, vol. 3, Industrial Design – Graphic Design, 2nd edn. (Basel/Boston: Birkhäuser, 1987), 38–49.

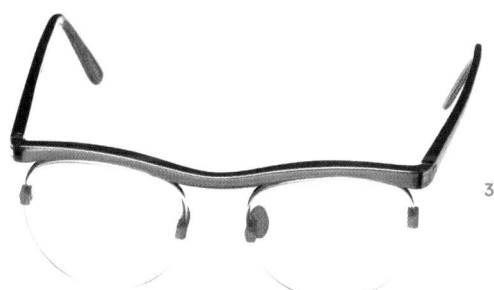

3

Vorwort Teilprojekte
/Foreword Subprojects

Pia Jerger \ Eine Vielzahl von Produkten und Dienstleistungen umgibt uns täglich – sie sind zur Normalität in einer globalen Konsumgesellschaft geworden. Diese verlangt nach einer stets wachsenden Bandbreite an Marken und Produkten. Und gestaltet? Das ist auf den ersten Blick alles Materielle, das uns täglich begleitet. Geht es um die Vermarktung der Produkte, sind Kinder, Heranwachsende und junge Menschen als Zielgruppen zunehmend interessant geworden – nicht nur, weil gerade sie rundum vernetzt und empfänglich für Marketingbotschaften aller Art sind. Doch Werbekampagnen und Produktgestaltungen spiegeln häufig nicht die Vielfalt unserer Gesellschaft und die entsprechenden Bedürfnisse wider. Stattdessen verweisen sie auf ein binär geprägtes Geschlechtersystem und tragen zu einer Teilung zweier konstruierter Welten bei – eine in Pink und eine Blau, wie gerne im Bereich der Spielwelt für Kinder referenziert wird. Um dieses Denken in Stereotypen aufzubrechen und uns dem Ziel einer offenen Gesellschaft anzunähern, arbeiteten wir für das Ausstellungsprojekt »Nicht mein Ding« mit verschiedenen Akteur*innen zusammen, ließen deren Perspektiven einfließen und sichtbar werden.

    Das Verständnis von Ausstellungen als Ort des lebendigen Austauschs war für uns der Ausgangspunkt der Konzeption. Seit geraumer Zeit werden in Museen partizipative Projekte durchgeführt – einhergehend mit einer zunehmenden Hinwendung zu Gegenwarts- und Alltagsthemen. Die aus unserer Sicht virulenten Gegenwartsfragen hierzu liegen auf der Hand: Wie wollen wir leben? Wie sollen die Dinge gestaltet sein, mit denen wir uns umgeben? Wie beeinflussen Design und Gestaltung unser Denken, Handeln und gesellschaftliche Entwicklungen?

Every day we are besieged by a multitude of products and services – they have become a normality in global consumer society. And there is an incessant demand for an ever-growing spectrum of brands and products. And design? At first glance, it is part of everything material that accompanies our daily lives. When it comes to the marketing of products children, adolescents, and young adults have become increasingly interesting target groups – not least because they are networked all-round and particularly receptive for advertising messages of all types. But marketing campaigns and product designs often do not reflect the diversity of our society and the corresponding needs. Instead, they refer to a binary gender system that divides into two constructed worlds – one in pink, the other blue – which is happily employed in the world of children's toys. In an attempt to interrupt this thinking in stereotypes and to strive for an open society, we worked together with a diverse range of protagonists for »Not My Thing – Gender in Design« and allowed their perspectives to flow into the exhibition project and become visible.

    Our departure point was the idea of exhibitions as sites of lively exchange. For quite some time now, participative projects are being organised in museum contexts – in connection with a growing focus on contemporary and everyday topics. In our eyes, they arise from fundamental questions: How do we want to live? How should the things that surround us be designed? How does design influence our thoughts, actions, and developments in society?

Ausgehend von diesen übergeordneten Fragen und der Überzeugung, dass die Themen Gender und Design als gesellschaftlich relevante Aspekte des Alltags nicht nur fruchtbaren Boden für eine vielseitige Auseinandersetzung bieten, wurden mit Blick auf die im Februar 2019 in Ulm eröffnete Ausstellung vier Teilprojekte initiiert, welche eine umfassende und perspektivenübergreifende Diskussion über Gender im Design anregten. Dafür galt es mit verschiedenen Zielgruppen zu arbeiten, die Betreffenden nicht nur zum kritischen Denken zu ermutigen, sondern ihre Rolle als Beobachter*innen von Gestaltungsstrategien und gesellschaftlichen Dynamiken sowie die eigene Position in diesem Feld zu stärken. Durch die Vielfältigkeit und kollaborative Struktur der Projekte erforderte jedes der Teilprojekte unter Berücksichtigung der spezifischen Kompetenzen, die die Akteur*innen mit- und einbrachten, und der unterschiedlichen Arbeitsweise individuelle und mitunter intensive Aushandlungsprozesse.

Im Oktober 2018 starteten zwei der vier Teilprojekte. Bereits im September reiste die kanadische Designerin Olivia Daigneault Deschênes als erste Stipendiatin des von Katharina Kurz initiierten Designer in Residence-Programms des HfG-Archivs an. Das Programm, gefördert von der Stiftung HfG Ulm, gibt jungen Gestalter*innen die Gelegenheit zur persönlichen und kreativen Weiterentwicklung und ermöglicht zugleich, die Sammlung des Archivs anhand zeitgenössischer Themen zu befragen. Für drei Monate lebte und arbeitete Olivia Daigneault Deschênes auf dem Campus der ehemaligen HfG Ulm. In Form einer angewandten Designforschung erarbeitete sie zu den Themen Essen und Tischkultur sowie der damit verbundenen Ausübung von Geschlechterrollen das Projekt »Zeig' mir wie du isst und ich sag' dir wer du bist«. Aus einer feministisch-kritischen Perspektive und bezugnehmend auf die Sammlungsbestände des HfG-Archivs befördern die Resultate über gestalterische Mittel eine höchst anregende Perspektive auf ein banal wirkendes Alltagsthema.

Eine Woche lang arbeiteten 22 Schüler*innen einer 9. Klasse der Realschule Dornstadt in der ehemaligen Hochschule für Gestaltung. Einem Ort, der den Jugendlichen bis dahin nicht vertraut war. Die Arbeit mit ihnen war insofern besonders spannend, als dass sie sich als Heranwachsende in einer Phase befinden, in der sie ihre eigene Identität formen, wozu auch ganz wesentlich die geschlechtliche gehört. Gesellschaftlich geprägte Geschlechterbilder werden bewusst wahrgenommen, gebildet und modifiziert. Angeleitet von Susanne Umscheid (Produktdesignerin) und Fabian Karrer (Kommunikationsdesigner) erforschten sie in den fünf Tagen nicht nur die Relevanz von Design als Gegenstand des täglichen Lebens, sie untersuchten gender-codierte Produkte und deren Gestaltungssprache und entwarfen selbst Produktideen – von der beheizbaren Tasse über

With these deliberations in mind and the conviction that gender and design – as aspects of the everyday with particular social relevance – could offer fertile ground for a multifaceted exploration, four subprojects were initiated in the run-up to the exhibition, which inspired a comprehensive and multiperspectival discussion about gender in design. They involved working with different target groups and encouraging participants to critical thinking, but also strengthening their role as observers of design strategies and social dynamics. In light of the diversity and collaborative structure of the projects, each subproject required individual and sometimes profound processes of negotiation, which took into account the different ways of working and specific competences the actors possessed and contributed.

Two of the four subprojects commenced in October 2018. But already in September, the Canadian designer Olivia Daigneault Deschênes arrived as the very first scholar in the Designer in Residence programme of the HfG-Archiv, initiated by Katharina Kurz. Supported by the HfG Ulm Foundation, the programme provides emerging designers with a unique opportunity for personal and creative development, while facilitating a survey of the HfG-Archiv collections on the basis of contemporary approaches. Olivia Daigneault Deschênes worked and lived on the campus of the former Ulm School of Design for three months. In the form of an applied design research, she developed the project »Show me how you eat, I will tell you who you are« on the subject of eating and table culture and the interdependent performance of gender roles. From a critical feminist perspective that also referenced the inventory of the HfG-Archiv, her results made creative use of design to convey a highly inspiring perspective on a seemingly banal aspect of daily life.

Over the course of a week in October 2018, 22 pupils from the 9th grade of Realschule Dornstadt worked in the former Ulm School of Design, a place the youth were not familiar with previously. The cooperation with the pupils was particularly exciting as they are in a phase in which they are forming their own identity, wherein gender plays a significant role. Socially constructed gender roles were consciously perceived, applied, or modified. Guided by Susanne Umscheid (product designer) and Fabian Karrer (communication designer) for the five days, they explored the role of design as a subject of day-to-day life but also gender-coded products, their design language, and even developed their own product ideas – from heatable cups and a series of cosmetics packages to shoes with wheels controlled via an app. What started out with questions like »What does it actually mean to design something?« led to an understanding of the role of designers in society, acknowledging

eine Reihe von Kosmetikverpackungen bis hin zu Schuhen mit Rollen, die über eine App gesteuert werden können. Waren es zu Beginn hauptsächlich Fragen wie »Was bedeutet es eigentlich, etwas zu designen?«, wurden im Verlauf der Projektwoche vermehrt die gesellschaftliche Rolle von Designer*innen deutlich sowie Fabian Karrer und Susanne Umscheid als Vorbilder anerkannt und Rollenklischees mehr und mehr hinterfragt. Die Projektwoche wurde großzügig gefördert von »lab.Bode – Initiative zur Stärkung der Vermittlungsarbeit in Museen«, einem Programm, das insbesondere mir durch regelmäßige Fortbildungsmodule im »Denklabor« im Berliner Bode-Museum immer wieder wertvolle Impulse lieferte und Perspektiven für das Projekt eröffnete, ohne die es in der Form nicht stattgefunden hätte.

Die Kollegiat*innen des Aicher-Scholl-Kollegs (vh ulm), eines Studiums Generale für Schulabsolvent*innen zur beruflichen Orientierung, erarbeiteten im Produktdesignkurs unter dem Fokus »Gender im Design« Modelle, Objekte und Installationen, die Ansätze aus der Gestaltung aufgreifen und teilweise künstlerisch reflektieren. Ein Trimester lang, von Oktober bis Dezember (2018), recherchierten sie unter der Anleitung von Designer Uli Häussler intensiv zum Thema und erhielten einen Begriff davon, welche komplexen Prozesse hinter der Gestaltung im Allgemeinen stehen. Als junge Erwachsene galt es, ihnen nicht nur eine Berufsperspektive aufzuzeigen, sondern ihnen ein tieferes Verständnis von dem Wert von Design und der gesellschaftlichen Verantwortung, die Gestalter*innen tragen, zu vermitteln.

Der Idee folgend, dem Thema im Stadtraum Ulm / Neu-Ulm Sichtbarkeit zu verschaffen, zeigte die PUTTE als Off-Space Arbeiten Juliane Peils, die ihre Sichtweisen auf die Beziehung zwischen Gender und öffentlichem Raum visuell dokumentierte. Mittels der Fotografie legt sie bestehende Strukturen im Stadtraum offen und gibt zugleich ihren subjektiven Blick durch die Linse preis. Als Schaufenster – und zwar als Erweiterung der Ausstellungsräume des HfG-Archivs im städtischen Raum und als inhaltliche Anknüpfung an die Verschmelzung zwischen öffentlichem Raum und Aufmerksamkeit heischender Schaufenstergestaltung – zeigte sich die PUTTE als ausgezeichneter Ort, nicht zuletzt wegen der zwei eigenen großen »Schaufenster«, die ebenfalls einbezogen wurden.

Die Ergebnisse der Projekte waren nicht nur Ausgangspunkt zur Reflexion und Diskussion für Ausstellungsbesucher*innen, sondern nahmen im Verlauf des Projekts Einfluss auf kuratorische Entscheidungen. Neben der Herausforderung, sich im Zuge der Ausstellungsvorbereitung auch auf Planungsunsicherheiten einzulassen und vielfältige Austauschprozesse zu begleiten, galt es zudem zuzulassen, kuratorische Erzählweisen zugunsten einer Vielstimmigkeit aufzubrechen. Durch die Ausstellungsgliederung in Alltagsbereiche sowie das Nebeneinander von Leihgaben, Sammlungsbeständen und Projektarbeiten wurden multiple Anknüpfungspunkte geschaffen. Während somit einerseits eine

Fabian Karrer and Susanne Umscheid as role models, and an increased questioning of gender clichés. The Project Week was generously supported by lab.Bode – Initiative to Strengthen Museum Education in Museums, a programme that time and again has provided me, in particular, with valuable impulses in the framework of further education modules in the »think-tank« at the Bode Museum in Berlin. It also revealed new perspectives for the exhibition project without which it couldn't have happened in this form.

In the product design course with the focus »Gender in Design«, students of Aicher-Scholl-Kolleg (vh ulm), a general studies programme for secondary school graduates for professional orientation, developed models, objects, and installations that employed and – some quite artistically – reflected upon design methods. In a trimester from October to December 2018 they thoroughly researched the theme under the guidance of designer Uli Häussler and acquired insights into the complex world of design. The objective was not only to reveal a professional perspective to the young adults but also to convey a deeper understanding of the importance of design and the social responsibility that designers bear.

With the aim of drawing attention to the exhibition theme in the urban space of Ulm and Neu-Ulm, the off-space PUTTE presented an exhibition of works by Juliane Peil, who visually documented her perspective on the relationship between gender and public space. Her photography captured such hidden and overt manifestations in urban space, while offering her own subjective view through the lens. Serving as a public display window – an innercity satellite of the more remote HfG-Archiv exhibition spaces, with a thematic fusion of attention-grabbing shop window design and public space – PUTTE proved to be an excellent location, owed not least to its own two large shop windows.

The results of the subprojects incited reflection and discussion amongst exhibition visitors, but they were also quite influential upon curatorial decisions throughout the project. Besides the challenge of being open to planning uncertainties in the run-up to the exhibition and assisting in the multifaceted exchange processes, we also felt the need to let curatorial narratives give way to this polyphony of perspectives. By structuring the exhibition into thematic areas of the everyday and juxtaposing loaned exhibits, items from the HfG-Archiv collections, and works from the subprojects, we were able to offer multiple access points for visitors. Although this approach generated a coherent and at the same time heterogeneous narration, only during the practical realisation phase did it become clear that certain contributions could not be easily embedded in such a structure. The decision to present these results and thereby grant insights into the participants' mindsets and viewpoints, while

stringente und gleichzeitig umfassende Narration möglich wurde, zeigte sich erst während der praktischen Umsetzung, dass sich Beiträge hier und da nicht einfach in diese Struktur einbetten ließen. Die Entscheidung zu treffen, diese Ergebnisse einerseits zu zeigen und damit einen Einblick in die Denk- und Sichtweisen der Teilnehmer*innen zu gewähren, andererseits aber beispielsweise Skizzen nicht zusätzlich auszustellen, erforderte eine notwendige Sorgfalt, um trotz aller Grenzverwischungen sinnvolle Linien zu ziehen. Gerade darin liegen zugleich das Potenzial und die Herausforderung einer kuratorisch-vermittelnden Praxis. Die Tatsache, dass wir bei allen Teilprojekten als Vermittlerinnen agierten und das Feld verschiedenen kompetenten Workshopleiter*innen überließen, ermöglichte uns wiederum auch kritische Impulse zu geben und den Überblick zu behalten. Die Gleichwertig- und Vielfältigkeit zwischen kuratorischem Anspruch und Projektergebnissen zu kommunizieren, wurde wiederum Aufgabe einer entsprechenden Präsentationsform. Darunter fällt nicht nur eine einheitliche Ausstellungsgestaltung, umgesetzt von Fabian Karrer, sondern auch das Schaffen von Beteiligungsmöglichkeiten für Besucher*innen, wie z. B. Postkarten mittels Aicher-Piktogrammen zu bestempeln oder sich an der Abstimmung über Wirkungsweisen von »Stuhlikonen« der Designwelt zu beteiligen.

Das Vertrauen in die Kreativität und Fähigkeiten der Teilnehmer*innen hat sich nicht nur gelohnt, sondern alle Teilprojekte haben auf ihre Weise das Großprojekt bereichert. Die Einlassung aller Beteiligten darauf kann nicht hoch genug geschätzt werden, denn es ist klar, dass solche Vorhaben nur dann gelingen, wenn die Bereitschaft sich für Neues zu öffnen gegeben ist – ganz in diesem Sinne gilt unser Dank nochmal den Schüler*innen der Realschule Dornstadt, den Kollegiat*innen des Aicher-Scholl-Kollegs, Olivia Daigneault Deschênes und Juliane Peil.

Wie die Ausstellung möchte auch die Publikation u. a. den Blick darauf richten, dass hinsichtlich der Herausforderungen von Gegenwart und Zukunft junge Menschen gehört und einbezogen werden wollen – sie sollten die Welt, in der sie leben, aktiv mitgestalten können. Es sind auch sie, die dazu beitragen können, stereotype Bilder in unseren Köpfen abzubauen und für Vielfalt einzutreten. Gerade am Feld der Gestaltung lassen sich soziokulturelle Dynamiken nachvollziehen, verhandeln und transformieren. Es gilt verschiedenen Akteur*innen dafür einen Raum zu bieten, sie zu gesellschaftlichen Aushandlungsprozessen einzuladen und – besonders als Kulturinstitution – diese zu begleiten.

not additionally exhibiting explanatory sketches, for instance, required a necessary diligence in order to draw clear, sensible lines despite the blurred thematic borders. Precisely herein resides both the potential and the challenge of curatorial-educational practice. The fact that we played the role of mediators in all of the subprojects and left the field to diverse competent workshop leaders enabled us, in turn, to insert critical impulses and maintain an overview. The task of communicating the equality and diversity between the curatorial intention and the project results required an appropriate presentation format. This included developing a uniform exhibition design, which was implemented by Fabian Karrer, but also creating participation formats for visitors, such as stamping postcards with Aicher pictograms or rating the gender associations of »chair icons« in contemporary design history.

The trust invested in the creativity and abilities of the participants not only paid off – each of the subprojects enriched the greater exhibition project in their own way. The engagement of all of the involved cannot be praised highly enough, for it is certain that such projects only work when there is a readiness to open yourself to something new. In this spirit, we would like to once again thank the pupils from Realschule Dornstadt, the students from Aicher-Scholl-Kolleg, Olivia Daigneault Deschênes, and Juliane Peil.

Like the exhibition, this publication aims to draw attention to the fact that, in light of the challenges in the present and future, young people want to be involved and be heard – and they should be given every opportunity to actively shape the world they live in. It is also they who can make a contribution to deconstructing the stereotypical images in our heads and take a stand for diversity. Precisely in the realm of design, sociocultural dynamics can be identified, negotiated, and transformed. This calls for spaces where a variety of different actors are invited to social processes of negotiation and where we – especially as a cultural institution – accompany them.

Schulprojekt mit einer 9. Klasse der Realschule Dornstadt / School project with 9th grade pupils from Realschule Dornstadt

Schulprojekt mit einer 9. Klasse der Realschule Dornstadt / Projektwoche (22. – 26.10.2018), Lehrerin: Michaela Settele-Jakob, Konzeption und Durchführung: Susanne Umscheid (Produktdesignerin) / Fabian Karrer (Grafikdesigner), gefördert von lab.Bode – Initiative zur Stärkung der Vermittlungsarbeit in Museen

Tag 1 / Führung durch das HfG-Archiv mit Katharina und Pia, die Designer Suse und Fabian stellen sich vor.

Tag 2 / Was ist typisch männlich – typisch weiblich? Wir stellen eine Collage von uns selbst her. »Es hat uns Spaß gemacht, vor allem unsere fertigen Werke zu betrachten.« Alicia, Hanna, Vanessa, Kim »Es hat Spaß gemacht, eine eigene Collage zu gestalten, und es war cool, dass wir so viele Materialien zu Verfügung gestellt bekommen haben.« Meike

Tag 3 / Gegenderte Produkte werden »untersucht«. Praktische Aufgabe: Herstellung eines genderneutralen Puzzles für 3- bis 6-Jährige. »Wir fanden die Gruppenarbeit cool, weil sie uns zum Singen animiert hat«. Yannick, Moritz

Tag 4 / Kann man Produkte klug gendern? Wir erfinden und stellen ein Produkt her, das sowohl für den Mann und die Frau ist. »Uns hat die Teamarbeit sehr viel Spaß gemacht. Es war sehr interessant, dass wir etwas mit dem anderen Geschlecht zusammen entwerfen sollten. Das war auf jeden Fall mal etwas anderes, und es hat auch Spaß gemacht.« Ella, Meike, Lea, Laura

Tag 5 / Wir entwerfen ein Plakat für unser fertiges Produkt. Dies soll nun aber gegendert sein! »Die Nachbesprechungen haben uns besonders gefallen, da sie uns animiert haben, mehr zu leisten. Daneben hat es uns Spaß gemacht, unsere Produkte den anderen vorzustellen.« Robin, Damian »Wir fanden gut, dass man einen Blick fürs Gegenderte bekommen hat. Uns hat das Projekt sehr gut gefallen, wir würden dort gerne nochmal vorbeischauen, um Sachen zu designen und zu gendern.« Lauri, Samuel, Benjamin

A school project with 9th grade pupils from Realschule Dornstadt / Project Week (October 22–26, 2018), school teacher: Michaela Settele-Jakob, concept and realisation: Susanne Umscheid (product designer) / Fabian Karrer (graphic designer), supported by lab.Bode – Initiative to Strengthen Museum Education in Museums

Day 1 / Tour through the HfG-Archiv with Katharina and Pia, the designers Susanne and Fabian introduce themselves.

Day 2 / What is typical male – typical female? We make a collage about ourselves. »We had fun, it was especially nice to see our finished projects.« Alicia, Hanna, Vanessa, Kim »It was interesting to make a collage about myself. And it was cool that we had so many materials to work with.« Meike

Day 3 / We »investigate« gendered products. Practical task: Create a »gender-neutral« puzzle for 3 to 6-year-olds. »We found the group work cool because it animated us to sing.« Yannick, Moritz

Day 4 / Can you cleverly gender products? We invent and design a product that is for men as well as women. »We really enjoyed the team work. It was really interesting that we should design something together with the other gender. In any case, that was something new and a lot of fun.« Ella, Meike, Lea, Laura

Day 5 / We design a poster for our finished product. But now it should be gendered! »We really liked the talks at the end because they motivated us to try harder. It was also fun to present our products to the others.« Robin, Damian »It was good to develop an eye for gendering. We really enjoyed the project. We would definitely like to pass by again to design things and gender them.« Lauri, Samuel, Benjamin

Susanne Umscheid \ **Rückblick** \ Nach der Schule noch schnell shoppen gehen, vielleicht ein neues Deo, ein T-Shirt oder einfach nur ein Getränk kaufen – Jugendliche treffen in ihrem Alltag zahlreiche Kaufentscheidungen. Indem sie das tun, wählen sie aus und gestalten sich selbst. Das Shirt tailliert oder gerade geschnitten? »Vanille-, Himbeere-« oder »Alaska-Wildness-Deo«? Diese Kaufentscheidungen beeinflussen, welches Geschlecht andere und ich mir selbst zuordne. Damit gehen zeitgleich Schätzungen darüber einher, ob man beispielsweise handwerklich und ∕ oder mathematisch begabt, witzig und ∕ oder empathisch ist. Wenn Jugendliche in diesen Kategorien lesen und gelesen werden, haben sie in meinen Augen ein Recht darauf, erklärt zu bekommen, wie diese Kategorien entstehen und wie sie selbst diese bewusst nutzen können. Um zu erklären, was Jahrtausende an Zivilisation und Jahrzehnte an Design mit ihrem Alltag zu tun haben, war das Format einer Projektwoche ein guter Anfang.

Was damit begann zu verstehen, was eigentlich hinter den Begriffen Design und Gender steckt, führte zum Erforschen des eigenen Leseverhaltens von Schriften, Formen und Farben in Bezug auf Gender und der Frage, wie man aus dem eigenen Leseverhalten wieder herauskommt, um ein Produkt für andere (Geschlechter) zu gestalten. Gemeinsam mit Grafiker Fabian Karrer bestand bis zum ersten Tag mehrheitlich Neugier, wie potenzieller Designnachwuchs mit diesem komplexen Thema umgehen würde – und bereits am Nachmittag unseres ersten Tages war ich beeindruckt von der Ambivalenz aus Stereotypen und Wachheit, die mir gegenüber saß.

Männer sind mehr als Holzhacken und Autos, Frauen mehr als sexy und Mutter, das war den Teilnehmenden einerseits klar, und dennoch sprachen viele ihrer Entwürfe und Ideen genau das Gegenteil aus. Schminke und zarte Farben für die Mädels, Traktoren und kräftige Farben für die Jungs.

Den Weg, den wir begleiteten, war von buchstäblichem Glitzer, vielen Fragen und Hunger auf das Themenfeld gesäumt. Schlussendlich beschlich mich der Eindruck, die Ambivalenz der Schüler*innen zumindest für diese greifbarer gemacht zu haben. So beschrieben sie einerseits, wacher zu sein, was ihre Umgebung anbelangte und zeitgleich reproduzierten sie für sich selbst dennoch stereotype Geschlechterbilder. Letztere sind bereits andere als noch in der Generation vor ihnen, und dennoch existiert die Aufteilung in aktive und passive Charakterzüge im Bezug auf Geschlechter: Mädels schauen Netflix, sind modisch und emotional, Jungs zocken Videospiele, sind sportlich und selbstbewusst. So zeigten auch die während der Projektwoche erarbeiteten Produktmodelle sehr individuelle Auffassungen der Begriffe weiblich, männlich oder unisex.

Für mich war dieses Geschlechterbilder aus- und erleben, gestalten und annehmen eine willkommene Beobachtungssituation, wirft sie für mich in meiner Arbeit als Produktgestalterin doch die Frage auf, wie meine Gestaltung und das Design insgesamt persönlichen Generationen-Bias bearbeiten kann und sollte.

Review \ A bit of quick after-school shopping, perhaps a new deodorant, a t-shirt, or maybe just a drink – youth make numerous purchasing decisions in their everyday. In doing so, they are making selections and designing themselves. Does the t-shirt have a fitted waist or is it straight cut? »Vanilla-Strawberry« or »Alaska-Wilderness« deodorant? These purchasing decisions influence which gender others and I personally associate with myself. This is paired with conjectures whether, for instance, one is talented in crafts and ∕ or mathematics, funny and ∕ or empathetic. When youth are read and read others in these categories, they have the right, in my mind, to an explanation where these categories originate and how they can consciously use them themselves. To explain what millennia of civilisation and decades of design have to do with their everyday, the format of a Project Week was a good starting point.

Beginning to understand what is actually behind the words »gender« and »design« led to an investigation of one's own interpretation of typefaces, forms, and colours in connection with gender and to the question of how to step out of one's own interpretative mode in order to design a product for another (gender). Together with graphic designer Fabian Karrer, curiosity had built up about how the potential up-and-coming designers would deal with this complex topic – and already in the afternoon of our first day, I was impressed by the ambivalence of stereotypes and awareness seated before me.

Men are more than just chopping wood and racing cars; women are more than just sexy and mothers – that was clear to the participants, yet many of their designs and ideas expressed the complete opposite. Make-up and soft colours for the girls, tractors and strong colours for the boys.

The path we ultimately pursued was literally lined with glitter, great inquisitiveness, and a hunger for the topic. In the end I had the impression we had made the pupils' ambivalent positions more tangible, at least for themselves. For example, they spoke about being more alert about their surroundings, but at the same time they reproduced stereotypical gender images for themselves. Even though these images already differ from the ones in the generation before them, there exists a division into active and passive character traits in relation to gender: girls watch Netflix, they're fashion-minded and emotional; boys play video games, they're sporty and confident. The product designs developed during the Project Week also reflected very personal perceptions of the terms feminine, masculine, or unisex.

For me, this living out and experience of gender images, their designs and assumptions, were a welcome observation – for my work as a product designer, it indeed poses the question of how my design activities and design in general can and should address these personal generation biases.

Materialkoffer / *Material box* / **Arbeit an einem Puzzle für Kindergartenkinder** / *Working on a jigsaw puzzle for nursery school children* / Projektwoche / *Project week* 2018

Ergebnis einer Feedbackrunde / *Result of a feedback session* / **Arbeit am Puzzle** / *Working on a jigsaw puzzle* / Projektwoche / *Project week 2018*

»Was macht mich aus?« Erstellen kreativer Collagen über sich selbst / »Who am I?« Creating creative collages about oneself
Arbeit am Puzzle / Working on a jigsaw puzzle / Projektwoche / Project week 2018

Brainstorming zu Geschlechterstereotypen: Was wird als typisch männlich, typisch weiblich angesehen? / *Brainstorming on gender stereotypes: What is considered typically male, typically female?* / **Arbeit am Puzzle** / *Working on a jigsaw puzzle* / Projektwoche / *Project week* 2018

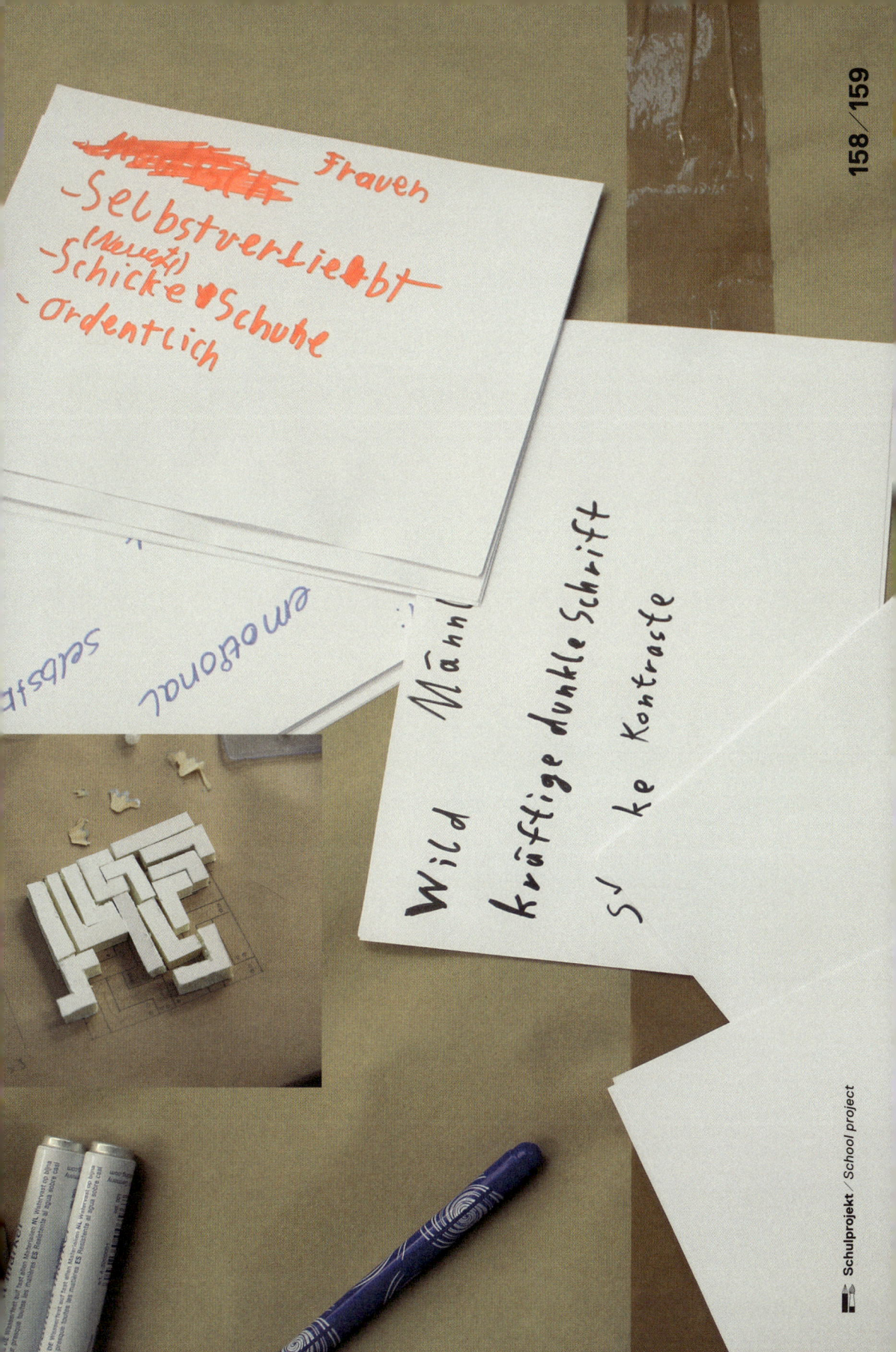

Arbeit am Produkt und Werbeplakat
/ *Working on a product and ad* /
Projektwoche / *Project week* 2018

Präsentation der gestalteten »gender-neutralen« Produkte / *Presentation of the designed »gender-neutral« products* / **Gegendertes Werbeplakat für das fertige Produkt, Slogan »Dich verfolgt deine Männlichkeit bis unter die Dusche«** / *Gendered ad for the designed product, slogan: »Your manhood hunts you down even under the shower!«* / **Projektwoche** / *Project week* 2018

Interview mit Michaela Settele-Jakob \ Michaela Settele-Jakob ist Deutsch- und Kunstlehrerin an der Realschule Dornstadt und begleitet die Projektwoche mit 22 Schüler*innen der Jahrgangsstufe 9 der Realschule Dornstadt als betreuende Lehrkraft.

Die Schüler*innen waren zum Zeitpunkt der Durchführung in der 9. Klasse zwischen 13 und 16 Jahre alt. Wie haben sie aus deiner Sicht auf das Thema Gender und Design reagiert als du ihnen das Projekt vorgestellt hast?

Der Begriff Gender war den Schüler*innen nicht geläufig und der Bezug zu Design völlig fremd. Anhand von Beispielen war jedoch schnell klar, wo überall Gender im Design anzutreffen ist und die Vorfreude auf das Projekt war schnell geweckt.

Wie passte das Thema Gender und Design für dich in die Lebenswelt und den Alltag deiner Schüler*innen?

Als junge Heranwachsende sind die Schüler*innen diesem Thema in sämtlichen Medien, von Instagram bis Facebook, ausgesetzt. Für mich war es wichtig, zu sehen, wie sich ein kritischer Umgang mit diesem Thema langsam entwickelte.

Die Projektwoche fand in den Räumen der ehemaligen HfG Ulm statt. Die Schüler*innen kamen aus Dornstadt und anderen umliegenden Ortschaften und hatten zum Teil eine lange Anreise. Auch die Versorgungssituation vor Ort war nicht optimal, geeignete Räumlichkeiten mussten von uns für die Projektwoche geschaffen werden. Warum hat dich das Projekt dennoch überzeugt? Und was waren deine Erwartungen?

Mit einer Schulklasse die gewohnte Umgebung zu verlassen, bedeutet immer Mehrarbeit für Schüler*innen und Lehrerin. Aber der Gewinn, welcher durch außerschulische Veranstaltungen entsteht, ist durch nichts zu ersetzen.

Die Schüler*innen kommen aus unterschiedlichen Klassen, kannten das HfG-Archiv nicht und waren mit den Begriffen Gender und Design wenig vertraut. Was hat dich überrascht? Wie hast du die Schüler*innen wahrgenommen? Hast du neue Talente bei deinen Schüler*innen entdecken können?

Beeindruckend war, wie natürlich sich die Klasse dem Thema näherte. Von Berührungsängsten oder Vorurteilen war nichts zu spüren. Team-, und Kritikfähigkeit sowie kreative Kompetenzen kamen deutlich zum Ausdruck.

Wie hast du deine Position als betreuende Lehrkraft innerhalb des Projekts wahrgenommen und ausgeführt?

Eine Klasse als stille Beobachterin zu begleiten, war eine völlig neue Erfahrung. Schnell wurden die Designer zum Ansprechpartner Nr. 1 bei Fragen der kreativen Umsetzung.

Interview with Michaela Settele-Jakob \ Michaela Settele-Jakob is a German and art teacher at Realschule Dornstadt and was the supervisor of the Project Week with 22 pupils from the 9th grade.

At the time of the Project Week the pupils were in the 9th grade and between the ages of 13 and 16. How did they respond to the topic of gender and design, in your view, when you introduced the project?

The pupils were not familiar with the term »gender«, and the connection with design was completely foreign. But given a few examples, it was quickly clear that gender in design can be encountered in a lot of places and on various occasions, and that instantly aroused enthusiasm for the project.

In your opinion, how did the topic of gender and design fit into the daily lives and surroundings of the pupils?

As adolescent youth, the pupils are exposed to these topics in all types of media, from Instagram to Facebook. For me, it was important to see how a critical approach to these themes gradually evolved.

The Project Week took place in the rooms of the former HfG Ulm. The pupils came from Dornstadt and other surrounding towns, some had a long journey to get there. The provisions on site were not ideal either; we had to create suitable spaces for the Project Week. Why did the project still win you over? And what were your expectations?

Leaving familiar surroundings together with a school class always implies extra work for the pupils and the teacher. But the benefits you gain through extracurricular activities are indispensable.

The pupils came from different classes, didn't know the HfG-Archiv, and were hardly familiar with the topics of gender and design. What surprised you? How did you perceive the pupils in this context? Did you discover new talents in your pupils?

I was impressed that the class engaged with the topic so naturally. There were no signs to see of any reservations or prejudices. There were clear expressions of team skills and dealing with criticism as well as creative competences.

How did you see and perform your position as the supervising teacher in the project?

Supervising a class as a quiet observer was a totally new experience. The designers quickly became the number one contact for questions about the creative process.

The Project Week was led and realised by Susanne Umscheid, a product designer, and Fabian Karrer, a communication designer. To what extent did their professions play a role for the pupils and, from your point of view, how did the pupils perceive them?

The class was in awe about being »instructed«

Die Projektwoche wurde von Susanne Umscheid, einer Produktdesignerin, und Fabian Karrer, einem Kommunikationsdesigner, geleitet und durchgeführt. Inwiefern waren deren Berufe für die Schüler*innen ein Thema und wie wurden die Beiden aus deiner Sicht von den Schüler*innen wahrgenommen?

Die Klasse war begeistert, von zwei Designern »angeleitet« zu werden. Die Schüler*innen genossen es sehr, im Rahmen einer Schulveranstaltung, von externen Spezialisten begleitet zu werden. Besonders interessant war es für die Klasse, »echte Designer« hautnah zu erleben und gemeinsam mit ihnen arbeiten zu dürfen. Bei dem ein oder anderen Schüler*in hat sich durch die Zusammenarbeit der Wunsch verstärkt, nach dem Realschulabschluss einen kreativen Beruf anzustreben.

Wie schätzt du die Freiräume und Möglichkeiten ein, die die Schüler*innen zur Mitgestaltung im Verlauf des Projekts hatten?

Ziel der Projektwoche war es, ein Verständnis für die Konstruktion von Geschlechterrollen durch Designobjekte zu bekommen, diese in Einzel-, Partner- oder Gruppenarbeit anzuwenden und somit die gesamte Bandbreite eines klassischen Gestaltungsprozesses zu durchlaufen. Bei dieser Arbeit hatten die Schüler*innen innerhalb eines festgesteckten Rahmens sehr große Freiräume, mit denen sie unterschiedlich gut zurecht kamen. Da die Gruppenzusammensetzungen aber stets sehr heterogen waren, entstanden äußerst kreative Lösungen.

Nun hat die Projektwoche nicht nur thematisch, sondern auch räumlich getrennt von dem vertrauten Schulort stattgefunden. Inwieweit hat so eine Projektwoche längerfristig einen Einfluss auf die Schüler*innen? Welche »Nachwirkungen« konntest du zurück im Schulalltag beobachten?

Auch in diesem Schuljahr habe ich diese Klasse weiterhin als Zehntklässler in Bildende Kunst. Die erste Frage im neuen Schuljahr: »Machen wir dieses Jahr wieder ein Projekt an der HfG?«

Wie wurde das Projekt, insbesondere die Tatsache, dass die Resultate der Schüler*innen in der Ausstellung gezeigt wurden, von den Schüler*innen selbst, Eltern und Kolleg*innen aufgenommen?

Die Anerkennung von allen Seiten war riesig. Die Beteiligung bei der Vernissage am Abend durch Schüler*innen mit Eltern war sehr groß. Auch das Interesse, die ausgestellten Objekte nach der Ausstellung wiederzubekommen, ist ungebrochen.

Das Projekt wurde finanziert von lab.Bode – Initiative zur Stärkung der Vermittlungsarbeit in Museen und setzt sich besonders für die enge Zusammenarbeit zwischen Museen und Schulen und für innovative Vermittlungskonzepte ein. Welche Bedeutung hatte das Projekt für die Realschule Dornstadt?

by two designers. They really enjoyed being guided by external specialists in the framework of a school event. It was especially interesting for the class to have a first-hand experience with »real designers« and to be able to work together with them. For one or the other pupil, the cooperation might have spurred the desire to pursue a creative profession after graduation.

What is your assessment of their freedom and opportunities to participate in the design process during the project?

The aim of the Project Week was to convey an understanding of the construction of gender roles through design objects, to apply it in individual, partner, or group projects, and thereby experience the complete spectrum of a classical design process. In this task the pupils had a lot of freedom within a stipulated framework, which each of them dealt with in his or her own way. But as the group constellations were always quite heterogeneous, it led to extremely creative solutions.

The Project Week was not only thematically but spatially separated from the familiar school environment. To what extent did the Project Week have an effect for the pupils on a longer term? Which »after-effects« did you observe in the daily school life?

This year I have the group once again as a grade 10 art class. The first question was: »Are we going to do another project at the HfG this year?«

How did the pupils, their parents and friends, react to the project and especially to the fact that their works were presented in the exhibition?

The appreciation from all directions was amazing. A lot of pupils and their parents came to the evening of the vernissage. And the interest to have the exhibited objects back has been unbroken.

The project was financed by lab.Bode – Initiative to Strengthen Museum Education in Museums, which strongly advocates close cooperations between museums and schools as well as innovative educational concepts. What significance did the project have for Realschule Dornstadt?

The lab.Bode initiative made it possible for our class to enjoy a more than interesting Project Week, free of charge, under the guidance of the designers Susanne and Fabian. The class seized the opportunity to explore the role of design in everyday life, and it was impressive to experience how stereotypical, gender-coded products can be put to question. Did it have a sustained effect on the development of a critical awareness? That would be desirable.

Durch die lab.Bode-Initiative war es uns als Klasse möglich, unter Anleitung der Produktdesignerin Susanne Umscheid und dem Kommunikationsdesigner Fabian Karrer, kostenfrei eine mehr als interessante Projektwoche erleben zu dürfen. Die Schüler*innen nutzten die Gelegenheit, die Relevanz von Design als Gegenstand des täglichen Lebens zu erkunden und es war beeindruckend zu erleben, wie stereotype, gendercodierte Produkte hinterfragt wurden. Ob sich dabei nachhaltig ein kritisches Bewusstsein entwickelt hat? Es wäre wünschenswert.

Schüler*innen mit ihren entworfenen Produkten vor der HfG / *Students with their designed products in front of the HfG* / **Präsentation der Produkte** / *Presentation of the products* / Projektwoche / *Project week* 2018

Wiedersehen in der Ausstellung: Wie würden die Schüler*innen die Ausstellung kuratieren?
Follow-up at the exhibition: How would the students curate the exhibition? **Follow-up 2019**

Produktdesignkurs des Aicher-Scholl-Kollegs /
Product design course of the Aicher-Scholl-Kolleg

Aicher-Scholl-Kolleg (vh ulm) / Produktdesignkurs im 1. Trimester (10. – 12. 2018), Dozent: Uli Häussler
»Zu Beginn des Projekts war schnell klar: Gender und Design sind immer präsent und doch fällt es schwer, sich bewusst und konkret damit auseinander zu setzen. Die Frage, wann Genderanpassungen im Design sinnvoll oder nötig sind, ist dabei von zentraler Bedeutung. Im Laufe des Projekts war es uns deshalb besonders wichtig, spielerisch und mit etwas Humor eben diese *Anpassungen* kritisch zu hinterfragen.« Judith Hoerder, Jessy Tieu

Aicher-Scholl-Kolleg (vh ulm) / Product design course in the 1st trimester (10.–12.2018), instructor: Uli Häussler
»At the beginning of the project it was quickly clear: Gender and design are always all around us, but they are difficult to fathom in a conscious and concrete manner. The question whether adaptations based on gender make sense or are necessary in design was central. Hence, during the course of the project it was important that we critically question these 'adaptations', playfully and with a touch of humour.« Judith Hoerder, Jessy Tieu

Interview mit Judith Hoerder, »Küche vs. Werkstatt« mit Jessy Tieu

Du hast zusammen mit Jessy gearbeitet. Euer Thema hattet ihr schnell gefunden! Wie seid ihr darauf gekommen?

Wir sollten uns zunächst ja mit Themen und Dingen beschäftigen, die »typisch« Mann oder »typisch« Frau sind. Die (eigentlich) historische Rollenverteilung – die Frau in der Küche und der Mann in der Werkstatt – war dabei für mich ein wichtiger Aspekt, da besonders dieses Thema oft als nicht mehr zeitgemäß oder veraltet abgetan wird. Achtet man aber auf Werbung oder Zeitschriften, ist das nach wie vor in der Gesellschaft ein sehr gefestigtes Bild bzw. Klischee. Ich als (mehr oder weniger) kompetente Frau in beiden Räumen muss selbst beim Werkeln z. B. in der Schule Durchsetzungsvermögen haben, um beispielsweise auch mal bohren zu dürfen. Das Ganze war für mich also auch sehr persönlich. Betrachtet man rein optisch Bilder von eingerichteten Küchen und Werkstätten nebeneinander, ist der Vergleich ziemlich naheliegend – abgesehen von den Werkzeugen und Küchengeräten (die sich zum Teil sogar in ihrer Funktion ähneln), mit denen der jeweilige Raum ausgestattet ist, sind die beiden Umfelder sich sehr ähnlich.

Beschreibe euer Projekt in ein paar Sätzen.

Letztendlich geht es darum, eine Art Irritation zu kreieren, die zum Nachdenken anregt. Küche und Werkstatt sehen auf den ersten Blick ähnlich aus, trotzdem wird der eine Bereich dem männlichen Geschlecht und der andere dem weiblichen zugeordnet. Vertauscht man die Gegenstände aus den jeweiligen Räumlichkeiten, entsteht Verwirrung. An Stelle des Mixers liegt die Bohrmaschine in der Küche, der Mixer in der Werkstatt. Wo kann man jetzt welches Geschlecht (klischeemäßig) zuordnen? Der Betrachter oder die Betrachterin soll in den Raum kommen und auf den ersten Blick nichts Außergewöhnliches feststellen, erst auf den zweiten Blick merkt man, dass Küche und Werkstatt durch die vertauschte Einrichtung auch in ihrer Funktion verändert wurden. Was stimmt hier nicht? Die Irritation soll anregen.

In der Vorbereitung der Ausstellung hatte Katharina die Idee, die an den Ausstellungsraum angrenzende Küche für euer Projekt zu öffnen, was euch die Möglichkeit gab, diese zu bespielen. Welche Rolle hat das bei der Ausarbeitung der Installation für euch gespielt?

Es hat, würde ich sagen, das Ganze nochmal intensiviert und sogar erst möglich gemacht. Dadurch, dass wir speziell diesen Raum mit der Küchenzeile zur Verfügung bekommen haben, konnten wir die Szene erstens viel realistischer darstellen und zweitens die »Küchenwerkstatt«, also die mit Küchengeräten eingerichtete Werkstatt, direkt einander gegenüberstellen. Der Effekt wird dadurch, glaube

---

Interview with Judith Hoerder, »Kitchen vs. Workshop« *with Jessy Tieu*

You worked with Jessy on this project – and you were quick to find your topic! How did you come up with the idea?

First, we wanted to work on themes and objects that are seen as either »typically« male or »typically« female. I felt it was important to look at the (supposedly) historical allocation of gender roles – women in the kitchen and men in the workshop – because it is often dismissed as outdated or no longer relevant. But if you look at advertising and magazines today, it becomes clear that these stereotypes and clichés are still being promoted in society. As a woman, who is (more or less) capable in both the kitchen and the workshop, I had to be assertive enough, for instance in the school shop, to be allowed to use a drill, so the whole thing is very personal, too. If you look at a picture of a fully kitted out kitchen next to one of a workshop, aside from the tools and appliances (which in some cases have similar functions), it's incredible how alike the two environments actually are.

Describe your project in a few words.

Ultimately, it's about causing a confusion that makes people think. Kitchens and workshops might look similar at first glance, but one is considered male, and the other one female. Swapping objects between the two spaces – putting a food mixer in a workshop or a drill in a kitchen – leads to this puzzlement: Which gender (stereotype) belongs where? Upon entering the room, viewers – male or female – should not notice anything unusual; only later should they realise that the function of each space has changed due to this switching of appliances. Their unease should make them wonder: What's wrong here?

While preparing for the show, Katharina had the idea to make the kitchen next to the exhibition space available as a part of your project. What role did that play in developing the installation?

I would say it intensified the whole thing and even made it all possible in the first place. To use this space with real kitchen units allowed us, firstly, to make the installation more realistic, and secondly, to contrast it directly with the other space, the »kitchen workshop« equipped with kitchen appliances. I think it really helped amplify the effect. You walk into the room and, at first, you're confused; it gives you something to think about once you leave.

How has your view of designing objects used in everyday life and/or the design profession itself changed?

To examine the whole thing in such detail really opens your eyes. Now I notice things in magazines and in adverts that didn't catch my eye before. And, above all, it's made me much more critical of what

ich, wirklich verstärkt. Man läuft in den Raum und ist erst mal verwirrt, man läuft raus und hat etwas zum Nachdenken.

Inwiefern hat sich dein Blick auf Gestaltung von Dingen im Alltag und ∕ oder den Designberuf verändert?

    Durch die intensive Auseinandersetzung mit dem Ganzen werden einem die Augen einfach weiter geöffnet. Mir fallen jetzt Sachen in Zeitschriften oder in der Werbung auf, die mir vorher nicht so ins Auge gestochen sind. Und vor allem gehe ich viel kritischer mit dem um, was ich jetzt sehe. Vorher waren die Dinge eben so, es war normal, dass Küchengeräte in der Werbung mit Frauen dargestellt werden. Jetzt regt es mich auf, wenn so ein stereotypes Bild vermittelt wird. Aber ehrlich gesagt war ich immer schon relativ sensibel, was das Thema Rollenverteilung angeht.

I see. Before, that was just how things were. It was normal to see kitchen appliances advertised using women. Now, it annoys me when I see these stereotyped images. But, to be honest, I've always been quite sensitive about the gendering of roles in general.

Recherche zum Thema und Ausarbeitung erster Ideen ∕ *Doing research on the topic and development of preliminary ideas*

»Küche vs. Werkstatt« in der Ausstellung
∕ *»Kitchen vs. Workshop« at the exhibition*

Präsentation der Projektideen und Objekte
Presentation of the project ideas and objects

Präsentation der Projektideen und Objekte
/ *Presentation of the project ideas and objects*

Arbeiten am Comic / *Working on the comic*

Interview mit Anna-Lotta Dechow, Comic
»Das pinke Rennauto«

Am Aicher-Scholl-Kolleg könnt ihr zwischen vielen unterschiedlichen Kursen und Themen wählen. Was hat dich an diesem Kurs angesprochen?
　　Bevor ich den Kurs gewählt habe, hatte ich schon einige Zeit mit dem Gedanken gespielt, beruflich etwas mit Design zu machen. Daher habe ich möglichst viele Kurse in diesem Bereich am ASK belegt.

Welche Grundidee hattest du und welche Möglichkeiten hat dir die Umsetzung deiner Idee in der Form eines Comics gegeben?
　　Meine Grundidee war es vor allem aufzuzeigen, wie sehr die Vorurteile und Erwartungen, die wir im Bezug auf Männlichkeit und Weiblichkeit haben, gesellschaftlich projiziert und somit auch anerzogen werden. Die Idee in Form eines Comics umzusetzen, hat es mir ermöglicht eigentlich komplexere Zusammenhänge sehr vereinfacht darzustellen und somit den Fokus auf das Thema »Gender Design« zu setzen. Darüber hinaus habe ich im Comic die Geschichte zweier Personen erzählt und hoffe dadurch bei den Besucher*innen der Ausstellung einen gewissen Grad von Identifikation mit der Geschichte und somit auch mit der Thematik erreicht zu haben.

Im Gästebuch wurde dein Comic von Besucher*innen positiv kommentiert. Wie war es für dich, deinen Comic »Das pinke Rennauto« in der Ausstellung zu sehen? Und inwiefern hat es deine Umsetzung beeinflusst, zu wissen, dass das Ergebnis ausgestellt wird?
　　Besonders weil die Auseinandersetzung mit dem Thema »Gender Equality« so aktuell und so wichtig ist, war es schön zu sehen, dass mein Comic zu der Ausstellung beigetragen hat. Abgesehen davon hat das Wissen darüber, dass am Ende der Unterrichtseinheit eine Ausstellung steht, natürlich sehr motiviert, das Projekt fertigzustellen.

Inwiefern hat sich dein Blick auf Gestaltung von Dingen im Alltag und / oder den Designberuf verändert?
　　Da wir uns viel mit alltäglichen Produkten auseinandergesetzt haben, bin ich auch im Alltag aufmerksamer geworden. Mir fällt es seit der Mitwirkung an der Ausstellung viel häufiger auf, wenn die Gestaltung eines Produkts zum Beispiel von der Anatomie des weiblichen Körpers inspiriert ist. Auch Missstände wie »Pink Tax« sind jetzt noch präsenter als sie es vorher sowieso schon waren und ich finde mich häufig in Debatten in Bezug auf das Thema »Gender (In-)Equality« wieder.

Interview with Anna-Lotta Dechow, Comic
»The Pink Racing Car«

There are lots of different courses to choose from at Aicher-Scholl-Kolleg (ASK). What made you choose this one?
　　Before choosing this course, I already thought I might want to do something in the design field later on. That's why I've taken as many design courses as possible at ASK.

What was your initial idea and what possibilities did turning it into a comic allow you?
　　My initial idea was mainly to show the extent to which the prejudices and expectations we have regarding masculinity and femininity are projected socially and thus instilled in us. Realising my idea in the form of a comic made it possible for me to present actually very complex relationships in a simplified way and thereby focus on the topic of »Gender in Design«. Furthermore, my comic tells the story of two individuals, who I hope visitors to the exhibition can relate to, as well as the issues that are addressed through these characters.

Visitors wrote some very positive comments about your comic in the guest book. How did you feel seeing your comic The Pink Racing Car exhibited in the show? And how did knowing that it would be exhibited affect your approach to developing it?
　　It was great to see my comic in the exhibition, especially because the subject of »gender equality« is so relevant and important today. Apart from that, knowing that there would be an exhibition at the end of the course naturally motivated me to complete the project.

How has your view of designing objects used in everyday life and/or the design profession itself changed?
　　As we worked a lot with everyday objects, it has made me more attentive in everyday life. Since taking part in the exhibition, I'm much more aware of products having been designed with, for example, the anatomy of the female body in mind. I'm also much more aware of injustices, such as the »Pink Tax«, for example, and often find myself in debates about »gender (in-)equality«.

Interview mit Tabea Wegelin, »Killing Boys, Killing Girls« mit Anne-Sophie A.

Ihr seid zu Inspirationszwecken durch die Spielzeugwarenabteilung der Kaufhäuser gestreift. Welche Beobachtungen habt ihr in Bezug auf die Produktgestaltung dabei gemacht?

Zuerst ist uns aufgefallen, dass die ganze Spielwarenabteilung streng nach Jungen und Mädchen aufgeteilt ist. Als nächstes, dass Farben eine sehr wichtige Rolle spielen. Spielzeug für Jungen ist meistens blau, grau oder schwarz, während Mädchenspielzeug eher weiß, rosa oder allgemein hell ist. Spielzeug für Jungen soll oft auch gefährlich wirken durch »Laser«, »Flammen«, etc., während Mädchenspielzeug oft glitzert, weich und flauschig ist oder mit Motiven wie Blumen und Herzen verziert ist.

Was hat euch dazu bewegt, das Thema der Spielzeugwaffe zu wählen?

Kinder sind sehr leicht zu beeinflussen und nehmen sehr viel unterbewusst auf. Deswegen haben wir uns dazu entschieden, uns gegendertes Design im Bereich Spielzeug genauer anzuschauen. Für die Waffen haben wir uns entschieden, weil wir sie als Kinderspielzeug unangebracht und ein Stück weit makaber finden, und sie so zu einem interessanten Gegenstand für ein solches Experiment werden. Aber auch weil es eigentlich eher ein Jungen-Spielzeug ist, das in unserem Fall recht neutral gestaltet ist. Es gibt aber auch ziemlich ähnliche Waffen, die so gestaltet sind, dass sie Mädchen ansprechen sollen.

Beschreibt eure Vorgehensweise in ein paar Sätzen.

Wir haben uns drei gleiche Spielzeugpistolen besorgt, die ursprünglich für Jungen designed waren. Wir haben eine der Waffen weiß angesprüht um zu beobachten, welchen Effekt das auf die Waffe hat. Ist die Waffe nun »neutral« oder kann man immer noch anhand der Form erkennen, dass dieses Produkt für Jungen gestaltet wurde? Die anderen beiden Waffen haben wir so dekoriert, dass sie eindeutig einem Geschlecht zugeordnet werden können. Dafür haben wir auf die Beobachtungen im Laden zurückgegriffen. Wie zum Beispiel die Farbwahl, dass die Pistole für Mädchen glitzert und weiche Federn schießt und die Pistole für Jungen eher realistisch und gefährlich aussieht. Der Griff ist aus Leder, weil wir im Kurs anhand von Möbeln herausgefunden haben, dass dieses Material eher männlich konnotiert ist.

Eure Waffen wurden neben dem Projekt einer Designerin, Dominique Gehrke, gezeigt, die das Softair-Gewehr für Mädchen, eine weiße mit rosa Blüten überzogene Waffe, sowie eine Thor-Frisierpuppe für Jungen entworfen hat. Welche Nähe seht ihr zu eurem Projekt und inwiefern sind eure Ansätze verschieden?

Interview with Tabea Wegelin, »Killing Boys, Killing Girls« mit Anne-Sophie A.

For inspiration, you wandered through the toy departments of different large stores. What observations did you make about product design there?

First, we noticed that every toy department is strictly divided into boys' and girls' sections. Second, that colours play a very important role: Boys' toys are mostly blue, grey, or black, while girls' toys tend to be white, pink, and generally more brightly coloured. Toys for boys are often made to look dangerous through the use of lasers and flames, etc. Girls' toys, on the other hand, often sparkle, are soft and fluffy, or come decorated with motifs such as flowers and hearts.

What made you decide to the subject of toy weapons?

Children are easily influenced and absorb a lot subconsciously. That's why we decided to explore gendered design through toys in more detail. We chose toy weapons because we find them inappropriate and a bit morbid as children's toys – though this is what makes them interesting to use in such an experiment. We also chose them because, as a stereotypical boys' toy, we could adapt them to make them look more neutral. Still, there are similar weapons designed to appeal to girls as well.

Describe your approach in a few words.

We got three of the same toy guns originally designed for boys. We sprayed one of the weapons white to see what effect it had: Does it make the weapon »neutral« or is it still possible to tell from the shape that this object was designed for boys? We decorated the other two weapons so that they could clearly be assigned to a specific gender. To do this, we used what we'd learned from the toy stores we'd visited: Using a gendered choice of colours, we made a glittery gun that shoots soft feathers for the girls, and a more realistic and threatening-looking gun for the boys. We covered the grip on the boys' toy gun in leather because we learned, while looking at furniture design on this course, that leather has a more male connotation.

Your toy weapons were shown alongside designer Dominique Gehrke's project – she designed a white airsoft rifle covered with pink flowers for girls, and a Thor hairdressing doll for boys. What are the similarities between the two projects and how did your approaches differ?

Both our approach and Dominique Gehrke's approach are similar in terms of making a gun for girls. We all noticed that weapons are more of a boys' toy because they exude danger, which fits the stereotype of masculine behaviour. Dominique Gehrke wanted to show that it is the gun's dark colour and square-edged, angular appearance that makes it seem like a boys' toy. We, on the other hand, wanted to show that shape is secondary, though of course not completely negligible.

Unser Ansatz und der Ansatz von Dominique Gehrke sind sich, was die Mädchenpistole angeht, ein Stück weit ähnlich. Uns allen ist aufgefallen, dass Waffen eher Spielzeuge für Jungen sind, weil sie eine gewisse Gefahr ausstrahlen, was gut zum männlichen Rollenbild und stereotypischen Verhalten passt. Dominique Gehrkes Ansatz ist, dass das kantige und eckige Aussehen und die dunkle Farbgebung der Pistolen dafür sorgen, dass diese eher als Jungs-Spielzeug wahrgenommen wird. Wir hingegen wollten mit unserem Experiment zeigen, dass die Form zweitrangig, aber natürlich auch nicht komplett zu vernachlässigen ist. Da es bereits Mädchen-Pistolen zu kaufen gibt, wollten wir auch kein neues Produkt erschaffen, wie Dominique Gehrke mit der Thor-Frisierpuppe, sondern an ein- und demselben Produkt zeigen, was für einen Unterschied Farbe, Materialien und Texturen machen.

Inwiefern hat sich dein Blick auf Gestaltung von Dingen im Alltag und / oder den Designberuf verändert?

Ich denke, dass Gender an sich schon ein komplexes Thema ist, und natürlich nochmal mehr im Zusammenhang mit Design. Es ist ein bisschen wie die Frage, was zuerst da war, das Huhn oder das Ei. Bedient Design nur unsere schon vorhandenen Geschlechterrollen, oder ist Design mit daran schuld, dass es weiterhin so fest bestehende Geschlechterrollen gibt? Ich denke, es ist ein bisschen von beidem. In unserer heutigen Gesellschaft sind strenge Geschlechterrollen nicht mehr notwendig, da es nicht mehr darum geht, wer der Stärkste ist und sich um das Überleben kümmern muss, sondern wer am klügsten ist. Und da gibt es meiner Ansicht nach keinen Unterschied zwischen Geschlechtern. Designer sollten daher dazu beitragen diese Geschlechterrollen aufzubrechen, idealerweise durch »neutrale« Produkte. Ich habe während des Projekts jedoch gelernt, dass sowas einfacher klingt als es ist, weil nahezu alles entweder männlich oder weiblich konnotiert ist.

Because girls' guns are already available to buy on the market, we didn't want to create a new product, like Dominique Gehrke's Thor hairdressing doll; instead, we wanted to use a product that already exists to show what difference colour, materials, and textures make.

How has your view of designing objects used in everyday life and/or the design profession itself changed?

I think that gender, in and of itself, is a very complex topic, and even more so when it relates to design. It's a bit of a chicken-or-the-egg situation: Does design simply respond to existing gender roles, or can design be partly blamed for perpetuating these gender roles? I think it's a bit of both. In today's society strict gender roles are no longer necessary because it is no longer about who's the strongest and needs to ensure survival, rather it's more about being the smartest. And, in my view, there is no difference between the genders. Designers should, therefore, help break these gender stereotypes, ideally, by designing »neutral« products. However, I've learnt while working on this assignment that it's a lot easier said than done because almost everything has either male or female connotations.

Killing Boys, Killing Girls /
drei Versionen einer Spielzeugpistole
/ *three variations of a toy gun*

Interview mit Anton Sievert, »Ulmer Hocker«

Welche Überlegungen gingen den Entwürfen voraus?
Im Rahmen der Aufgabe »Gender im Design« untersuchten wir verschiedene Geschlechterstereotypen und inwiefern diese Klischees das Design beeinflussen. Meine Idee war, einen neutralen Gegenstand so umzuformen, dass er Geschlechterrollen und geschlechtsspezifischen Gewohnheiten entspricht. Dabei sollte die Umsetzung möglichst schlicht, aber trotzdem praktisch und nutzbar sein. Zudem sollte anhand der Abänderungen klar werden, ob das Design weiblichen oder männlichen Stereotypen entspricht. Das Vorbild, der Ulmer Hocker, sollte in seinem Konzept klar erkennbar und in der Grundform erhalten bleiben. Meine Überlegung war, das unterschiedliche Sitzverhalten von Männern und Frauen durch Gestaltung zu verdeutlichen.

Beschreibe die vier Varianten in ein paar Sätzen.
Im Sitzverhalten gibt es klare Unterschiede zwischen den Geschlechtern. Männer sitzen gerne breit und beanspruchen viel Platz. Entsprechend sind die Hocker kantig und wuchtig. Eine Variante bietet eine Lehne, auf der man sich vorbeugen und abstützen kann. Die andere Variante betont ihre wuchtige Form durch hohe Armlehnen. Im Gegensatz dazu fallen Entwürfe für Frauen filigraner, runder und auf keinen Fall kantig aus. Die Sitzfläche ist bei einem der Hocker-Entwürfe leicht nach innen gewölbt, im anderen Fall sogar mit einem Kissen gepolstert, um die Bequemlichkeit zu unterstützen.

Inwiefern hat sich dein Blick auf Gestaltung von Dingen im Alltag und/oder den Designberuf verändert?
Der Ulmer Hocker ist klar und einfach in seiner Form. Dennoch ist es mir gelungen geschlechterspezifische Varianten daraus abzuleiten, ohne dass die Funktionalität als Hocker verloren geht. Die Formensprache ist nach wie vor einfach. Eine Erkenntnis ist, wie der gleiche Gegenstand männliche und weibliche Attribute unterstützen kann. Ich achte mehr auf die Wechselwirkung von Gender und Design. Das Bestechende am Ulmer Hocker und den Varianten liegt in der Einfachheit der Formen. Dennoch ist Funktionalität gegeben und eine klare Beziehung zu den Geschlechtern wird deutlich. Ich habe mich gefragt, ob Design nicht häufig auch überflüssigen »Ballast« in der Gestaltung mit sich trägt, anders als es bei dem Ulmer Hocker der Fall ist. Dies ist für mich durch eine Beschäftigung mit Design überhaupt klar geworden.

Interview with Anton Sievert, »Ulm Stool«

What considerations did you bring to the design process?
For the »Gender in Design« assignment, we examined various gender stereotypes and the extent to which these clichés influence design. My idea was to redesign an existing »neutral« object to make it correlate with gender roles and certain gender-specific expectations. The end product had to be simple, but also practical and usable. Additionally, it had to be clear on the basis of the changes made whether the design corresponds with male or female stereotypes. The neutral object I chose to work with was the Ulm Stool. I had to make sure the stool's basic concept and shape remained clearly recognisable. My idea was to use design to illustrate the differences between men and women's sitting styles.

Describe your four design variants in a few words.
There are clear differences in the way males and females sit.
As men tend to sit spread out and take up a lot of space, the male stools are boxy and bulky. One model allows you to lean forward and rest on a support. Another model has high armrests that emphasise its bulky shape. In contrast, the stools designed for women are rounder and more delicate, they have nothing boxy about them at all. The seat on one of these stools is curved slightly inwards; on another, it is padded with a cushion for comfort.

How has your view of designing objects used in everyday life and/or the design profession itself changed?
Despite the Ulm Stool's plain and simple design, I managed to derive gender-specific variants without losing its functionality as a stool. The formal language remains simple. One thing I learnt from this exercise is that the same object can be made to include male and female attributes. I'm more attentive to the connections between gender and design. The striking thing about the Ulm Stool, and the different versions of it, is the simplicity of its forms. It is functional yet the relationship to each gender is made very clear. I was wondering whether, in contrast to the Ulm Stool, designs often carry unnecessary »dead weight«. This was something that I came to realise through my engagement with design more generally.

Arbeiten an verschiedenen Miniaturvarianten des Ulmer Hockers / *Working on miniature models as variations of the Ulm Stool*

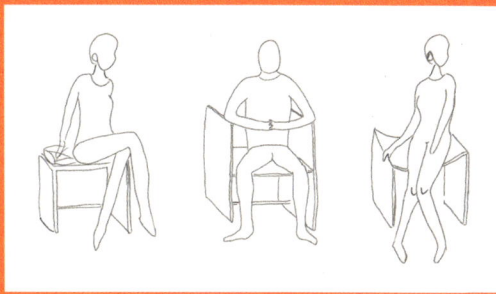

Designer in Residence / Stipendiatin: / *Resident:* Olivia Daigneault Deschênes

Dreimonatiges Stipendium (15.09. – 15.12.2018), Residence-Stipendiatin: Olivia Daigneault Deschênes, Designerin (Vancouver / Kanada), gefördert durch die Stiftung Hochschule für Gestaltung HfG Ulm und das HfG-Archiv / Museum Ulm

»Für drei Monate auf dem HfG-Campus zu leben erlaubte mir, mich in einem inspirierenden Umfeld verstärkt mit den Themen Feminismus und Architektur zu beschäftigen. Auf Grund meines Interesses, mittels Design patriarchiale Strukturen des Alltags offenzulegen, entschied ich mich dafür, auf das Thema Essen und dessen Verhältnis zu *Gender* zu fokussieren. Am meisten inspiriert hat mich dazu die Gestaltung der HfG-Mensa von Max Bill. Für eine feministisch-kritische Perspektive wende ich in meinem Projekt *Zeig' mir wie du isst und ich sag' dir, wer du bist* Performance und ›critical thinking‹ als Designmethoden an.«
Olivia Daigneault Deschênes

A three-month scholarship (15.09. – 15.12.2018), resident: Olivia Daigneault Deschênes, designer (Vancouver, Canada), supported by the HfG Ulm Foundation and the HfG-Archiv / Museum Ulm

»Living and working at the HfG Ulm complex for three months allowed me to pursue my reflections on feminism and architecture in an inspiring environment. Interested in developing ways to use design to unfold manifestations of patriarchy in everyday life, I decided to focus on eating and its relation to gender. I was most inspired by Max Bill's design of the HfG canteen. My project ›Show me how you eat, I will tell you who you are‹ explores critical thinking and performance as design methods towards a critical-feminist practice.« Olivia Daigneault Deschênes

Olivia Daigneault Deschênes \ **Zeig' mir wie du isst und ich sag' dir, wer du bist.** Wie kann Architektur dem feministischen Anliegen dienen, patriarchale und geschlechtsspezifische Unterdrückungsmechanismen zu durchbrechen? Diese Frage bildet die Grundlage meiner Arbeitspraxis und war auch das Leitmotiv für meine Projekte, die ich als erste Stipendiatin des Designer in Residence-Programms im HfG-Archiv Ulm im Jahr 2018 produzieren durfte.

Meine Zugänge entlang der Schnittstellen von Feminismus und Architektur sind weitgehend von den Arbeiten der Architekturhistorikerin Jane Rendell beeinflusst. Auf Basis ihrer Analysen von zeitgenössischen Entwürfen schlägt sie spezifische Terminologien, Konzepte und Arbeitszugänge vor, die eine feministische »critical spatial practice« [kritische räumliche Praxis] formen. Diese stellen nach meinem Verständnis eine Assemblage von Methoden an der Schnittstelle zwischen Theorie und Praxis dar, die, getrieben von dem Wunsch nach sozialem Wandel, eher auf eine selbstkritische Transformation als auf eine einfache Analyse abzielen (Rendell 2018). Mein Ziel ist es, zu demonstrieren, wie aus einer kritischen Perspektive heraus angewandte architektonische Gestaltungsmethoden zu feministischer Wissensproduktion beitragen können. In einer Abkehr vom in der konventionellen Architekturpraxis so etablierten, auf Problemlösung ausgerichteten Ansatz, behaupte ich, dass Architektur in bestimmten Kontexten in der Lage ist, komplexe Manifestationen von Machtstrukturen und gesellschaftlichen Normierungen offenzulegen und zu analysieren.

Der Fokus der Residency 2018 bestand in der Erkundung des Themas »Gender Design«. Wenngleich der Anspruch auf Nutzungsneutralität innerhalb des gestalterischen Berufsfelds mittlerweile weitgehend beherzigt wird, lehrt uns der Feminismus, dass unsere Gesellschaft den weißen westlichen Mann als wirkmächtige Stimme installiert hat, dessen Sichtweise als Norm gilt. Vor diesem Hintergrund bedeutet Genderneutralität häufig schlicht ein Zugang aus männlicher Perspektive, auch wenn sie nicht als solche erkannt wird. Demgegenüber stellt allein schon der Begriff Gender Design als solcher das Konzept einer Neutralität infrage, indem ein feministischer Blickwinkel auf den geschlechtsspezifischen Charakter der uns umgebenden Dinge eingenommen wird. Somit verstehe ich das Thema Gender Design als Bestandteil feministischer Arbeit.

Ausgehend davon, dass Alltagsgegenstände und -räume im Zusammenspiel zwischen Nutzer*innen, Artefakten und sozialen Normen hergestellt werden, widmete sich mein Projekt dem Essen als einem performativen Akt von Geschlechtsidentitäten (Abb. 1–3). Im Entwurfsprozess kombinierte ich Archivrecherche, das Anfertigen von Prototypen und performative Formate und arbeitete mit Kolleg*innen innerhalb des HfG-Campus', dem Schreiner des Museum Ulm, Freiwilligen des Verschwörhauses sowie dem Albrecht Catering Team zusammen. Während meines Residence-Aufenthalts verschmolzen mein Alltag am HfG-Campus, meine Arbeit und

Show me how you eat, I will tell you who you are. How can architecture serve the feminist agenda of dismantling patriarchy and gender-based oppression? This question is the premise of my practice and the main guidance for the work produced as the first Designer in Residence at the HfG-Archiv Ulm in 2018.

My approach to the intersection of feminism and architecture is widely influenced by the work of architectural historian Jane Rendell. Through analysis of contemporary work, Rendell suggests specific terms, concepts and modes of practice that form feminist critical spatial practice, which I understand as an assembly of methods at the intersection of theory and practice that seek to transform in a self-critical matter rather than simply analyse, driven by a desire for social change (Rendell 2018). My goal is to demonstrate how architectural design methods applied in a critical perspective can contribute to feminist knowledge production. In a given context, rather than taking the problem-solving approach so establish within conventional architectural practice, I suggest that architecture can unfold and analyze complex manifestations of power structures and social orders.

The 2018 residency called for investigating the theme »Gender Design«. While the neutral user approach is largely adopted in design professions, feminism teaches us that our society has constructed the white western man as the dominating voice, and presents their perspective as the norm. In that regard, a gender-neutral approach is in practice often simply an approach based on men's perspective, although without being identified as such. The very notion of gender design challenges the idea of neutrality, adopting a feminist lens that highlights the gendered nature of our artefacts. In this sense, I understand the theme »Gender Design« to take part in feminist work.

Approaching the making of everyday objects and spaces as taking place in the interactions of the user, the artefact and social norms, my project investigated eating as a performative act of gender identities (fig. 1–3). The design process combined archival research, prototyping and performances and involved collaboration with colleagues from the HfG building complex, carpenters from Museum Ulm, volunteers from the Verschwörhaus and the Albrecht catering team. Inside the framework of the residency, my everyday life in the HfG building complex, my work and my research became interdependent and almost indistinguishable. The proximity to the Ulm School of Design (HfG-Ulm) legacy not only influenced my work but also led me to think of the residency as a performance in itself in which I took part as the embodied subject (fig. 4). The investigation of performance as a design method allowed me to work at the intersection of everyday life and research work, the banal day-to-day in an out of the ordinary environment, and to capture the residency program's greatest potential as a catalyst for emerging ideas in contemporary design research.

meine Forschung allmählich zu einem großen Ganzen. Die räumliche Nähe zum Erbe der HfG Ulm beeinflusste nicht nur meine Projekte, sondern brachte mich auch dazu, die Residency als Performance an sich zu denken, an der ich als verkörpertes Subjekt teilnahm (Abb. 4). Performativität als Designmethode zu untersuchen, erlaubte es mir, mich an den Rändern zwischen Alltag und Forschung zu bewegen, ein triviales Tagaus, Tagein in einer außergewöhnlichen Umgebung zu leben und das Potenzial des Residence-Programms als Katalysator für neue Ideen in der zeitgenössischen Designforschung voll auszuschöpfen.

Auch die in der Ausbildung an der damaligen HfG Ulm herrschende systematische Herangehensweise zur Artikulation kritischer Argumente fand Niederschlag in meinen Projekten. So ist etwa Ernst Möckls Diplomarbeit »Die Gestalt von Essgeräten als Ergebnis ihrer Gebrauchsfunktion« (1958), ein Produktdesignprojekt zu einem Essbesteck, das die unterschiedlichen Gesten des Mundes und der Hände als funktionale Vorgaben für das Essen diverser Gerichte analysierte. Möckl legte seinen Entwurfsprozess mittels Tabellen, Zeichnungen und Fotografien dar (Abb. 5–6). Für den Entwurf von zwei Bestecksets als Paar, das der binären Geschlechterlogik folgt, fertigte ich ähnliche Tabellen an: Über sie werden bestimmte sozial geprägte Erwartungshaltungen in Bezug auf das Verhältnis von Essen und Geschlecht als funktionale Grundbedingungen für gestalterische Entscheidungen rationalisiert und abgeleitet (Abb. 7). Funktionalität wird hier nicht als neutrales Gestaltungsprinzip übersetzt, sondern ist vielmehr eine Strategie der Übertreibung und Absurdität, die sich eher an der Vorstellung stereotyper statt universeller Nutzer*innen orientiert. Ein wichtiger Teil dieses Experiments war es, in der HfG-Mensa während unserer täglichen Mittagspausen mit den Besteck-Prototypen zu essen. Sicherlich diente mir das wiederholte Ausprobieren dieser Bestecke zur Verbesserung des Designs, aber mehr noch war es dadurch auch anderen möglich, mich beim Essen zu beobachten – der Akt war nun eher Performance als simple Demonstration. Diese täglichen Mittagessen-Performances provozierten Reaktionen der Anwesenden und forderten sie heraus, ihr eigenes Festhalten an oder Ablehnen einer solchen konstruierten Binarität zu reflektieren (Abb. 8).

Das Performen als Teil des Projekts fußte auf dem theoretischen Konzept der performativen Konstitution von Gender, wie es von der politischen Philosophin Judith Butler (Butler 1991) beschrieben wurde. Kurz zusammengefasst behauptet Butler, dass Geschlecht und sexuelle Identitäten durch das Tun und Machen [doing and making], und nicht durch das Sein [being] gesellschaftlich konstruiert werden (Bonnevier 2007, 35).

Throughout the project, I was drawn by the systematic approach prevailing in HfG-Ulm design education to articulate critical arguments. Ernst Möckl's diploma »The Shape of Eating Utensils as a Result of their Function of Use« (1958) is a product design project of a cutlery set investigating the different gestures conducted by the mouth and hands to serve the functional constraint of eating various foods. His design process was demonstrated in charts, drawings and photographs (fig. 5–6). In designing two cutlery sets as a binary, I created similar charts in order to rationalise the design moves according to identified social expectations around food and gender, presented as functional constraints (fig. 7). Here, functionality is not rendered as a neutral design principle but is rather paired with strategy of exaggeration and absurdity, thinking of stereotypical users rather than a universal one. An important part of this experiment was to eat with cutlery prototypes, during our daily lunch break in the HfG canteen, or »Mensa« in German. Certainly, eating with the cutlery allowed me to improve the design through iterations but more so, it allowed others to observe my eating, which made the act a performance rather than a simple demonstration. These daily lunch performances provoked reactions from others and triggered them to reflect on their own adherence or rejection of such constructed binary (fig. 8). Performing as part of the project referred to the theoretical concept of gender performativity, as explained by political philosopher Judith Butler (Butler 1999). In short, Butler defends that gender and sexual identities are socially constructed by doing and making, rather than being (Bonnevier 2007, 35). After deconstructing how the concept of gender as binary translates into eating behavior, I oriented the work towards queer construction of gender. Thinking of seating as part of the act of eating, I altered the Ulm Stool, called Ulmer Hocker, with simple geometric transformations, in order to influence the way one sits on it (fig. 9). Similar to Michelle Christensen and Florian Conradi's project »practical theory«, my experiment of queering the Ulm Stool aimed to explore how the interaction between things and body performs identities. In both projects, the designed seats guide or force the seated position and say: »think about how you perform your gender as a ritualised act« (Christensen and Conradi 2017, 55). Unlike the cutlery as binary, the altered Ulm Stool can be turned around and encourages a range of seated positions dissociated from stereotypical references (fig. 10–12).

Working with the Ulm Stool to speak of queer identities was also drawn by the metaphorical idea of performing it as a subject with multifaceted identities. The original design's particularity of shifting was maintained to refer to gender identities as multiple, active and forever shifting. In this instance, the performative aspect of the work was taken by the objects themselves. A table designed with a flexible top and adjustable legs served for stools to gather around and re-enact the way bodies negotiate their

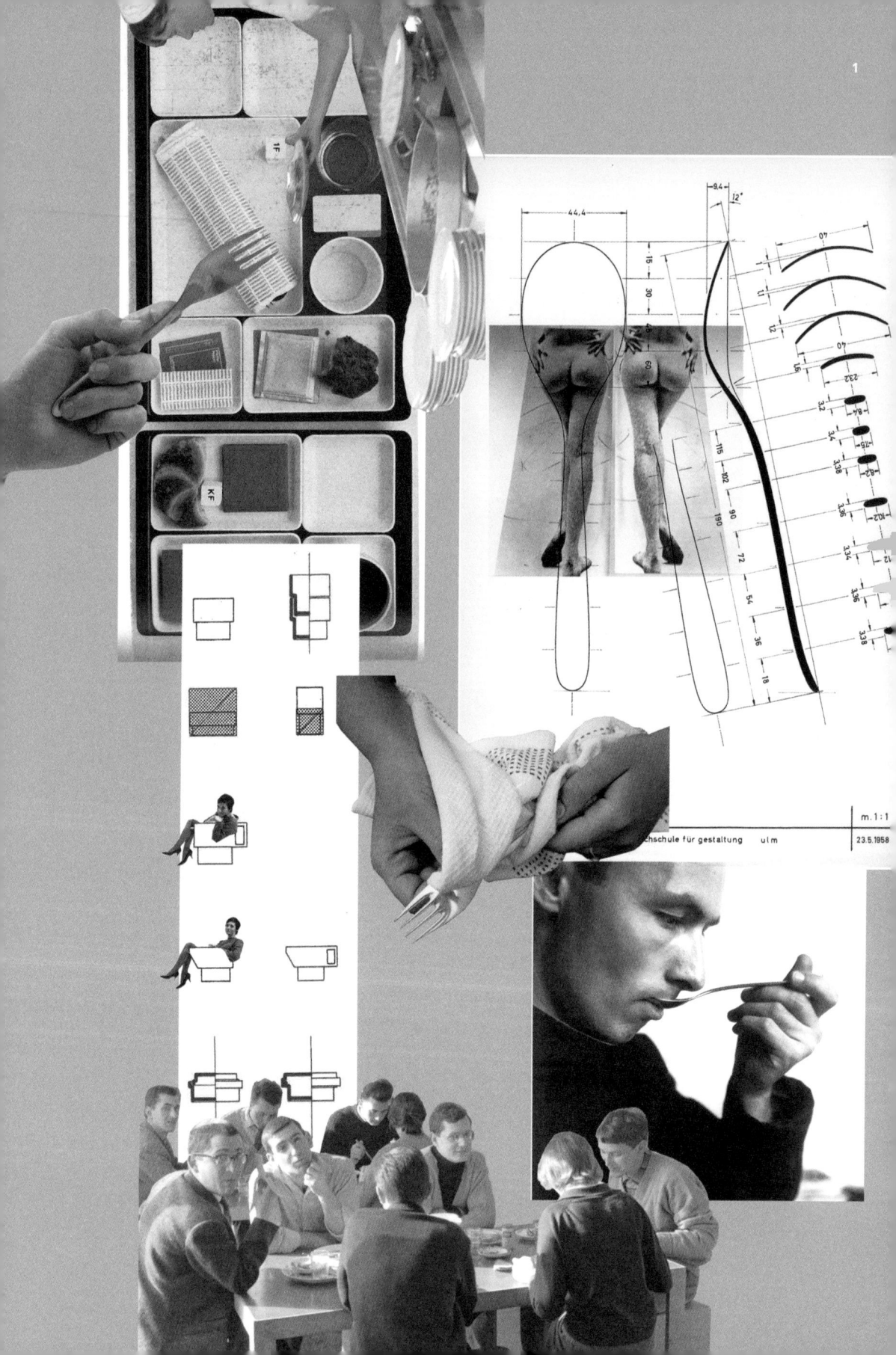

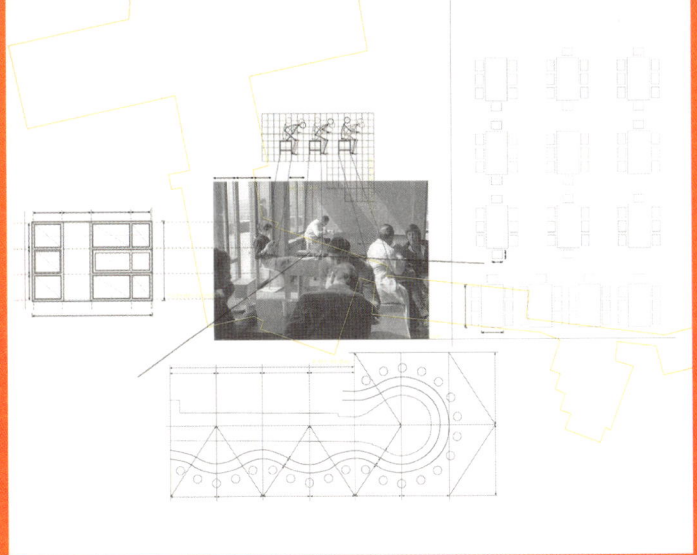

3

1 Meine Archivrecherche fokussierte sich auf das Design von Besteck und Geschirr, die HfG-Mensa und die Fotografiesammlung. Diese erste konzeptionelle Collage entstand aus im Archiv vorgefundenen Materialien, die mit dem Forschungsthema Essen und Gender zu tun haben. / My archival research focused on cutlery and tableware design, the HfG canteen (»Mensa«) and the photography collection. This early conceptual collage was made of materials found in the archive, which spoke of the research topic of eating and gender.

2–3 Konzeptzeichnungen von der Mensa, die mein Interesse als Raum für soziale Zusammenkünfte und des Alltagsgeschehens weckte, damals wie heute, sowie als räumliche Manifestation für viele Gestaltungsprinzipien der HfG Ulm. / Conceptual drawings representing the canteen, which I got interested in as the space of social gatherings and everyday life both then and now and as the spatial demonstration of many of HfG-Ulm design principles.

2

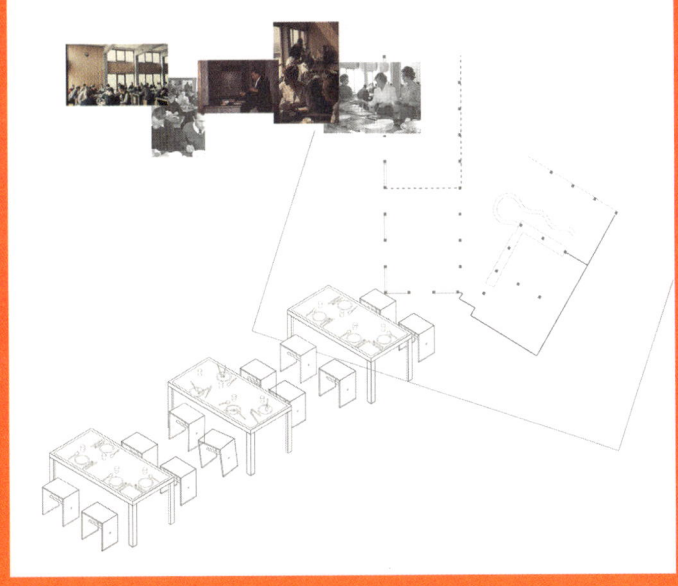

Nachdem ich dekonstruiert hatte, wie das binäre Konzept von Geschlecht auf das Essverhalten übertragen wird, orientierte ich die Arbeit an einer queeren Auslegung von Gender. Unter Einbeziehung des Sitzens als Teil des Mahlzeitenrituals modifizierte ich den sogenannten Ulmer Hocker durch einfache geometrische Eingriffe, um zu beeinflussen, wie jemand darauf sitzt (Abb. 9). Ähnlich wie das Projekt »praktische Theorie« [practical theory] von Michelle Christensen und Florian Conradi, versuchte ich mit meinem Experiment des Queering des Ulmer Hockers herauszustellen, wie in der Interaktion zwischen Dingen und Körpern eine Performativität von Identität zum Ausdruck kommt. In beiden Projekten lenken oder erzwingen die gestalteten Sitzobjekte die Sitzposition, als würden sie sagen: »Denke darüber nach, wie du dein Geschlecht als ritualisierten Akt aufführst« (Christensen und Conradi 2017, 55). Im Gegensatz zu den binären Essbestecken können die abgewandelten Ulmer Hocker gekippt und gedreht werden und begünstigen eine Reihe von Sitzpositionen, gelöst von stereotypen Vorbildern (Abb. 10–12).

Anhand des Ulmer Hockers über queere Identitäten zu sprechen, war auch von der metaphorischen Idee getragen, ihn als ein Subjekt mit facettenreichen Identitäten auftreten zu lassen. Die besondere Wandlungsfähigkeit des Originalentwurfs wurde bewahrt, um Geschlechtsidentitäten als multipel, aktiv und in ständigem Wandel begriffen darzustellen. In diesem Fall wurde der performative Aspekt des Projekts von den Objekten selbst inspiriert. Die Gestaltung eines Tisches mit flexibel beweglicher Platte und verstellbaren Beinen wurde in Bezug zu den Hocker-Versionen gesetzt, um sich an dem Tisch zu versammeln und die Art und Weise nachzuahmen, wie Körper ihre Position im Raum aushandeln. Um es mit Leslie Weisman zu sagen: wir verstehen, wer wir sind, dadurch, wo wir sind und mit wem (Weisman 1992). Das Anpassen des Tisches an die verschiedenen Hockersitzhöhen macht die Verhandlung und Affirmation von Macht im gesellschaftlichen Akt der Zusammenkunft rund um eine Mahlzeit greifbar (Abb.13).

Wie zuvor erwähnt, ist die Überschneidung meines Alltagslebens in Ulm mit der Arbeit als Designerin in Residence für mich von großer Bedeutung. Meine abschließende gestalterische Untersuchung war von der täglichen Einnahme einer warmen Mahlzeit in der HfG-Mensa motiviert. Während mir dies das Vorbereiten von Lunch Boxes, eine ganz übliche Notwendigkeit in der kanadischen Kultur, ersparte, war mir die politische Dimension, sich für ein solches Angebot zu entscheiden, sehr wohl bewusst; sie trägt zur Arbeitsteilung bei, die an Geschlechter- und Klassenbeziehungen gebunden ist. Nach einiger Betrachtung der Mensa-Architektur entschied ich mich, die Wand zwischen Küche und Speisesaal als Manifestation der Arbeitsteilung und räumliche Schwelle zwischen Kochen und Essen in meine Arbeit einzubeziehen. Ich dokumentierte die vom Albrecht Catering Team ausgeführten Kochvorgänge in der Küche, fotografierte die arbeitenden

position in space. To paraphrase Leslie Kane Weisman, one understands who they are based on where they are and who they are with (Weisman 1992). The table's adjustment to the different stool heights made the negotiation process and affirmation of power in the social act of gathering around food tangible (fig. 13).

As mentioned before, I find important the crossing of my everyday life in Ulm and the work produced as designer in residence. The last design exploration was motivated by my daily purchase of a cooked meal at the canteen. While this brought me the freedom of not having to prepare lunchboxes, which is most common in Canadian culture, I was well aware of the political load of such decision; contributing to labor division, tied to gender and class relations. Looking at the canteen's architecture, I decided to work on the wall dividing the kitchen from the dining space, as the materialisation of labor division, and the interstice between cooking and eating. I documented the performed labor of cooking the kitchen of Albrecht catering where I took photographs of working arms repetitively chopping, stirring, cleaning and scooping, which was turned into a wallpaper pattern to apply on the kitchen wall (fig. 14). This way, the architecture speaks and leaves a trace of the cooking labor, forcing to reflect on the gender and class distribution between the dining hall and its kitchen (fig. 15).

Reflecting back, to work on the topic of eating in the specific environment of canteens was a deliberate choice of a seemingly anecdotal topic for gender design inquiry. This was motivated by a desire to challenge myself in finding manifestations of patriarchy in less contested terrains and tied to the belief that everything is political. The chosen topic responded directly to the sheltered and privileged format of the residency. As the context called for defining myself as the »Designer in Residence aus Kanada«, I performed the residency and I was able to fully grasp its format to appropriately shape my experience and my work. Early on, I understood the residency as a time of productive solitude for self-projection, where the history of HfG-Ulm served as a pillar for my contribution in contemporary critical work.

In the end, I see in my project as a re-enactment of everyday life at the former Ulm School of Design, both then and now (fig. 16). When revisiting my memories of my time in Ulm, I find in the banal day-to-day moments of magnitude that testified the potential of a design residency at the HfG-Archiv. While the institution today is mostly activated by researchers and art historians, my work and production as a designer certainly brought me closer to the school's initial activities, and consequently contributed in bridging the archival collection to contemporary matters in design. I remember, when working late in the archive, finding myself alone in the building and thinking of those who have done the same as design students in the 1950s and 60s. On these occasions, it felt as if the walls spoke and

Arme und Hände, die unermüdlich schnitten, rührten, säuberten und schöpften. Diese wurden als eine Art Wandtapetenmuster auf die dem Saal zugewandte Küchenwand im Architekturmodell appliziert (Abb. 14).

Auf diese Weise spricht die Architektur, sie zeigt Spuren von der geleisteten Arbeit des Kochens und drängt dadurch zum Nachdenken über Gender- und Klassenverteilung zwischen dem Speisesaal und angeschlossener Küche (Abb. 15).

In der Rückschau war die Beschäftigung mit dem Thema Essen in der spezifischen Umgebung von Mensen eine bewusste Entscheidung für eine scheinbar anekdotenhafte Episode im Rahmen einer Gender-Design-Studie. Dabei war ich von dem Anliegen motiviert, mich selbst herauszufordern und Manifestationen patriarchaler Mechanismen in weniger diskursbeladenen Terrains aufzuspüren, verbunden mit der Überzeugung, dass alles politisch ist. Das gewählte Thema reagierte somit direkt auf das geschützte und privilegierte Format der Residency. Indem der Kontext auch meine Selbstdarstellung als die »Designerin in Residence aus Kanada« bedingte, geriet auch die Residency zu einer Art Performance, wodurch es mir möglich war, das Programm in höchst passender Weise zu meiner Erkenntnisgewinnung und für meine Arbeitsergebnisse zu nutzen. Schon frühzeitig begriff ich den Aufenthalt als eine Zeit produktiver Einsamkeit zugunsten einer Selbstreflexion, in der die Geschichte der HfG Ulm als wichtige Stütze für meinen Beitrag zu einer zeitgenössischen kritischen Arbeit diente.

Letzten Endes sehe ich mein Projekt als Reenactment des Alltagslebens an der ehemaligen Hochschule für Gestaltung Ulm, damals wie heute (Abb. 16). Wenn ich meine Erinnerungen an die Zeit in Ulm Revue passieren lasse, muss ich an die vielen kostbaren Momente in den gewöhnlichen Alltagsabläufen denken, die das Potenzial eines Designer in Residence-Angebots am HfG-Archiv bezeugen. Obwohl die Institution heute vor allem von Forscher*innen und Kunsthistoriker*innen belebt wird, brachten mich meine Recherchen und Produktionen als Designerin auch den ursprünglichen Aktivitäten der Schule näher. Dies trug maßgeblich dazu bei, eine Brücke zwischen den Sammlungsbeständen und zeitgemäßen Fragestellungen im Design schlagen zu können. Ich erinnere mich daran, wie ich spätabends im Archiv arbeitete und merkte, dass ich mich allein im Gebäude befand, an diejenigen denken musste, die wohl das Gleiche als Designstudent*innen in den 1950er- und 1960er-Jahren getan hatten. In diesen Momenten fühlte es sich an, als könnten die Wände sprechen und mir ein flüchtiger Blick in die Vergangenheit der HfG Ulm ganz allein geschenkt war.

I was offered for a moment the memory of the HfG-Ulm all to myself.

Bibliografie / Bibliography: Bonnevier, Katarina. 2007. »Behind Straight Curtains: Towards a Queer Feminist Theory of Architecture.« Stockholm, Axl Books. ■ Butler, Judith. 1999. »Gender Trouble: Feminism and the Subversion of Identity.« New York, Routledge. ■ Christensen, Michelle and Florian Conradi. 2017. »Das Projekt: What we design, designs Us Back.« In Gender Design: Streifzüge zwischen Theorie und Empirie, Edited by Uta Brandes, p. 51–61. Basel, Switzerland, Birkhäuser. ■ Möckl, Ernst. 1958. Diplomarbeit / diploma, Abt. Produktgestaltung / Department Product Design: »Die Gestalt von Essgeräten als Ergebnis ihrer Gebrauchsfunktion« [EN: »The Shape of Eating Utensils as a Result of their Function of Use«]. Dozent: Max Bill, Koreferent / in: Prof. Dr. Max Bense, Prof. Maximilian Debus, Prof. Dr. Etienne Grandjean, Prof. Mia Seeger. Sign.: Diplom 58.6 © HfG-Archiv / Museum Ulm ■ Rendell, Jane. 2018. »Only Resist: A Feminist Approach to Critical Spatial Practice.« The Architectural Review, February 19th, 2018. ■ Rendell, Jane. 2011. »Critical Spatial Practices: Setting Out a Feminist Approach to some Modes and what Matters in Architecture.« In Feminist Practices, Interdisciplinary approaches to Women in Architecture, Edited by Lori A. Brown, p. 17–55. Surrey: Ashgate Publishing. ■ Weisman, Leslie Kanes. 1992. »Discrimination by design: A Feminist critique of the man-made environment.« Urbana, University of Illinois Press.

4 Auswahl von Fotografien aus einer systematischen Sichtung der Sammlungsbestände, die verschiedene Gesten der Hand und des Mundes während des Essens zeigen, in Zusammenschau mit Selbstporträts bei performativen Versuchen mit Besteck und Geschirr. / *Samples of photographs from a systematic survey of the archive's collection showing different gestures of the hand and mouth in the act of eating are paired with self-portraits from a series of performed explorations with cutlery and tableware.*

5 Ernst Möckls Diplomprojekt ist ein gutes Beispiel für funktionalistisches Design, das von einem systematischen Prozess angeleitet ist. Die hier gezeigte Tabelle für die Gestaltung einer Gabel bietet die rationale Grundlage für die formale Ausführung des Objekts. / *Ernst Möckl's diploma project is a great example of functionalist design led by a systematic process. Here, the design chart for the fork rationalises the formal expression of the object.* / Quelle: *Source:* Ernst Möckl, 1958, Sign.: Dipl. 58.6, HfG-Archiv / Museum Ulm.

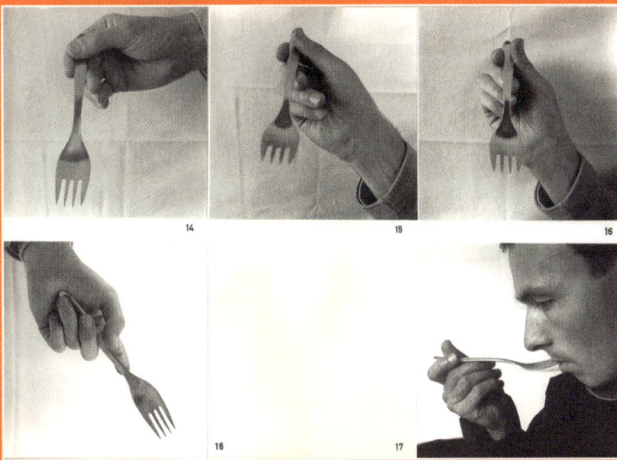

6

6 In Ernst Möckls Diplomprojekt demonstrieren Fotografien die Funktionalität des Entwurfs und fokussieren dabei auf die Gesten der Hand und des Mundes.
/ *In Ernst Möckl's diploma project, photographs demonstrate the design's functionality, with a focus on the hand and mouth gestures.* / Quelle: / *Source:* Ernst Möckl, 1958, Sign.: Dipl. 58.6, HfG-Archiv / Museum Ulm.

7

7 Die zwei Designtabellen für das Besteck als binäre Sets basieren auf den Erkenntnissen von sozialwissenschaftlichen Studien, die darauf hinweisen, wie Nahrungsmittel gegendert werden, um binäre Geschlechtsidentitäten und männliche Dominanz zu untermauern: Von Frauen wird Gemüse, Salat und kleiner Appetit erwartet, während Fleisch, Grillware und große Portionen Männlichkeit vermitteln.
/ *The two design charts for the cutlery as binary sets are based on findings from social science researches that point out how food is gendered in a way to maintain the gender binary and masculine domination: vegetables, salads and small appetites are expected from women while meat consumption, barbecue and large portions are expressions of manhood.*

Cutlery Set A

	Social Expectations/ Observed Facts	Fonction	Design
Arm	Take less space / Are quieter and smaller	Keep elbows close to the body and make minimum gestures with the arms.	Small size of cutlery set forces proximity between the user and the plate. Using two pieces of cutlery to shovel things forces arms to stay close to the body.
Hand	Eat light	Small grip and delicate position of the hand.	The handle's shape and size only allow a two fingers grip.
Mouth	Eat less / Eat in small bites	Minimum opening of the mouth and actions such as pinching, sucking and licking.	The «scoop» piece is small in depth and therefore forces user to put cutlery only so deep into the mouth. The «lick» piece forces to suck and lick due to its shape.
Food	Eat healty / Eat greens / Crave sweets and desert	Suitable for soft food and finely cut vegetables.	The «split» piece is more suitable to rip vegetables and make it almost impossible to cut meat. The size of the cutlery only allows small bites making it more appropriate to eat small portion and forces a slow paste of eating.

Cutlery Set B

	Social Expectations/ Observed Facts	Fonction	Design
Arm	Are bigger / Require more space	Should force to lift elbows and exaggerate the use of space by the arms.	Long and angled handle to force elbows to lift up.
Hand	Eat heavy / Eat solid food	Hand's position that has a good grip.	The handle's shape and size only allow a strong and full-hand grip.
Mouth	Eat more / Eat large portions	Should force large opening of the mouth, to allow big bites	The width of the «shovel» piece forces the mouth to open largerly. The «poke» piece only has two teeth to control a minimal sizebite.
Food	Eat less healthy / Eat meat / Need more carbs and more proteins for physical work	Suitable for eating large portions and cutting large pieces of meat.	The «chop» piece encourages hammering on the plate and chopping-like gestures.

8 Das finale Design der Essbestecke resultierte aus den wiederholten Einsätzen der Prototypen, die zu Gegenständen von Performances während der Mittagspausen in der Mensa wurden. Die aufgezeichneten Performances dokumentierten sowohl den Entwurfsprozess als auch dessen Einbettung in das informelle Alltagsleben am HfG-Campus. / *The final cutlery design was obtained by iterations where all prototypes became the subject of performances at lunch in the canteen. The recorded performances documented both the design process and its intersection with the informal life at the HfG building complex.*

10 Das Experiment des Ulmer-Hocker-Queerings spielt nicht mit Absurdität oder Ironie. Es ist vielmehr eine Reflexion über unser Vermögen, uns Gender als variable und sich immerfort wandelnde Identität vorzustellen. Die zahlreichen Fotografien, die ich von mir auf den modifizierten Hockern anfertigte, belegen meine unterschiedlichen Befindlichkeitsgrade während des Einnehmens von standardmäßigen bis zu provokanten Sitzpositionen im Rahmen meiner angenommenen Geschlechtsidentität. Sie zeigen auch das Potenzial des Hockers, einen subversiven Akt des Sitzens anzuregen. / *The experiment of queering the Ulm Stool doesn't play with absurdity or irony. Instead, it is a reflection on our ability to conceptualise gender as a mobile and ever-changing identity. The many photographs I took of myself sitting on the altered stools explored my level of comfort in performing normalised to provocative sitting positions, based on my appeared gender identity and tested the stools' ability to support subversion in the act of sitting.*

9 Wiederum in Anlehnung an eine systematische Herangehensweise sammelte ich Fotografien von Personen, die auf dem Ulmer Hocker sitzen, imitierte diese in Selbstporträts und reproduzierte die Posen schließlich in ergonomischen Figurenskizzen, die auf die Abstraktion von Körpern und Identitäten anspielen. / *Referring again to a systematic approach, I collected photographs of people seated on the Ulm Stool, imitated them in self-portraits and finally reproduced the postures in ergonomic figure drawings, playing with abstraction of bodies and identities.*

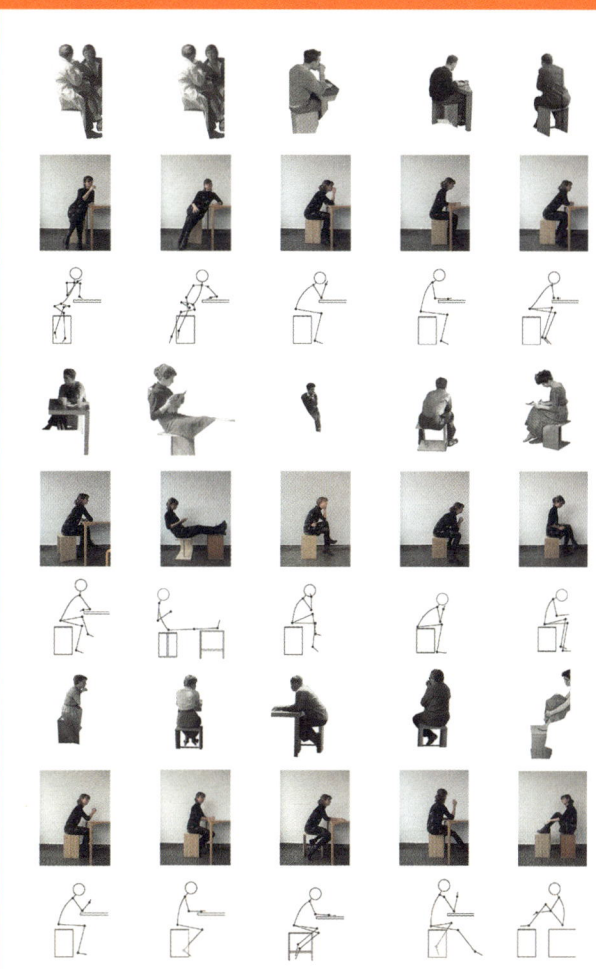

9

11 Die Serie von Selbstporträts im Sitzen auf dem gequeerten Ulmer Hocker bezieht auch die Betrachter*innen ein und stellt die Frage, wie diese die unterschiedlichen Sitzpositionen desselben Körpers wahrnehmen. »Wie reproduziert die Wahrnehmung anderer Geschlechtsidentitäten?« / *The series of self-portraits sitting on the queered Ulm Stool also engages with viewers and wonders how they perceive the different seated position performed by the same body: »How does the perception of the others reproduces gender identities?«*

12

12 1:1 Modelle der drei »queeren« Hockervarianten ∕ *1:1 models of the three queered Ulm Stool variations*

13 Fotografien aus dem Archiv, die zeigen, wie Körper interagieren, bestärkten meine Ideen über Machtverteilung und erlernte Identitäten als Prozess der Sozialisierung in informellen Zusammenkünften um einen Tisch. ∕ *Photographs from the archive showing how bodies interact supported my idea of power negotiation and learned identities as a process of socialisation, in informal gatherings around a table.*

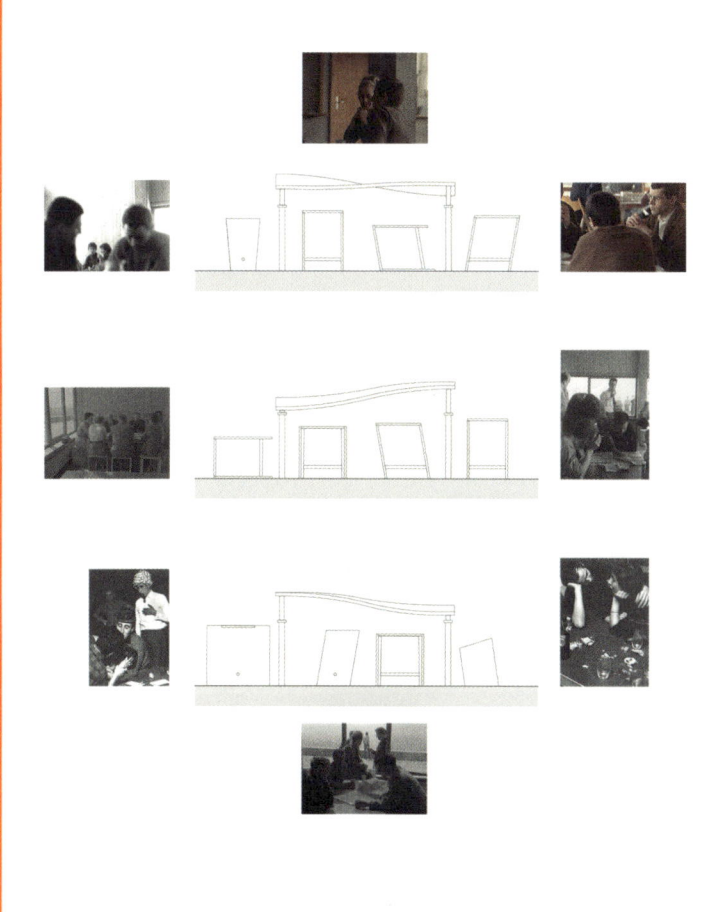

13

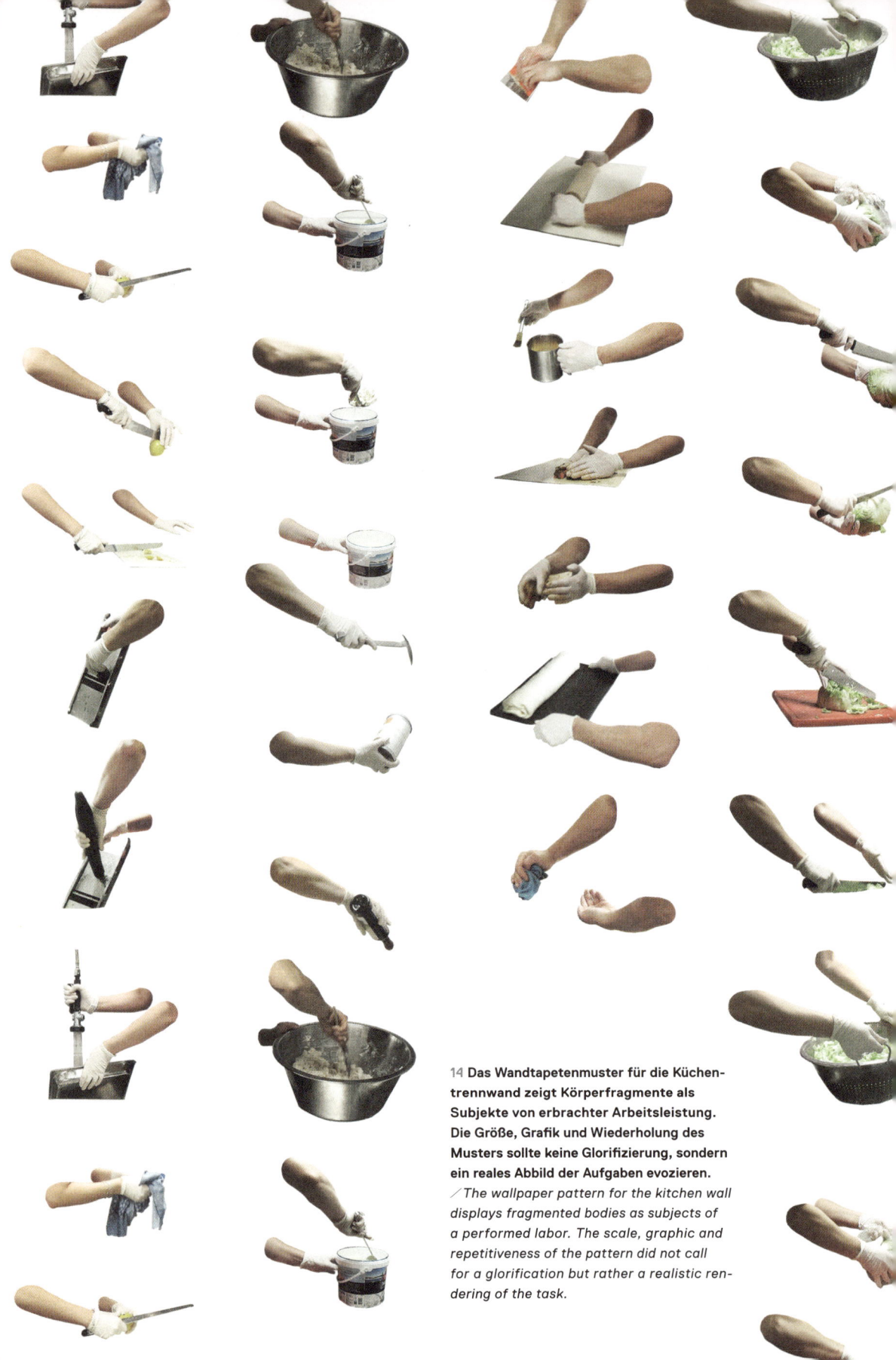

14 Das Wandtapetenmuster für die Küchentrennwand zeigt Körperfragmente als Subjekte von erbrachter Arbeitsleistung. Die Größe, Grafik und Wiederholung des Musters sollte keine Glorifizierung, sondern ein reales Abbild der Aufgaben evozieren.
/ The wallpaper pattern for the kitchen wall displays fragmented bodies as subjects of a performed labor. The scale, graphic and repetitiveness of the pattern did not call for a glorification but rather a realistic rendering of the task.

16 Plan der Mensa mit Darstellung des Essbestecks, der Hocker und Tischexperimente. Bildcollagen mit Szenen aus dem Alltag der ehemaligen HfG Ulm und vom Residence-Aufenthalt, in ein und demselben physischen Raum zusammengeführt. / *Plan of the canteen with the representation of the cutlery, stools and table experiments. Vignettes showing scenes of the everyday, from the former HfG-Ulm and from the residency, both embedded in the same physical space.*

15 Fotografie des finalen Präsentationsmodells mit einem Fragment der Mensa sowie der Wandtapete, des Tisches und des gequeerten Ulmer Hockers. / *Photograph of the final presentation model showing a fragment of the canteen, with the wallpaper, the table and the queered Ulm Stool.*

Gender – Space – Architecture
Ausstellung mit Fotografien von Juliane Peil in der PUTTE
/Exhibition with photographs by Juliane Peil in the PUTTE

Fotografie-Ausstellung ∕ PUTTE ∕ Neu-Ulm ∕ Laufzeit 13.04. – 05.05.2019 ∕ Leitung PUTTE: Axel Städter ∕ Fotografin: Juliane Peil

»Auf meinen fotografischen Streifzügen dokumentiere ich regelmäßig architektonische Formen und Strukturen. Gleichzeitig interessiere ich mich für die (Um-)Gestaltung des urbanen Stadtbilds und darin eingeschriebene Elemente, die nicht immer auf den ersten Blick sichtbar sind. Durch seinen ausschnitthaften Charakter erlaubt das Medium Fotografie es, die Wahrnehmung zu fokussieren. Für das Ausstellungsprojekt begann ich Anfang 2019, Aspekte von Geschlecht im öffentlichen Raum zu erkunden, wie etwa stereotype Darstellungsweisen von Männlichkeit und Weiblichkeit. Dabei empfand ich insbesondere die subtilen Nuancen von Geschlechterklischees, die uns im Alltag im Einzelnen aber auch im Nebeneinander begegnen, als äußerst spannend.« Juliane Peil

Photography exhibition ∕ PUTTE ∕ Neu-Ulm ∕ duration: 13.04. – 05.05.2019 ∕ Head of PUTTE: Axel Städter ∕ photographer: Juliane Peil

»On my photographic forays I often document architectural forms and structures. At the same time, I am also interested in the (re)design of the urban cityscape and the inscribed elements, which are not always visible upon first glance. Photography's excerpt-like character enables the medium to focus perception. At the beginning of 2019 I began investigating aspects of gender in public space for the exhibition project – for instance, the stereotypical representations of masculinity and femininity. In particular, I found the subtle nuances of gender clichés, which we encounter in specific details but also in juxtaposition, extremely interesting.« Juliane Peil

Axel Städter \ **Gender – ein Schaufenster in die Gesellschaft** \ Kern des Ausstellungsprojektes »Nicht mein Ding – Gender im Design« des HfG-Archivs Ulm war die Überprüfung von Gendernormierungen in Dingen und ihrer Gestaltung – und damit auch unseres Alltags. Als Projektraum für aktuelle Kunst war die PUTTE inhaltlich wie auch durch ihre Lage nahe der Stadtgrenze Ulm / Neu-Ulm prädestiniert für diese Kooperation. Die Ausstellung »Gender – Space – Architecture« bildete als Schaufenster eine Erweiterung von »Nicht mein Ding« in den Stadtraum hinein, der selbst in den letzten Jahren zu verschiedenen Gelegenheiten in den Fokus der Auseinandersetzung mit der Genderthematik rückte.[1]

Auch das Projekt in der PUTTE setzte, ähnlich wie »Nicht mein Ding«, bei alltäglichen Dingen und Situationen an. Die Fotografin und Kunsthistorikerin Juliane Peil begab sich auf eine Feldstudie durch die Städte Neu-Ulm und Ulm. Das gewählte Medium der Fotografie diente dabei als Werkzeug, um den konstanten Fluss der Eindrücke zu fokussieren. Als Flaneurin bewegte sich Peil bewusst durch den öffentlichen Raum und spürte offensichtlichen oder verborgenen Setzungen im Stadtraum nach. Diese Herangehensweise sowie die Thematik waren für die Präsentation in der PUTTE als Off-Space besonders reizvoll.

Was sieht der geschulte Blick? Was nehmen wir im Alltag in der so genannten Zweilandstadt vielleicht gar nicht (mehr) wahr? In Zeiten heutiger Konsum- und Verwertungslogik dominiert häufig die Außenwerbung feilgebotener Güter und Dienstleistungen. Durch ihre Omnipräsenz und die Normierung auf ein binäres Geschlechtersystem erhöht sich der Entscheidungsdruck auf die Menschen, ein »Dazwischen« wird selten bedient.[2] Zudem beschleicht einen das Gefühl, Männlichkeitsmerkmale würden strategischer in den Zeitgeist eingebunden. Hingegen war und ist das Bild der Frau, das gezeichnet wird, zumeist auf das Objekthafte reduziert.

Die Präsentation der Fotografien Juliane Peils gliederte sich in zwei (Alltags-)Bereiche. Inspiriert von der Idee des Schaufensters – zur Ausstellung »Nicht mein Ding« und zum Thema öffentlicher Raum – wurden im ersten Bereich Arbeiten gezeigt, die sich mit der Nutzung von Fenstern als Werbeflächen stereotyper Darstellung von Geschlechtszuweisung auseinandersetzen. Häufig wird durch die Normierungen, man könnte sie auch Codes nennen, eine bewusste Grenze mit der Intention gezogen, eine jeweils andere Gruppe gehöre nicht dorthin.

Mit der Bespielung der zwei großen Fenster der PUTTE durch die Illustratorin Jamila von Carnap wurde diese Idee wiederum gezielt aufgegriffen und diese »Schaufenster« mit einer ironischen Umkehrung nahezu archetypischer Logo-Gestaltung heute moderner »Barber Shops« und »Beauty Salons« versehen. In der Werbung eingesetzt, erscheint das Stilmittel der Umkehrung erfrischend-amüsant und verfehlte seine Wirkung auch bei den Ausstellungsplakaten von »Nicht mein Ding« nicht.

Gender – A Display Window into Society \ The main intention of the exhibition project »Not My Thing – Gender in Design« by the HfG-Archiv Ulm was to investigate gender norms in things and their design – hence, our everyday lives as well. PUTTE, a project space for contemporary art, was predestined for this cooperation, both in terms of content and given its location nearby the Ulm / Neu-Ulm city limits. The exhibition »Gender – Space – Architecture« represented a display window to extend »Not My Thing« into urban space, which itself has become the focus of a discussion on gender issues on different occasions in the last years.[1]

Similar to »Not My Thing«, the project in PUTTE was anchored in everyday things and situations. Photographer and art historian Juliane Peil set off on a field study in the cities Neu-Ulm and Ulm. The chosen medium of photography served as a tool to channel the constant flow of impressions. Like a flâneur, Peil consciously navigated through public space, retracing obvious and hidden correlations in the cityscape. This artistic method and theme were particularly appealing for a presentation in the off-space PUTTE.

What does the trained eye see? Are there perhaps aspects of daily life that we don't perceive (anymore) in the so-called twin city? In our current age marked by the logic of consumption and profit, a predominant impression is often that of outdoor advertising for goods and services. Its omnipresence in combination with the normalisation to a binary gender system heighten people's decision-making pressure – an »in-between« is rarely offered.[2] What's more, you get the creeping suspicion that traits of manhood are more strategically incorporated into the zeitgeist. While the portrayed image of the woman still typically assumes an object-like character.

The presentation of Juliane Peil's photography was organised into two sections (of the everyday). Inspired by the idea of the display window – to the exhibition »Not My Thing« and the topic »Public Space« – in the first section, works were presented that dealt with use of windows as advertising surfaces for stereotypical representations of gender ascriptions. Normalisations, one could also call them codes, are often employed to consciously draw a border indicating that a respective other group does not belong here.

In the intervention on the two big windows of PUTTE by illustrator Jamila von Carnap, this idea was addressed in a bolder manner by furnishing this display window with an ironic reversal of almost archetypal logo designs for today's trendy barber shops and beauty salons. A strategy used in advertising, the reversal as a stylistic device has a refreshing surprise effect, and it also did not lose any of its power on the exhibition posters for »Not My Thing«. With Carnap's design for »Barbara's Shop« and its counterpart »The Gentlemen's Beauty Salon«, the windows of PUTTE became a vivid membrane

Frauenparkplätze für allein fahrende Frauen

Gender – Space – Architecture

Durch Carnaps Gestaltung von »Barbara's Shop« und dem Pendant »The Gentlemen's Beauty Salon« wurden die Fenster in der PUTTE verstärkt zur Membran zwischen Innen- und Außenraum: Damit also eine wichtige Schnittstelle, gleichzeitig aber auch Folie für viele Setzungen im öffentlichen Raum, die Geschlechternormen betreffend. Als Kunstwissenschaftler interessierte mich dabei gerade dieser Kern künstlerischen Schaffens, das bewusste Irritieren der Passant*innen und Ausstellungsbesucher*innen als Methode, Menschen aus dem Tritt zu bringen und dadurch einen frischen Blick zu ermöglichen.

Während im ersten Teil der Ausstellung Architektur, Raum und Werbeflächen miteinander verschmolzen, ging es im zweiten Teil einen Schritt weiter in den öffentlichen Raum. Die dort präsentierten Fotografien zeigten weder eindeutige Stereotype noch spezifische Verweise, sondern vielmehr subjektive Blicke in den Stadtraum Ulms und Neu-Ulms. Die Betrachter*innen waren durch die gewählten Ausschnitte aufgefordert, sich hinsichtlich der eigenen Haltung selbst zu befragen. Wie wirkt Stadtraum? Wie beeinflusst die Wahrnehmung der Umgebung die Lebenswelt der Einzelnen?

Das Ausschnitthafte des Mediums Fotografie zeigte hierbei seine Grenzen im buchstäblichen Sinne: Als eine Rahmung, aber auch als Verstärkung durch den Charakter der Momentaufnahme.

Es liegt auf der Hand, sich mit diesen Fragen nach sozial geprägter Geschlechtsidentität im persönlichen wie auch im öffentlichen Bereich auseinanderzusetzen.[3] Kunst trägt einen wichtigen Teil dazu bei.

Diese gesellschaftliche Aufgabe kann nicht allein durch Gesetzgebung geregelt werden, spätestens der freie Markt wird immer eigene Gesetze bedienen. Doch es gibt noch einen wichtigen Faktor auf dem Weg der Gleichberechtigung und Gleichbehandlung aller und das sind die Menschen selbst: Wir bestimmen, was gekauft wird und für beziehungsweise gegen was wir uns positionieren. Es steht und fällt mit einer einfachen und auf viele Bereiche übertragbaren Frage: Wie wollen wir leben?

[1] Dazu zählt etwa die Implementierung von Gender-Mainstreaming der Stadt Ulm bei der Planung des Wohnquartiers am Lettenwald im Jahr 2010. Ziel solcher Projekte ist es, die Bedürfnisse aller künftigen Nutzer*innen bereits in der Planung mitzudenken, zu eruieren und selbige gegebenenfalls hinzuzuziehen, vgl. Stadt Ulm (SUB – Stadtplanung, Umwelt und Baurecht), Beschlussvorlage »Bebauungsplan 'Wohnquartier am Lettenwald'«, GD 283/10, Ulm 15.06.2010.
[2] Dittrich, Monika: Gender studies. Getrennte Spielwelten (30.01.2018), https://www.deutschlandfunk.de/gender-studies-getrennte-spielwelten.724.de.html?dram:article_id=409544, zul. abgerufen am 02.19.2019.
[3] Zuletzt wurde der Themenkomplex der Gleichbehandlung, hier sind Gender Mainstreaming und Frauenförderung hervorzuheben, durch den Begriff des Diversity Managements erweitert. Vgl.: Gender Mainstreaming und Diversity Management im Kontext kommunaler Gleichstellungspolitik, Positionspapier des Deutschen Städtetages (01.12.2016), http://www.staedtetag.de/imperia/md/content/dst/veroeffentlichungen/mat/positionspapier_gender_mainstreaming_2016.pdf, zul. abgerufen am 02.19.2019.

between inside and outside – a dynamic interface that at the same time also served as a placeholder for the many correlations in public space, which have to do with gender norms. As an art historian, I was interested in precisely this element of artistic creativity: the intentional irritation of passersby and exhibition visitors as a method, a wake-up call that enables a fresh look at things.

While the first part of the exhibition resulted in a fusion of architecture, space, and advertising, the second part took a step further into public space. Here the presented photography did not depict clear stereotypes or specific references to gender, rather subjective views of Ulm and Neu-Ulm's cityscape. The selected details challenged observers to interpret them from their own stance. How does urban space affect us? How does perception of one's surroundings influence the life world of individuals? The excerpt-like quality of the photographic medium literally reveals its limits: as a frame, but also as an enhancement by the nature of the snapshot.

It goes without saying that these questions regarding socially constructed gender identity should be addressed in both personal and public realms.[3] Art can play an important role in this process.

This social task cannot be negotiated through policy-making alone – and certainly, the free market will always follow its own rules. But there is another important factor on the road to equal rights and treatment of all, and that is the people themselves: We decide what is purchased and what we position ourselves for or against. It all relies on a simple question, which can be applied in many areas: How do we want to live?

[1] This includes, for example, the implementation of gender mainstreaming by the City of Ulm in the planning of the Lettenwald residential area in 2010. The aim of such projects is to involve, determine, and consult the needs of future users already in the planning phase. Cf. Stadt Ulm (SUB – Stadtplanung, Umwelt und Baurecht), Beschlussvorlage »Bebauungsplan 'Wohnquartier am Lettenwald',« GD 283/10, Ulm, June 15, 2010.
[2] Monika Dittrich, »Gender Studies. Getrennte Spielwelten,« Deutschlandfunk, Jan. 30, 2018, https://www.deutschlandfunk.de/gender-studies-getrennte-spielwelten.724.de.html?dram:article_id=409544.
[3] Recently, the thematic field of equal treatment, with emphasis on gender mainstreaming and the advancement of women, was expanded with the term »diversity management«. Cf. »Gender Mainstreaming und Diversity Management im Kontext kommunaler Gleichstellungspolitik,« German Association of Cities policy paper, December 1, 2016, http://www.staedtetag.de/imperia/md/content/dst/veroeffentlichungen/mat/positionspapier_gender_mainstreaming_2016.pdf.

Biografien / *Biographies*

Dr. phil. Stefanie Dathe, geboren 1968 in Frankfurt / Main, studierte Kunstgeschichte, Philosophie, Ethnologie und Alt-Amerikanistik in Mainz, Bonn und Zürich. Forschungsaufenthalte in Spanien. 1999 Promotion zur mittelalterlichen Architekturgeschichte Spaniens. Seit 1994 berufliche Tätigkeit im Galerie-, Kunsthandels- und Ausstellungswesen in der Schweiz, in Österreich und Deutschland. Zahlreiche Veröffentlichungen zur zeitgenössischen Kunst. Freiberufliche Kunsthistorikerin und Ausstellungskuratorin. 2005–2008 Kuratorin an der Städtischen Galerie Ravensburg. 2008–2016 Leiterin des Museums Villa Rot, Burgrieden-Rot. Seit Dezember 2016 Direktorin des Museums Ulm. *Stefanie Dathe (Dr. phil.), born 1968 in Frankfurt / Main, studied art history, philosophy, ethnology, and Early American studies in Mainz, Bonn, and Zurich. Following periods of research in Spain, she completed her doctorate on the history of medieval Spanish architecture in 1999. She has worked in the gallery, art market, and exhibition sector in Switzerland, Austria, and Germany since 1994. Dathe has written numerous publications on contemporary art and is a freelance art historian and curator: in 2005–2008 curator at the Städtische Galerie Ravensburg (Municipal Gallery Ravensburg); in 2008–2016 director of the Museum Villa Rot in Burgrieden; since December 2016 director of the Museum Ulm.*

Olivia Daigneault Deschênes studierte Architektur an der University of British Columbia in Vancouver, der University of Montreal sowie an der Lund Universität in Schweden (2012–2018). In ihrer Masterarbeit wandte sie »feminist critical spatial practice« als eine Methode an, um verborgene, patriarchale Manifestationen im Raum sowie bei der Durchführung der gynäkologischen Routineuntersuchung offenzulegen. Außerdem forschte sie zur Geschlechtergleichstellung am Beispiel der Architekturschule und von Architekturbüros in Vancouver. Diese Ergebnisse stellte sie 2017 auf dem »Dearq International Symposium Women in Architecture« an der University de Los Andes in Bogota, Kolumbien, vor. Im Herbst 2018 wurde sie vom HfG-Archiv Ulm, von der Stiftung für Gestaltung HfG Ulm und von Prof. Dr. em. Uta Brandes (themenspez. Jurymitglied) als erste Stipendiatin des Residence-Programms ausgewählt und eingeladen. Zurzeit arbeitet sie als Trainee in einem Architekturbüro in Montreal. *Olivia Daigneault Deschênes studied architecture at the University of British Columbia in Vancouver, the University of Montreal, Canada, and Lund University in Sweden (2012–2018). In her master's thesis she used »feminist critical spatial practice« as a method to abstract and reveal manifestations of patriarchy in the space and performance of the gynecological routine exam. In addition, she researched gender equality both in the school of architecture and in architecture offices of Vancouver. She presented these results in 2017 at the »Dearq International Symposium Women in Architecture« at the University de Los Andes in Bogota, Colombia. In fall 2018 she was selected and invited by the HfG-Archiv, the HfG Ulm Foundation, and Uta Brandes (theme-specific member of the jury) as the very first scholar of the Designer in Residence programme. She is currently working as a trainee in an architectural practice in Montreal.*

Pia Jerger studierte Literatur-, Kunst- und Medienwissenschaft an den Universitäten Konstanz und Prag sowie Kunstgeschichte mit Schwerpunkt Kunstvermittlung an der Heinrich-Heine-Universität Düsseldorf. Neben einer Lehrtätigkeit an einer Grundschule für gehörlose Kinder, Hazaribagh (Indien), arbeitete sie bei FUTURA. Centre for Contemporary Art in Prag als kuratorische Assistenz und bei den Skulptur Projekten Münster 2017 in der Presse- und Öffentlichkeitsarbeit. Im Bereich der Kulturvermittlung sammelte sie Erfahrungen in verschiedenen Einrichtungen (z. B. »Junge Nacht« im Museum Kunstpalast, Galerie Ludorff, KRASS e.V.). Im Rahmen des von der Kulturstiftung des Bundes und der Staatlichen Museen zu Berlin gemeinsam geförderten Programms »lab.Bode – Initiative zur Stärkung der Vermittlungsarbeit in Museen« war sie wissenschaftliche Volontärin im Museum Ulm. Seit 2019 ist sie dort als Kuratorin für Vermittlung tätig. *Pia Jerger studied literature, art, and media studies at the University of Konstanz and the University of Prague; she also studied art history, with a focus on art education, at the Heinrich Heine University in Düsseldorf. In addition to teaching at a primary school for deaf children in Hazaribagh, India, she has worked at the Futura Centre for Contemporary Art in Prague as curatorial assistant, and, in 2017, for the Münster Sculpture Projects press and public relations department. Jerger has gained experience as a cultural mediator in various institutions, including the Museum Kunstpalast (for the Young Night event), the Ludorff Gallery, and the KRASS Culture for Children Foundation. Through the lab.Bode – Initiative to Strengthen Museums Education in Museums programme, which is jointly funded by the German Federal Cultural Foundation and the Staatliche Museen zu Berlin, she worked as a junior research assistant at Museum Ulm. She joined the museum as curator for art education in 2019.*

Fabian Karrer studierte Mediendesign an der Dualen Hochschule Ravensburg. Er ist selbstständig als Designer tätig. Sein Fokus liegt auf grafischen Arbeiten – oft im Spannungsfeld zwischen Design und Kunst. Neben seinen Design-Projekten in den Bereichen Szenografie, Corporate Design, Grafik- und Editorial Design, Leitsysteme, Digital und Film, arbeitet er an einer Vielzahl freier, selbst initiierter Projekte. Er unterrichtet zudem an der Dualen Hochschule Ravensburg, im Kapuziner Kreativzentrum Ravensburg und der Höheren Fachschule für Künste, Gestaltung und Design, St. Gallen. Eine Auswahl seiner Arbeiten ist auf studioerika.de zu sehen. *Fabian Karrer studied media design at Ravensburg University of Cooperative Education and works as a freelance designer. His focus is on graphic work which often navigates various terrains between design and art. In addition to set design, corporate design, graphic and editorial design, signage, digital and film assignments, he works on many of his own self-initiated projects. He teaches at Ravensburg University of Cooperative Education, the Capuchin Creative Centre Ravensburg, and the St. Gallen Centre of Vocational Education and Training. A selection of his work can be viewed at: studioerika.de*

Katharina Kurz studierte Materielle Kultur, Philosophie und Museum und Ausstellung an der Carl von Ossietzky Universität Oldenburg sowie Art Education (Curatorial Studies) an der Zürcher Hochschule der Künste (2011–2017). Sie arbeitete als kuratorische Assistenz von Angeli Sachs im Museum für Gestaltung Zürich. Über einen zusätzlichen Forschungsaufenthalt in der dortigen Designsammlung knüpfte sie mit ihrer Masterarbeit »Objektkarrieren im Museum« an, abgefasst anhand des Vorlasses von Textildesigner Erich Biehle. Neben jüngsten Vorträgen auf dem Deutschen Kunsthistorikertag oder an der PH Karlsruhe, lehrte Kurz an der HfG Schwäbisch Gmünd Kommunikationstheorie. Im HfG-Archiv initiierte sie das Designer in Residence-Programm und kuratierte die Ausstellung »Nicht mein Ding – Gender im Design«. Kurz war als wissenschaftliche Volontärin im HfG-Archiv / Museum Ulm (2017–2019) zugleich Mitglied des VolkswagenStiftung geförderten Forschungsprojekts »Gestaltung ausstellen. Die Sichtbarkeit der HfG Ulm: Von Ulm nach Montréal«. *Katharina Kurz studied material culture, philosophy, and museum and exhibition studies at the Carl von Ossietzky University of Oldenburg as well as art education (curatorial studies) at Zurich University of the Arts (2011–2017). She was curatorial assistant to Angeli Sachs at the Museum für Gestaltung Zürich before staying on at the museum's design collection to research her master's thesis entitled »Object Careers in the Museum«, explored on the basis of the estate of textile designer Erich Biehle. In addition to recent lectures at the Congress of German Art Historians and Karlsruhe University of Education, Kurz has also taught communication theory at the University of Applied Sciences Gmünd. At the HfG-Archiv she established the Designer in Residence programme and curated the »Not My Thing – Gender in Design« exhibition. Kurz was a junior research assistant for the HfG-Archiv / Museum Ulm from 2017 to 2019, while also working on the Volkswagen Foundation-funded research project »Exhibiting Design: The Visibility of the Ulm School of Design, From Ulm to Montreal.«*

Axel Städter studierte Kunstgeschichte und Kunstwissenschaft an der Universität Karlsruhe (TH) und der TU Berlin mit einem Fokus auf Kunsttheorie und -praxis sowie Medienkunst. Seit Herbst 2015 ist er verantwortlich für die Presse- und Öffentlichkeitsarbeit der MEWO Kunsthalle in Memmingen und kuratierte dort im Herbst 2018 die Ausstellung »Forest. Enter. Exit.«. Im November 2018 übernahm er zusammen mit Carolina Pérez Pallares die künstlerische Leitung der PUTTE – Projektraum für aktuelle Kunst e.V. in Neu-Ulm. *Axel Städter studied art history and fine arts at Karlsruhe University and the Technical University of Berlin, focusing on art theory and practice as well as media art. Since autumn 2015 he has managed the press and public relations for MEWO Art Gallery Memmingen, where he curated the exhibition »FOREST. ENTER. EXIT.« In November 2018, together with Carolina Pérez Pallares, he took over as artistic director of PUTTE – Projektraum für aktuelle Kunst e.V. (project space for contemporary art) in Neu-Ulm.*

Susanne Umscheid ist diplomierte Industriedesignerin mit dem Schwerpunkt Gender und Design und begann bereits während ihrer Studienzeit an der Kunsthochschule Kassel, als selbstständige Grafikerin und Multiplikatorin zu arbeiten. Für ihre Diplomarbeit »Das Geschlecht der Dinge« erhielt sie im November 2019 eine Anerkennung des bf-Preises. Derzeit ist sie eine interdisziplinäre Auf-Vielen-Hochzeiten-Tänzerin: So ist sie Koordinatorin beim LSBT*IQ Netzwerk des Landes Hessen, freie Grafikerin u. a. für das Staatstheater Kassel, organisiert achtsame Kultur- und Freizeitveranstaltungen und vermittelt deren Notwendigkeit durch Fortbildungen. Ihren Schwerpunkt in den Bereichen Gender und Design baut sie insbesondere im Bezug auf UI/UX-Design und die Gestaltung digitaler Produkte aus und verstärkt dessen Intersektionalität in Bezug auf soziale Nachhaltigkeitsfelder. Susanne Umscheid hat bereits erfolgreich einige Workshops für Kinder, Jugendliche und Erwachsene konzipiert und durchgeführt, wie auch 2018 die Projektwoche mit einer 9. Stufe der Realschule Dornstadt für das Ausstellungsprojekt »Nicht mein Ding – Gender im Design«. *Susanne Umscheid has a degree in industrial design with a focus on gender and design. She began working as a freelance graphic designer and educator while still a student at Kassel School of Art and Design. In November 2019 she was awarded a bf-Prize for her diploma thesis »The Gender of Things«. She currently works across a range of interdisciplinary fields: as coordinator for the LSBT*IQ Network in the State of Hesse, as a freelance graphic designer for, among others, Kassel State Theatre, as well as organising mindful cultural and recreational events that she advocates for through further training. She is currently broadening her focus on gender and design, particularly with regard to UI/UX design and the design of digital products, and is working to strengthen its intersectionality in terms of social sustainability. Umscheid has successfully conceived and conducted a number of workshops for children, young people, and adults, including for the group of 9th grade pupils from Realschule Dornstadt in 2018 as part of the Project Week for the »Not My Thing – Gender in Design« exhibition.*

Christiane Wachsmann, geb. 1960, studierte im Anschluss an eine Tischlerlehre die Fächer Architektur und Design an der Staatlichen Akademie der Bildenden Künste in Stuttgart (1981–1986). Danach absolvierte sie ihr Redaktionsvolontariat bei den Stuttgarter Nachrichten (1987–1989). Es folgten Leitung und Aufbau des Archivs der Hochschule für Gestaltung Ulm (HfG-Archiv). In dieser Zeit entstanden zahlreiche Kataloge zum Thema HfG Ulm, darunter über Hans Gugelot als Lehrer, Walter Zeischegg, die Anfänge der HfG und den Unterricht von ehemaligen Bauhäuslern in Ulm. 1997–2008 Familienphase. Zeitgleich Gründung und Leitung der Schreibwerkstatt an der Ulmer Volkshochschule (bis 2018). 2008–2017 verantwortlich für Inventarisierung und Digitalisierung im HfG-Archiv. Seit 2018 ist sie Kuratorin und stellvertretende Leiterin des HfG-Archivs. Im Juni 2018 erschien ihr Buch »Vom Bauhaus beflügelt – Menschen und Ideen an der Hochschule für Gestaltung Ulm«. *Christiane Wachsmann, born 1960, studied architecture and design at the State Academy of Fine Arts in Stuttgart (1981–1986) following a carpentry apprenticeship. She then completed an editorial traineeship at Stuttgarter Nachrichten (1987–1989) before setting up and managing the archives of the Ulm School of Design (HfG-Archiv). During this time, she produced numerous catalogues on the subject of Ulm School of Design, including on former teacher Hans Gugelot, Walter Zeischegg, the beginnings of the HfG Ulm, and the teaching of former Bauhaus members in Ulm. The years 1997–2008 saw Wachsmann take time out to raise a family. During this period, she founded and managed (until 2018) the Ulm Adult Education Centre writing workshops. In the years 2008–2017 she was responsible for the inventory and digitisation of the HfG-Archiv, before taking up her current role as curator and deputy director in 2018. Her book »Vom Bauhaus beflügelt: Menschen und Ideen an der Hochschule für Gestaltung Ulm« was published in June 2018.*

Literatur / *Literature*

Allgemein / *General* Becker, Ruth und Beate Kortendiek, Hrsg. 2010. Handbuch Frauen und Geschlechterforschung: Theorie, Methoden, Empirie. 3. Aufl. Wiesbaden: VS, Verlag für Sozialwissenschaften. ■ Brandes, Uta. 2017. Gender Design: Streifzüge zwischen Theorie und Empirie. Basel: Birkhäuser. ■ Brandes, Uta und Sigrid Metz-Göckel, Hrsg. 2017. »Gender und Design: Zum vergeschlechtlichten Umgang mit dem gestalteten Alltag«. Für GENDER. Zeitschrift für Geschlecht, Kultur und Gesellschaft / Journal for Gender, Culture and Society, 9 (3). Opladen: Barbara Budrich. Netzwerk Frauen- und Geschlechterforschung NRW. ■ Buchmüller, Sandra. 2018. Geschlecht Macht Gestaltung – Gestaltung Macht Geschlecht: Der Entwurf einer machtkritischen und geschlechterinformierten Designmethodologie. Berlin: Logos. ■ Buchmüller, Sandra und Gesche Joost. 2009. »Der Schein bestimmt das Sein. Zum Verschleierungsmechanismus der kulturellen Gestaltung von Geschlecht«. In Oberflächen/Untersichten, Neuwerk, Zeitschrift für Designwissenschaft, Schriftenreihe der Burg Giebichenstein, Hochschule für Kunst und Design Halle, Eva Kristin Stein und Florian Walzel (Hrsg.): Bd. 1, S. 73–83. DOI: https://doi.org/10.11588/neuw.2009.0.30477. ■ Feige, Daniel Martin. 2018. Design: Eine philosophische Analyse. Berlin: Suhrkamp. ■ Gesser, Susanne, Martin Handschin, Angela Jannelli und Sibylle Lichtensteiger, Hrsg. 2014. Das partizipative Museum: Zwischen Teilhabe und User Generated Content. Neue Anforderungen an kulturhistorische Ausstellungen. Bielefeld: transcript. ■ Hepworth, Kate. 2016. »Gender and Design«. In The Bloomsbury Encyclopedia of Design, Vol. 2, hrsg. v. Clive Edwards, 74–77. London / New York: Bloomsbury. ■ John, Hartmut und Anja Dauschek, Hrsg. 2008. Museen neu denken: Perspektiven der Kulturvermittlung und Zielgruppenarbeit. Bielefeld: transcript. ■ Kortendiek, Beate, Birgit Riegraf und Katja Sabisch, Hrsg. 2019. Handbuch Interdisziplinäre Geschlechterforschung. Wiesbaden: Springer VS. ■ Mareis, Claudia. 2011. Design als Wissenskultur: Interferenzen zwischen Design- und Wissensdiskursen seit 1960. Bielefeld: transcript. ■ Mareis, Claudia. 2016 [2014]. Theorien des Designs: Zur Einführung. 2. Aufl. Hamburg: Junius. ■ Mörsch, Carmen, Angeli Sachs und Thomas Sieber, Hrsg. 2016. Ausstellen und Vermitteln im Museum der Gegenwart. Bielefeld: transcript. ■ Piontek, Anja. 2017. Museum und Partizipation: Theorie und Praxis kooperativer Ausstellungsprojekte und Beteiligungsangebote. Bielefeld: transcript. ■ Von Braun, Christina und Inge Stephan, Hrsg. 2006 [2000]. Gender Studien: Eine Einführung. 2. Aufl. Berlin u. Heidelberg: Springer. ■ Weller, Birgit und Katharina Krämer. 2012. Du Tarzan Ich Jane: Gender Codes im Design. Hannover: Blumhardt. ■ Züllich, Philipp und Internationales Design Zentrum Berlin e.V., Hrsg. 2008. Universal Design: Unsere Zukunft gestalten / Designing Our Future. Berlin: IDZ.

Öffentlicher Raum / *Public Space* Aicher, Otl und Martin Krampen. 1996 [1977]. Zeichensysteme der visuellen Kommunikation: Handbuch für Designer, Architekten, Planer, Organisatoren. Stuttgart: Koch; Berlin: Ernst & Sohn [Neuausgabe]. ■ Christian, Alexander. 2017. Piktogramme: Tendenzen in der Gestaltung und im Einsatz grafischer Symbole. Köln: Halem. ■ Eitler, Pascal. 2005. »Das Stripteaselokal«. In Orte der Moderne: Erfahrungswelten des 19. und 20. Jahrhunderts, hrsg. v. Alexa Geisthövel und Habbo Knoch, 248–256. Frankfurt / Main: Campus. ■ Krampen, Martin, Michael Götte und Michael Kneidl. 2007. Die Welt der Zeichen: Kommunikation mit Piktogrammen. Ludwigsburg: avedition. ■ Rathgeb, Markus. 2006. Otl Aicher. London / New York: Phaidon Press. ■ Sarnow, Melanie. 2013. Sex im Alltag – Die Entwicklung des Umgangs mit Sexualität seit den 1960er Jahren in Deutschland und den USA. Hamburg: Bachelor + Master Publishing. ■ Senatsverwaltung für Stadtentwicklung und Umwelt, Hrsg. 2011. Gender Mainstreaming in der Stadtentwicklung, Berliner Handbuch. Berlin: Kulturbuch. PDF verfügbar unter: www.stadtentwicklung.berlin.de/soziale_stadt/gender_mainstreaming/download/gender_deutsch.pdf, zul. abgerufen am 11.10.2018. ■ Stadtentwicklung Wien, Hrsg. 2013. Handbuch Gender Mainstreaming in der Stadtplanung und Stadtentwicklung. Werkstattbericht Nr. 130, Wien: Stadtentwicklung und Stadtplanung. PDF verfügbar unter: https://www.wien.gv.at/stadtentwicklung/studien/pdf/b008290.pdf, zul. abgerufen am 11.10.2018.

Spielen und Erziehung / *Play and Education* Adams, Annmarie. 2010. »The Power of Pink: Children's Bedrooms and Gender Identity«. In FKW: Zeitschrift für Geschlechterforschung und visuelle Kultur, Nr. 50, 58–69. Johnson, Derek. 2014. »Chicks with Bricks: Building Creativity Across Industrial Design Cultures and Genderes Construction Play«. In LEGO Studies: Examining the Building Blocks of a Transmedial Phenomenon, hrsg. v. Mark J. P. Wolf, 81–104. New York u. London: Routledge. ■ Knudsen, Gry Høngsmark und Erika Kuever. 2015. »The Peril of Pink Bricks: Gender Ideology and LEGO Friends«. In Consumer Culture Theory, 171–188. DOI: http://dx.doi.org/10.1108/S0885-211120150000017009. ■ Konzack, Lars. 2014. »The Cultural History of Lego«. In LEGO Studies: Examining the Building Blocks of a Transmedial Phenomenon, hrsg. v. Mark J. P. Wolf, 1–14. New York u. London: Routledge, Taylor & Francis. ■ Lange, Alexandra. 2018. The Design of Childhood: How the Material World Shapes Independent Kids. London: Bloomsbury. ■ Schmiedel, Stevie und Pinkstinks Germany e.V., Hrsg. 2019. Rosa für Alle!?: Gendersensible Erziehung in der Kindertagesstätte und Zuhause. 2. Aufl., Hamburg: Pinkstinks Germany. ■ spiel gut Arbeitsausschuß Kinderspiel + Spielzeug e.V., Hrsg. 2012. Vom Spielzeug und vom Spielen: Ratgeber für gutes Spielzeug. 20. Überarbeitete und erweiterte Ausgabe. Ulm: wie Hrsg. ■ Umscheid, Susanne. 2018. »Der Aufstieg des pinken Steins«. In Das Geschlecht der Dinge, unveröff. Diplomarbeit S. Umscheid, 36–45. Kunsthochschule Kassel.

Medizin und Gesundheit / *Medicine and Health* Bösl, Elsbeth. 2017. »Medizintechnik und Lifestyle-Produkt: Milchpumpen, Muttermilchdiskurs, Stilldiskurs und Konzepte von Mutterschaft«. In Mutterschaften sichtbar machen: Sozial- und kulturwissenschaftliche Beiträge, hrsg. v. Eva Tolasch u. Rhea Seehaus, Geschlechterforschung für die Praxis, Band 4, 43–57. Opladen / Berlin / Toronto: Barbara Budrich. ■ Bundesministerium für Familie, Senioren, Frauen und Jugend, Hrsg. 2018. Mutterschutzgesetz: Leitfaden zum Mutterschutz. 14. Aufl., Berlin. ■ Dinges, Martin. 2012. »Rauchen: gesundheitsgefährdend – und typisch ›männlich‹? Zum historischen Wandel geschlechtsspezifischer Zuschreibungen«. In Erziehung, Bildung und Geschlecht: Männlichkeiten im Fokus der Gender-Studies, hrsg. v. Meike Sophia Baader, Johannes Bilstein und Toni Tholen, 128–145. Wiesbaden: Springer VS. ■ Ehrnberger, Karin, Minna Räsänen, Emma Börjesson, Anne-Christine Hertz und Cristine Sundbom. 2017. »The Androchair: Performing Gynaecology through the Practice of Gender Critical Design«. In The Design Journal, 20:2, 181–198. Routledge, Taylor & Francis. DOI: 10.1080/14606925.2016.1261510. ■ Ehrnberger, Karin, Emma Börjesson, Anne-Christine Hertz und Cristine Sundbom. 2015. »The Andro-Chair. Designing the Unthinkable: Men's Right to Women's Experience in Gynaecology«. In Nordes: Design Ecologies, No. 6 (2015), Stockholm. PDF unter: https://archive.nordes.org/index.php/n13/article/view/399/377, zul. abgerufen am 10.10.2018. ■ Freudenschuß, Ina. 2012. »Vom Recht auf Stillen zur Pflicht der Mutter: Elemente eines globalen Stilldiskurses«. In GENDER. Zeitschrift für Geschlecht, Kultur und Gesellschaft, 4 (3), 138–145. https://nbn-resolving.org/ urn:nbn:de:0168-ssoar-397283, zul. abgerufen am 27.09.2019. ■ Heininger, Luisa. 2013. Zum Wandel des Stillverhaltens in der BRD zwischen 1950 und 1990. Eine Oral History-Studie. Düsseldorf: Heinrich-Heine-Universität. ■ Hentschel, Manfred W. u. Petermann, Jürgen. »Wie gut«. In DER SPIEGEL, Nr. 4/1964, 22.01.1964, 60–68, Hamburg: Spiegel Verlag Rudolf Augstein. PDF abrufbar unter: https://www.spiegel.de/spiegel/ print/d-46162828.html, zul. abgerufen am 11.10.2019. ■ Herrmann, Jeremia. 2018. »Stillen«. In Gender Glossar / Gender Glossary, verfügbar unter: https://nbn-resolving.org/urn:nbn:de:bsz:15-qucosa2-320611, zul. abgerufen am 27.09.2019. ■ Keiner, Dirk. 2015. »Der kleine Unterschied«. In Pharmazeutische Zeitung, Ausg. 41, 15.10.2015. Eschborn: Avoxa – Mediengruppe Deutscher Apotheker GmbH, verfügbar unter: https://www.pharmazeutische-zeitung.de/ausgabe-412015/der-kleine-unterschied/, zul. abgerufen am 13.10.2019. ■ Levin, Richard I. 2005. »The Puzzle of Aspirin and Sex«. In New England Journal of Medicine. 352: 1366–1368. DOI: 10.1056/NEJMe058051. ■ Organisation for Economic Cooperation and Development (OECD). 2014. OECD Family Database, Child Outcomes (CO), Child Health (CO1.5): Breastfeeding Rates, last updated, 01.10.2009, hrsg. v. OECD – Social Policy Division – Directorate of Employment, Labour and Social Affairs. PDF verfügbar unter: http://www.oecd.org/els/family/43136964.pdf, zul. abgerufen am 26.09.2019. ■ Regitz-Zagrosek, Vera. 2014. »Geschlechterunterschiede in der Pharmakotherapie«. In Bundesgesundheitsblatt – Gesundheitsforschung – Gesundheitsschutz, 57 (9), 1067–1073. Berlin u. Heidelberg: Springer-Verlag. DOI: 10.1007/s00103-014-2012-6. ■ Thomas, Anita und Alexandra Kautzky-Willer. 2015. »Gendermedizin«. In Gender Glossar / Gender Glossary, verfügbar unter: https://nbn-resolving.org/urn:nbn:de:bsz:15-qucosa-221273, zul. abgerufen am 10.10.2019. ■ Von der Lippe, Elena, et. al. 2014. »Einflussfaktoren auf Verbreitung und Dauer des Stillens in Deutschland«. In Bundesgesundheitsblatt – Gesundheitsforschung – Gesundheitsschutz, 57 (7), 849–859. Berlin u. Heidelberg: Springer-Verlag. DOI: 10.1007/s00103-014-1985-5. ■ Villa, Paula Irene. 2019. »Sex – Gender: Ko-Konstitution statt Entgegensetzung«. In: Handbuch interdisziplinäre Geschlechterforschung, hrsg. v. Beate Kortendiek, Birgit Riegraf und Katja Sabisch, 23–33. Wiesbaden: Springer VS. ■ Weltgesundheitsorganisation (WHO). 2018. Infant and Young Child Feeding (Fact Sheets), 16.02.2018, verfügbar unter: https://www.who.int/newsroom/fact-sheets/detail/infant-and-young-child-feeding, zul. abgerufen am 13.10.2019. ■ Weltgesundheitsorganisation (WHO). 2007. Evidence on the Long-Term Effects of Breastfeeding: Systematic Review and Meta-Analyses. Bernardo L. Horta ... [et al.], WHO: Department of Child and Adolescent Health Development (CAH), Genf, verfügbar unter: http://whqlibdoc.who.int/publications/2007/9789241595230_eng.pdf, zul. abgerufen am 13.10.2019.

Haushalt und Wohnen / *Household and Living* Becker, Katja und Claudia Herling. 2017. »Der Einfluss von Gender im Entwicklungsprozess von digitalen Artefakten«. GENDER. Zeitschrift für Geschlecht Kultur und Gesellschaft. Vol. 9, Nr. 3 / 2017, 26–44. Opladen: Barbara Budrich. DOI: https://doi.org/10.3224/gender.v9i3.03. ■ Christensen, Michelle und Florian Conradi. 2017. »Open-Source Cyborgs and DIY Data: Chances and Challenges for a Democratisation of Gender«. In GENDER. Zeitschrift für Geschlecht Kultur und Gesellschaft, 9 (3), 81–90. Opladen: Barbara Budrich. DOI: https://doi.org/10.3224/gender.v9i3.06. ■ Ehrnberger, Karin, Minna Räsänen und Sara Ilstedt. 2012. »Visualising Gender Norms in Design: Meet the Mega Hurricane Mixer and the Drill Dolphia«. In International Journal of Design, vol. 6, No. 3, 85–98. ■ Günter, Bettina. 1996. »Geschlechtsspezifische Aneignungsformen des Wohnens in den fünfziger Jahren zwischen selektiver Bescheidenheit und Teilhabe am Konsum«. In RaumStationen: Kulturwissenschaftliche Beiträge zu Konzeptionen von Geschlecht, Architektur und Raum. Frauen. Kunst. Wissenschaft [seit 2007 FKW: Zeitschrift für Geschlechterforschung und visuelle Kultur], Nr. 22, 29–44. ■ Krejci, Jessica. 2018. »Weibliche Intelligenz: Giving It Her Voice«. In form Design Magazine: Embodiment of Design. No. 279, Sept / Oct 2018, 46–53. Frankfurt / Main: form.

Kosmetik und Gender-Marketing / *Cosmetics and Gender-Marketing* Antidiskriminierungsstelle des Bundes, Hrsg., Iris an der Heiden und Prof. Dr. Maria Wersig. 2017. Preisdifferenzierung nach Geschlecht in Deutschland: Forschungsbericht. Baden-Baden: Nomos. ■ Auster, Carol J. und Claire S. Mansbach. 2012. »The Gender Marketing of Toys: An Analysis of Color and Type of Toy on the Disney Store Website.« In Sex Roles: A Journal of Research, Nr. 67 (7–8), 375–388. DOI: 10.1007/s11199-012-0177-8. ■ Klatt, Jo und Günter Staeffler, Hrsg. 1990. Braun + Design Collection. Braun Produkte von 1955 bis heute. Hamburg: Braun + Design. ■ Kreienkamp, Eva unter Mitarbeit von Gerda M. Frisch und Regina Buchholz. 2007. Gender Marketing: Impulse für Marktforschung, Produkte, Werbung und Personalentwicklung. Landsberg a. L.: mi. ■ Plank, Liz. 2019. For the Love of Men: A New Vision for Mindful Masculinity. New York: St. Martin's Press. ■

Van Oost, Ellen. 2003. »Materialized Gender: How Shavers Configure the User's Feminity and Masculinity«. In How Users Matter: The Co-Construction of Users and Technology, hrsg. v. Nelly Oudshoorn und Trevor Pinch, 193–208. Cambridge: MIT Press.

Design: Ausbildung und Beruf / *Design: Education and Profession* Becker, Katja und Claudia Herling. 2017. »Der Einfluss von Gender im Entwicklungsprozess von digitalen Artefakten«. In GENDER. Zeitschrift für Geschlecht Kultur und Gesellschaft. Vol. 9, Nr. 3 / 2017, 26–44. Opladen: Barbara Budrich. DOI: https://doi.org/10.3224/gender.v9i3.03. ■ Breuer, Gerda und Julia Meer. 2012. Women in Graphic Design 1890–2012. Berlin: Jovis. ■ Brandes, Uta, Sandra Buchmüller und Sonja Stich. 2001/2003. »Über die unbewusste und bewusste Vergeschlechtlichung von Produkten. Eine (meta)morphologische Studie in zwei Teilen« (unveröff.). Auszüge in Gender & Design. Leitfragen, hrsg. v. Zentrum Frau in Beruf und Technik, ZfBT, 2006, 22–23. Castrop-Rauxel, wie Hrsg. PDF verfügbar unter: http://www.zfbt.de/veroeffentlichungen/dokumente/gender_design_2.81%20Leitfragen%20final.pdf, zul. abgerufen am 12.10.2017. ■ Dissel, Julia-Constance, Hochschule Darmstadt / University of Applied Sciences, Hrsg. 2019. Zeitgenössische Designerinnen: Design + Gender. IDF-Papers, Institut für Designforschung der Hochschule Darmstadt, Nr. 2. DOI 10.26082/idfp.g.19/002.d.1. ■ Grossmann, Yves Vincent. 2018. »Frauen im Industriedesign«. In Von der Berufung zum Beruf: Industriedesigner in Westdeutschland 1959–1990, 237–242. Bielefeld: transcript. ■ Krieger, Inga. 2015. »Weibliches Formen«. In DIE ZEIT, Zeitmagazin, Nr. 41/2015, 08.10.2015, verfügbar unter: https://www.zeit.de/zeit-magazin/2015/41/frauen-design-objekte-gestaltung, zul. abgerufen am 08.10.2019. ■ Levick-Parkin, Melanie. 2017. »The Values of Being in Design: Towards a Feminist Design Ontology«. In GENDER. Zeitschrift für Geschlecht Kultur und Gesellschaft. Vol. 9, Nr. 3 / 2017, 11–25. Opladen: Barbara Budrich. DOI: https://doi.org/10.3224/gender.v9i3.02. ■ Lindinger, Herbert. 1987. »Was hat Gugelot bewegt?« In System-Design Bahnbrecher: Hans Gugelot 1920–65, hrsg. v. Hans Wichmann, Band 3 Industrial Design – Graphic Design, 2. Aufl., 38–49. Basel / Boston: Birkhäuser. ■ Müller, Ulrike. 2016 [2014]. Bauhaus-Frauen: Meisterinnen in Kunst, Handwerk und Design. 2. Aufl. Berlin: Insel. ■ Müller-Krauspe, Gerda. 2007. Selbstbehauptungen: Frauen an der hfg ulm. Frankfurt / Main: Anabas. ■ Landesgewerbeamt Baden-Württemberg / Design Center Stuttgart, Hrsg., Oedekoven-Gerischer, Angela. 1989. Frauen im Design: Berufsbilder und Lebenswege seit 1900. / Women in Design: Careers and Life Histories since 1900. Band 1 u. 2, Ausstellungskatalog. Stuttgart: Design Center Stuttgart, Haus der Wirtschaft. ■ Staatliche Kunstsammlungen Dresden, Tulga Beyerle und Klara Nemeckova, Hrsg. 2018. Gegen die Unsichtbarkeit. Designerinnen der Deutschen Werkstätten Hellerau, 1898 bis 1938. München: Hirmer. ■ Otto, Elisabeth und Patrick Rössler. 2019. Bauhaus Women: A Global Perspective. London: Bloomsbury / Herbert Press.

Bildnachweise
/ Image Credits

Das HfG-Archiv / Museum Ulm ist bemüht, alle zur Veröffentlichung notwendigen Genehmigungen entsprechender Rechteinhaber*innen zu erhalten. Personen oder Institutionen, die möglicherweise nicht ermittelt beziehungsweise erreicht wurden und Verwertungsrechte an verwendeten Abbildungen beanspruchen, werden gebeten, sich mit dem HfG-Archiv / Museum Ulm in Verbindung zu setzen. / *The HfG-Archiv / Museum Ulm endeavours to obtain all necessary permissions from the respective copyright holders for publication. Persons or institutions who may not have been identified or reached and claim copyrights to the images used are requested to contact the HfG-Archiv / Museum Ulm.*

S. / pp. 15; 57–58; 62; 96; 104–105; 116; 118–119; 139, 146–147; 156 (Hintergrund / *background*); 169 (unten / *bottom*); 172 (Comic); 175; 177 (unten: Modelle / *bottom: models*); 190–191 (oben / *top*): Fabian Karrer

S. / pp. 19; 21–23; 48; 50; 88–89; 113; 136; 138: Fabian Karrer © HfG-Archiv / Museum Ulm

S. / p. 24: Benedikt Groß, Daniel Utz, CC BY-SA 4.0

S. / pp. 26–27: Bingyan Liu

S. / pp. 28–29: Marija Gašparović © studio 52hours

S. / pp. 30–31; 197–203: © Juliane Peil

S. / pp. 32–33: Paul Guddat, Matthias Grund, Alicia Shao

S. / pp. 34–35: © Nike

S. / pp. 36–39; 182–183; 186–193: Olivia Daigneault Deschênes © HfG-Archiv / Museum Ulm

S. / pp. 43–44: © JeongMee Yoon

S. / pp. 46; 49; 51; 77–78; 87; 90; 127; 129; 155 (oben / *top*); 157 (oben / *top*); 159 (Hintergrund / *background*); 160 (oben / *top*); 169–172; 177 (oben / *top*): © HfG-Archiv / Museum Ulm

S. / p. 53: Hinz, Weller, Krämer, Rajabi (oben / *top*); Simon Hellwig (unten / *bottom*)

S. / p. 54: © Anita Sarkeesian, feminist frequency

S. / p. 55: © Dominique Gehrke

S. / pp. 56; 155 (unten / *bottom*); 156 (Vordergrund / *foreground*); 157–159; 160; 163–165: Matthias Schmiedel © HfG-Archiv / Museum Ulm

S. / pp. 59; 144–145: Wolfgang Siol 1961 © HfG-Archiv / Museum Ulm

S. / pp. 60; 81 (rechts / *right*); 94–95; 140: Juliane Peil © HfG-Archiv / Museum Ulm

S. / p. 61: Zuzanna Kozerska-Girard, Playeress

S. / p. 63: © Jake Dypka, Hollie McNish

S. / p. 67: Martin Brunn © Martin Brunn & Carl Olof Berg

S. / p. 69: Anders Andersson © Emma Börjesson

S. / pp. 70–71: © Scholz & Friends

S. / p. 72: © SQlab GmbH Taufkirchen

S. / pp. 74–75: © Elvie

S. / p. 79 (links / *left*): Brian, CC-BY.NC 2.0

S. / p. 81 (links / *left*): CC BY-NC-SA 2.0

S. / p. 93: © Virtue Nordic

S. / p. 97: Kent Johansson © Karin Ehrnberger

S. / pp. 98–99: Loove Broms © Karin Ehrnberger

S. / pp. 101–103: © Robert Bosch Power Tools GmbH

S. / pp. 109–110: Pinkstinks Germany e.V.

S. / p. 111: Privatarchiv G. Gugelot

S. / p. 112: © Procter & Gamble

S. / p. 115 (unten / *bottom*): © Wirtschaftswundermuseum

S. / p. 115 (oben / *top*): © Mäurer & Wirtz GmbH & Co. KG

S. / p. 116: © Beiersdorf AG

S. / p. 117: Saana Hellsten, Studio Hellsten

S. / p. 124: Ernst Hahn © HfG-Archiv / Museum Ulm

S. / p. 128: Eva Koch-Hörmann © HfG-Archiv / Museum Ulm

S. / p. 130: Gerda Müller-Krauspe, Ursula Wenzel

S. / p. 131: © notamuse

S. / pp. 132–133: Jaqueline Diedam

S. / p. 134: © AIGA Women Lead

S. / p. 137: Sylvie Fleury, Three Star Books

S. / p. 142 (Stuhl-Miniaturen / *Chair Miniatures*): Vitra International AG © Vitra International AG: DKR Wire Chair, LCM, Panton Chair, Vegetal; © Cassina: Zig Zag Stoel; © Knoll International: Tulip Chair; © Artemide: Selene; © Thonet: W1

S. / p. 143: © Conradi + Christensen

S. / pp. 186 (unten / *bottom*); 187 (oben / *top*): Ernst Möckl © HfG-Archiv / Museum Ulm

Piktogramme unterliegen dem Urheberrecht. Die in dieser Ausarbeitung gezeigten Piktogramme von Otl Aicher dürfen weder vervielfältigt noch bearbeitet oder verfremdet werden. Die Wiedergabe bedarf der Genehmigung seitens der attoma Berlin GmbH, Helmholtzstraße 2-9, 10587 Berlin, Deutschland. Inhaber der Urheberrechte ist die ERCO GmbH, Brockhauser Weg 80-82, 58507 Lüdenscheid, Deutschland. www.otl-aicher-piktogramme.de

Dank / *Acknowledgements*

An alle Beteiligten der Kooperationsprojekte / *To all participants of the cooperation projects:* **Projektwoche** / *Project week:* den Schüler*innen / *the students,* Michaela Settele-Jakob und / *and* Martin Böhnisch (Bühl Realschule Dornstadt), Susanne Umscheid und Fabian Karrer, gefördert von / *funded by* lab.Bode – Initiative zur Förderung der Vermittlungsarbeit in Museen ▪ **Produktdesignkurs** / *Product design course:* den Kollegiat*innen / *the students* und / *and* Andreas Lörcher (Aicher-Scholl-Kolleg, vh ulm) und / *and* Uli Häussler ▪ **Designer in Residence-Programm** / *Programme:* Uta Brandes, Alexander Wetzig und / *and* Julia Hanisch (Stiftung Hochschule für Gestaltung HfG Ulm), Martin Mäntele (HfG-Archiv) sowie / *and* Olivia Daigneault Deschênes ▪ **Ausstellung** / *Exhibition* »Gender – Space – Architecture«: Axel Städter (PUTTE) und / *and* Juliane Peil

Für Leihgaben und Informationen / *For loans and information:* AIGA (US) ▪ Anita Sarkeesian (feminist frequency, US) ▪ Benedikt Groß, Daniel Utz (HfG Schwäbisch Gmünd) ▪ Bingyan Liu (Neuötting) ▪ Carl Olof Berg (Stockholm, SE), Chiaro Technology Ltd. and Elvie (London, GB) ▪ Dominique Gehrke (Köln) ▪ Emma Börjesson, Anne-Christine Hertz, Cristine Sundbom (Halmstad, SE) ▪ Gerda Müller-Krauspe, Petra Keller, Ursula Wenzel (Frankfurt) ▪ Gisela Kasten, Hans (Nick) Roericht (Ulm) ▪ Guus Gugelot (Hamburg) ▪ Herr Zopfs Friseurmuseum (Neu-Ulm) ▪ Ivana Preiss, Filip Vasić (52hours, Prag, CZ) ▪ Jake Dypka, Hollie McNish (London, GB) ▪ JeongMee Yoon (Seoul, KR) ▪ Jaqueline Diedam (Köln), Uta Brandes (Köln) ▪ Jörg Bohn (Wirtschaftswundermuseum, Rheinberg) ▪ Kai-Alexander Gehrmann (otl-aicher-piktogramme.de, attoma GmbH, Berlin) ▪ Karin Ehrnberger (Stockholm, SE) ▪ Katharina Krämer, Birgit Weller (Berlin/Hannover) ▪ Mäurer & Wirtz (Köln) ▪ Michelle Christensen, Florian Conradi (Berlin) ▪ Nike Deutschland GmbH (Berlin) ▪ Paul Guddat, Matthias Grund, Alicia Shao (Köln) ▪ Pinkstinks Germany e.V. (Hamburg) ▪ Procter & Gamble (Cincinnati, US) ▪ Robert Bosch GmbH (Stuttgart) ▪ Saana Hellsten (studio Hellsten, Helsinki, FI) ▪ Sandra Reckers (Schorndorf) ▪ Scholz & Friends (Berlin), The Female Company (Stuttgart) ▪ Three Star Books (Genf, CH) ▪ Silva Baum, Claudia Scheer, Lea Sievertsen (notamuse, Hamburg/Berlin) ▪ SQlab GmbH (Taufkirchen) ▪ Virtue Nordic (Kopenhagen, DK) ▪ Vitra Design Museum (Weil am Rhein) ▪ Zuzanna Kozerska-Girard (Playeress, Warschau, PL).

Für weitere Unterstützung / *For further support:* Burak Ertem, Werner Zingler (branddezign) ▪ Daniel Ries (HQ Print) ▪ Gisela Kasten (Ulm) ▪ Juliane Peil (Chemnitz) ▪ Martin Gerster (MdB) ▪ Matthias Schmiedel (Schmiedel.Photography) ▪ Miriam Albrecht, Robert Albrecht (albrecht.catering) ▪ Oliver Lang (Neu-Ulm) ▪ Petra Beckmann, Andreas Schulze (Landesvertretung Baden-Württemberg) ▪ Petra Kiedaisch (avedition, Stuttgart) ▪ PlayWood (Reggio Emilia, IT) ▪ Stefan Kaufmann (Verschwörhaus, Stadt Ulm) ▪ Susanne Dickel (Köln) ▪ Katharina Bühler, Tanja Schomaker, Sandra Soltau (lab.Bode – Initiative zur Stärkung der Vermittlungsarbeit in Museen) ▪ Thomas Gress, Michael Rupf (Stiftung HfG Ulm) ▪ sowie sehr herzlich dem Team des / *and also very warmly the team of the* HfG-Archiv / Museum Ulm.

Impressum / *Imprint*

Nicht mein Ding – Gender im Design
/ *Not My Thing – Gender in Design*

HfG-Archiv
Museum Ulm

Eine Ausstellung und Publikation des
/ *An exhibition and publication of the*
HfG-Archiv / Museum Ulm

Kuratorium / *Curatorship:*
Katharina Kurz (Ausstellung / *Exhibition*)
Pia Jerger (Vermittlung / *Education*)

Publikation / *Catalogue:*
Konzept und Redaktion / *Concept and editing:*
Pia Jerger, Katharina Kurz

Katalogtexte / *Texts:* **Katharina Kurz**

Mit Beiträgen von / *With contributions from:*
Olivia Daigneault Deschênes, Pia Jerger,
Axel Städter, Susanne Umscheid,
Christiane Wachsmann

Bildrecherche und Mitarbeit
/ *Image research and assistance:*
Viktoria Heinrich, Jasmin Al-Kuwaiti

Übersetzung / *Translation:*
Peter Blakeney & Christine Schöffler,
Charlotte Maconochie & Clemens Marschall

Lektorat (Deutsch) / *Copyediting (German):*
Martin Mäntele

Gestaltung / *Design:* **Fabian Karrer**
Studio Erika, studioerika.de

Druck und Einband / *Printing and binding:*
Kösel GmbH & Co. KG, Altusried-Krugzell
Papier / *Paper:* 140 g Multi Offset mit 1,25 Volumen
Schrift / *Font:* Replica

Verlag und Vertrieb /
Publishing and distribution:
avedition GmbH
Senefelderstr. 109
D – 70176 Stuttgart
avedition.de

Copyright © 2020 **av**edition GmbH, Stuttgart
Copyright © 2020 HfG-Archiv / Museum Ulm
Copyright © 2020 for the texts with individual authors
Copyright © 2020 for the photos see image credits

Printed in Germany
Erste Auflage / *First edition*
ISBN: 978-3-89986-327-7

Alle Rechte, insbesondere das Recht der Vervielfältigung, Verbreitung und Übersetzung, vorbehalten. Kein Teil des Werkes darf in irgendeiner Form (durch Fotokopie, Mikrofilm, oder ein anderes Verfahren) ohne schriftliche Genehmigung reproduziert oder unter Verwendung elektronischer Systeme verarbeitet, vervielfältigt oder verbreitet werden. / *This work is subject to copyrights. All rights are reserved, whether the whole or part of the materials is concerned, and specifically but not exclusively the rights of translation, reprinting, reuse of illustrations, recitations, broadcasting, reproduction on microfilms or in other ways, and storage in data banks or any other media. For use of any kind, permission of the copyright owner must be obtained.*

Bibliographische Informationen der Deutschen Nationalbibliothek / Die Deutsche Nationalbibliothek verzeichnet diese Publikation in der Deutschen Nationalbibliografie; detaillierte bibliografische Daten sind im Internet über http://dnb.de abrufbar. / *Bibliographic information published by the German National Library / The German National Library lists this publication in the German National Bibliography; detailed bibliographical data are available on the internet at http://dnb.de*

Mit freundlicher Unterstützung von / *With the kind support of:* Rudolf und Clothilde Eberhardt-Stiftung / Stiftung Hochschule für Gestaltung HfG Ulm / Freunde des Ulmer Museums e. V. / Christina Bauernfeind / Marina Bauernfeind